Praise for *The Together Tea...*

"Master the art of productivity with Maia's book, which teaches the best practices of organizing your work and achieving maximum efficiency. Whether you're a seasoned pro or just starting out in your career, this book is the ultimate guide to optimizing your workflow and achieving success."

—**Christopher Hines,** Chief Operating Officer, Crescent City Schools

"Finally, a book about being 'Together' for all members of my team! This is a book that helps anyone operate effectively as an individual *and* as a part of a greater team!"

—**Jenny Tan,** Chief of Schools, KIPP Northern California

"As a Together Leader, I completed this book review timely and on my own terms, all while managing multiple personal and professional priorities and getting plenty of sleep. This could be you! Maia Heyck-Merlin has delivered another great guide to support teammates in high-performing organizations of all sizes."

—**Cate Swinburn,** Co-Founder, President, and CEO, YouthForce NOLA

"Maia has done it again! Through powerful tools, practical tips, and personal wisdom accumulated through a career as an educator and nonprofit leader, Maia demystifies the 'magic' behind getting things done. *The Together Teammate* fills the void in speaking to the unique challenges and pressures experienced by those in the vast workplace middle – not yet leading organizations, but nonetheless doing significant and complex work. This book is a must-read for any team member looking to increase their effectiveness, conquer the chaos, and experience the awesome feeling of Togetherness."

—**Dr. Michael Cormack,** Deputy Superintendent, Jackson Public Schools

"Maia and her team have been helping people in operational support roles for almost 20 years to be more Together and thoughtful in their day-to-day operations. This book takes what I learned in *The Together Leader* and helps me apply my Together Tools in a whole new way not only to my professional world, but in my personal life as well. *The Together Teammate* provides vital and life-changing support to anyone juggling multiple priorities, tasks, and audiences."

—**Fortunata Blecharczyk,** Operations Manager

"*The Together Teammate* will benefit any public service professional who must decide how to use their limited time to make the most impact. I was able to implement Maia's tools immediately to become a more efficient professional and leader."

–Daniel Heller, Independent Education Consultant

THE
TOGETHER
TEAMMATE

THE TOGETHER TEAMMATE

Build Strong Systems, Make the Work Manageable, and Stay Organized Behind the Scenes

Maia Heyck-Merlin
with Heidi Gross

JB JOSSEY-BASS™
A Wiley Brand

To Kendra Rowe Salas, cheers to ten years, and because you are the epitome of Togetherness to me and so many others.

CONTENTS

SECTION 3: GET THE TEAM TOGETHER: TEAMMATE TRICKS TO MOVE THE WORK FORWARD   207

Take Stock: Know Your Role and Set Your Priorities

CHAPTER 1

Introduction – The Who, What, and Why of Togetherness for Teammates

Welcome to the Together Universe, my friends! I'm so glad you're here, and I'm excited for our journey into the world of Togetherness. Perhaps you picked up this book because you're searching for solutions so that you can move away from having to put out fires all day. Or maybe you're seeking boundaries and balance. Or you're brand new in your role and want to start out with some clear structure and intention. Or you've been in your position for a long time and things are generally going just fine, but you are looking for a good old-fashioned Together Tune-up.

What is *The Together Teammate*, you may wonder. Well, after I wrote *The Together Teacher* and then *The Together Leader*, I kept seeing individuals show up in my classes who were not teachers or leaders. They also didn't necessarily work in schools; they were from nonprofits, social-justice–focused organizations, and even . . . corporate settings. Or they were leaders but had less autonomy and more reactive jobs than some other folks. These people, *you all,* kept appearing in my classes and the tenor of your challenges was similar to leaders and teachers, but also unique. Here are a few things I heard about what your days contain:

- The incessant email/voice message/Slack/Teams notifications for the laptop help desk
- The constant interruption of a school entrance buzzer all day long
- The tracking of scheduling preferences for a manager who changes their mind constantly
- The copier that broke right before a board meeting and the materials need to go out *now*
- The hiring manager who wants you to set up candidate interviews first thing tomorrow
- The vendor for the holiday party that simply won't get back to you
- The manager who calls you for an urgent data report *right at this minute*

And yet, while you (dear reader) were carefully playing whack-a-mole with the unexpected, the constant deluge, and the busy – all likely with a smile and careful customer service orientation – some other more long-term, perhaps more strategic, more systems-level work was getting pushed to the bottom of the list. And then you are in full-on task mode, which leads to more full-on task mode, which can result in the same patterns over and over. And that is just today. And so, here, I hope, is a text that will help you manage and juggle all of the above. But first, what is this Togetherness of which I speak?

WHAT IS TOGETHERNESS, ANYWAY?

Ahh, it's a familiar question: Is this just another book about how to be organized? Well, no, not exactly. Organization might be part of it, but I believe it's a little more than that. To me, Togetherness evokes a feeling. See if you can picture it. I'm sure you've heard the phrase "She/he just has their _____ together." That's the feeling we in the Together-verse are going for, specifically:

- You have a sense of everything on your plate, even if you don't complete it all today.
- You can communicate your priorities consistently, naming trade-offs if necessary, and your work reflects these priorities.
- You follow up on all items, both big and small, that are important to others.
- You plan ahead thoughtfully, allowing buffer time for emergencies.
- You block time for your most important priorities, but leave room for emergencies.

- You are considered reliably responsive, but not immediately playing whack-a-mole to everything.

- You create boundaries, if you choose, between work and life, and you honor those boundaries through careful communication.

All of these things combined equal what we call Togetherness. You may have your own definition, or things you would add or take away. But my headline is that I don't equate Togetherness with perfection. Instead, my focus is on intentionality, results, and impact. What I mean by this is it is possible to *appear* to be completely Together and not actually accomplish the things that matter. To create gorgeous deliverables that may look good, but not be user-friendly enough to get to the outcomes needed. Or to "get things done" without actively applying your own critical thinking lens to how these tasks serve the ultimate goal. To me, color-coding and formatting in a Google Sheet can be helpful strategies to get the work done well, but are never the end goal. I focus on prioritization, relationships, and making time for what matters most – which is entirely up to you, the reader, to define for yourself.

 Reader Reflection: What would Togetherness look like in your role? As we embark on this Togetherness Journey together, I do want you to keep a few things in mind:

- **Togetherness is a journey, not a destination.** There will not be a mountaintop moment where all of a sudden you magically hit Inbox Zero, every project is wrapped up neatly, and projects are delegated perfectly. I think of Togetherness as a set of small tweaks meant to make your work lives more effective and efficient – and, dare I say, joyful?!

- **Everything in this book is an offering.** It's a buffet of Togetherness, if you will. This book is not "must-read-then-implement-and-utilize-every-single-tool." Nope, not my thing, and shouldn't be yours either. Consider this a buffet – take a little of this, try a lot of that, reject all of that. Not everything is meant to work with all people in all contexts. Put Together your own Togetherness plate.

- **I assume you already have aspects of Togetherness in place.** Well, of *course* you do. You are functioning adults with jobs and personal responsibilities and more. If you have Togetherness practices that *work*, then by all means keep them. Use this book to enhance around the edges, pick up a few tips, and test out a few things.

FAQ: Does this text focus on work-life balance as well? To the extent you are interested in going there, I *do* focus on balance. Over the years my classes have naturally included some attention to your personal lives, including ensuring time for rest, leisure, family, and friends. We are each one human, with one calendar, and one life. Getting more Together at work will automatically reap benefits for the personal side of things. No more being awakened by your Anxiety Brain (coined by a member of the Together Team) in the middle of the night, finding yourself fumbling for a sticky note or your phone, or asking yourself if you *actually* sent that email or just composed it in your brain? All of those thoughts rattling around will eventually have a negative impact on your home life, whether that takes the form of distraction, irritation, or plain old exhaustion. My sincere hope is that, if your systems at work are written down and reviewed regularly, you will "trust" that your Together System has caught everything – thus freeing your mind to enjoy time away from work. That said, if you choose to read this book through a purely professional lens, we welcome that, and you will still find it effective.

WHY THIS BOOK MATTERS TO ME

Many people know me as Maia (Papaya), MHM, or simply That Together Lady. Seriously, the last one is what someone once called me on a plane when they recognized me!? Since 2012, I have released two titles, *The Together Teacher* and *The Together Leader,* and two micro books, *The Together Project Manager* and *The Together Work-From-Home Teacher*. Since 2005, my small-but-mighty team and I have conducted hundreds of trainings for schools, districts, and nonprofit organizations. I spend as much time in the field as possible, listening to and learning from people whose work usually involves important mission-driven outcomes, a heavy social justice component, and somewhat unpredictable environments. Combine that with passionate people trying to make the world a better place, and we have an occasional recipe for overwork and burnout. In almost every single training, I have a group of people who work, often behind-the-scenes, to make education and mission-driven entities function at a high level – people like human resource managers, district IT support, cafeteria managers, special education coordinators, executive assistants to CEOs, charter network recruiters, data managers, and so on. And I have a special place in my heart for these folks, the teammates.

I've always loved behind-the-scenes work – and making large ideas and events come to fruition through careful planning. I literally picked my college because, when I visited at age 16, I observed a massive joyful campus event (called Kids' Day at Tufts University) and thought, "I would like to run that community event one day." I was attracted to the moving pieces, the gathering of people, and the ultimate goal of welcoming the community onto a campus. And lo and behold – as a sophomore, I was elected to lead Kids' Day for the University. And while my career continued into direct service – as a teacher, as the leader of an intense summer teacher training experience, as an executive within an education organization, as a staff trainer, and then in my work directly with schools – I've always been the person who has asked the questions around *How* will we make this work?" Add in over five years of working on the operations side of schools and two decades of training people who work behind the scenes – from every single school secretary for Madison Public Schools to the assistants at YES Prep in Texas to all operations team members and staff for FIRST Inspires in New Hampshire – so at this point I have some unique insight into the skills, motivations, stressors, and success factors in these demanding roles. Seeing all of these dynamics at work has made me very excited to write a book specifically for those of you in support roles, and here you have it: *The Together Teammate* – the third title in what will now be a "Together Trilogy."

What I am utterly convinced of is that this behind-the-scenes work or "trains running on time," or however you define keeping the mechanics, operations, and logistics smooth is essential to making missions possible (Tom Cruise jokes aside). Without your detailed thinking, careful planning, strategic flexibility, and problem solving on the fly, the ultimate mission (for whomever your organization serves) is simply not possible. Maybe you are already there (and if so, congrats!), but imagine how fulfilling your work would be if:

- You roll out new software in your organization with a detailed training plan – and everyone follows the plan! The new software is up and running and making the organization's work more efficient.

- The school talent show runs flawlessly because you created a minute-by-minute plan so everyone knew where to be when. The students are so proud, and the parents so impressed!

- You distribute technology to every single staff member – and at the end of the year everything comes back! What a budget save!

- The board retreat has agendas distributed in advance, airtight audio, and a lunch menu that is appealing to all people. Now the board can make effective decisions to push the organization ahead.

- The hiring fair has a rotating cast of teammates all taking turns all day, gorgeous recruitment materials in hand, and the candidates are followed up with within 24 hours. What a win for hiring the right people!

You get the picture. You matter, your work matters, and I am passionate about helping you excel in this important work.

WHO, SPECIFICALLY, THIS BOOK IS FOR

I'll be honest. I grappled with this question of audience for years in the lead-up to this book, and even a bit while writing it. But after conducting dozens of interviews, this book emerged to fill the gap for roles such as:

- Nonprofit support staff, such as chiefs of staff, information technology associates, human resources professionals, finance analysts, marketing team members, project managers, recruiters, and other people in what are commonly known as functional areas

- School office staff, such as attendance clerks, secretaries, and assistants

- School professional staff, such as data analysts, budget managers, operations assistants, operations directors, and operations managers

- School district or education agency noneducation professionals, such as executive assistants, budget analysts, communications staff, finance assistants, grants and compliance teams, and so on

While the aforementioned groups are the focus of this book, I have seen my work easily fit into for-profit companies as well, so if you work for one of those, welcome. I'm glad you are here.

You may glance at the previous list, and think, "What do these people have in common and how does one book serve all of their Togetherness needs?" Well, the themes I've seen in Together Teammate roles are:

- You likely have a set of tasks that is proactive and predictable.

- You may also have a set of tasks that is reactive and customer-service focused – and not always predictable.

- You may directly interact with students, clients, or other stakeholders – or may be fully behind the scenes.

- You likely find yourself fielding last-minute requests or dealing with crises (hopefully this isn't a daily occurrence!).

- You may have mostly self-directed work or may spend your days responding to colleagues' requests.

- You sometimes do not manage others, but often need to influence your peers and managers.

- You ensure high levels of collaboration with other people to push projects ahead.

- Perhaps most challengingly, you balance a set of proactive, strategic projects while also dealing with reactive customer service work.

If any of these describes your work world, welcome to the world of Togetherness.

FAQ: Can I read this book if I am in operations, but I also manage others? Yes, absolutely. You may think about it for your own work, or skip ahead to Section 3 around mindsets and processes, especially if your Together Tools are already in place. Additionally, I have ended many chapters with what I call "Manager Moments" for anyone who wants to think about how they may want to use these tools and concepts as a leader of teammates.

WHY TOGETHERNESS MATTERS BEHIND THE SCENES

I certainly understand the temptation you may have to say, "Why on *earth* should I bother even trying to get Together? Have you seen how my day blows up? I am quite literally cleaning up after people all day long." And yet . . . Your Togetherness matters deeply, and over the past two decades, I've had the privilege of working with people in behind-the-scenes roles in nonprofits, schools, school districts, and occasionally large corporate settings. It is clear just how much you are juggling, and why getting and staying Together are mission-critical. These quotes from my Together course participants tell some of that story.

- "Togetherness matters to my specific role because I am responsible for ensuring that both schools run as efficiently as possible, which means that critical tasks from bus assignments to accounts payable need to be completed on a daily basis."

- "My team members and principals depend on me to prioritize for the team, get things done, and follow through on commitments. Togetherness is keeping the ball rolling and strategically prioritizing projects for my team."

- "I have to organize all students' special education paperwork and coordinate deadlines. I also have to balance this with managing, coaching, and evaluating five people. Togetherness matters so that I maximize the time I am at work and still have time at home to do the things I love and keep me balanced."

- ◼ "Togetherness in my role matters because having all the records and information is vital to our schools getting the proper funding and the mobility of our students."

- ◼ "I get constant interruptions from staff and families. That said, they are the priority and making sure their needs are met is of utmost importance. From needing a paper clip to a family emergency, it is important to that individual. The balance between taking care of staff and families and, say, entering payroll is the tricky part!"

I'm sure these quotes resonate with you, and that is why you selected this book. I hope you saw the themes such as "vital," "maximize," "balance," "prioritize," and "follow-through." It should be clear by now that I believe your roles as Together Teammates are unique! Through your careful attention to details, specific tasks, and behind-the-scenes concerns, you are ultimately supporters of a larger goal – whether that is achieving a certain mission or making greater impact in a certain area – or both. My favorite way of understanding the importance of your roles is this quote from a former colleague: "Smooth operations are like air. They are expected, and no one notices. But when operations are bumpy, it is a crisis – and everyone notices." To me, this speaks to the vital nature of your roles, the essential value of your work, and how necessary it is to enable the work to run smoothly.

I know your jobs are both demanding and rewarding, and my hope is that this text helps you find a way to be structured, yet spontaneous. Planned, yet flexible. Have the work be meaningful, yet manageable. Able to forecast events, but also focused in the moment. My wish is that this book unleashes your potential, gives you permission to plan, and helps you feel the value you add to your organization or team.

 Reader Reflection: Why does Togetherness matter in your role? Why did you pick up this book?

Now that you have jotted a few notes on why Togetherness matters, let's chat about what I call Together Try-Its. These are some particular habits I have observed the *most* Together Teammates exhibit and practice on a daily basis.

TOGETHER TRY-ITS

As I interviewed, shadowed, and reviewed samples from dozens of Together Teammates over the course of two years, a few habits kept bubbling to the surface. Whether these individuals were in nonprofit roles, school-based roles, or other supporting roles, the practices they exhibited throughout their workdays were similar. I call these Together Try-Its. In some cases, I have written entire chapters about them, and in all cases, I have woven them in throughout the text. Let's review these Try-Its together and define them. As you read them, consider how you do or could exhibit these in your work.

- **Pause to Plan.** While this Together Try-It is not limited to teammates, it is so important that I want to call it out. Take time at consistent intervals to pause and plan for the coming days, weeks, and months. Set an agenda and outcomes for this time, and recognize it as integral to your work.

- **Pivot Powerfully.** Discern when a pivot is needed and when it isn't. When a pivot is needed, waste no time in reworking your plan for the day, keeping the correct priorities at the forefront.

- **Close the Loops.** Track tasks through the process until completely resolved. You should be tracking every item you toss out into the world and pushing it ahead until it is complete and tied neatly in a bow.

- **Own the Outcome, Not the Task.** In many cases, you may be assigned a particular task, and it can be very easy to just complete the task and cross it off the list. Consider your work complete only when the desired outcome is accomplished, rather than the To-Do checked off.

- **Show Your Work.** Communicate consistently about your projects and tasks, preemptively answer questions, and provide information at the time people need it. Be prepared to show behind-the-scenes steps, if required.

- **Forecast Forward Frequently.** Be the person who is looking ahead on the calendar, identifying potential collisions, and backwards mapping for the team.

- **Be the Bird's-eye.** Often you will be the only person who sees the full picture of a project or task, and you can play a role in helping others see how all the pieces fit together.

- **Spot the Need for Systems.** As you see patterns of one-off requests and tasks, constantly consider the value of a system to solve the challenge – and then propose that system. Anything you can do to automate processes, make tasks predictable, and reduce decision-making fatigue will be deeply appreciated.

- **Stand in the Shoes of Others.** As you create documents and design plans, place yourself in the shoes of the end user. Picture others working through your directions and information and do your best to set them up to be successful.

- **Clear the Cobwebs.** You may have projects or tasks that are a bit . . . shall we say, murky? Your job as a Together Teammate is to synthesize information, get rid of the static, and ultimately help get situations to clarity. Break it into manageable pieces, discern key questions, and push those questions to get answered. Practice helping others do this with their work, too.

- **Keep it One-Click.** When providing information to others, consider how you can convey the information with the clearest context, the maximum information, and the decision point or key details at someone's fingertips.

- **Get Recommendation Ready.** You may think you are just here to execute what others dictate or delegate, but my hope is that you play a role in research and recommendations of the best possible outcomes for any upcoming decision. Instead of just saying, "What should we do for team holiday gifts?" align on parameters, generate options, and put forth a recommendation.

I know some of the Together Try-Its may feel impossible or not welcomed, and that is why I call them "Try-Its"! It is possible that some of them may not work in your organization, and that is fine. Consider them practices to experiment with and have in your Together Toolkit.

 Reader Reflection: Which of these Together Try-Its feel familiar or easy? Which feel like they might be harder to try?

Now that I've painted a picture of what habits a successful Together Teammate demonstrates, let's see how this book is organized to help you reach your peak Togetherness.

HOW THIS BOOK IS ARRANGED

This book is arranged in three main sections, and I generally recommend reading the text in order, though by all means, if certain chapters or sections jump out to you, start there! Within each of the sections, you will encounter some practical interludes to put the ideas into practice.

Section 1: Take Stock: Know Your Role and Set Your Priorities. The first section of the book focuses on making sure your role is clear to you and others. Then I work to help you establish clear goals and priorities to guide your time and work. Lastly, we focus on the Year-at-a-Glance to gain hold on the tasks and patterns throughout the year – something I promise you'll find useful even if you have been doing your job for a long time.

Together Teammate Self Assessment. Before you dive right in to building a bunch of Together Tools, I want you to pause, use my Self-Assessment to figure out your existing strengths, and identify a few areas for growth. This will also help direct your reading throughout this book.

Section 2: Get Yourself Together: Create Your Together Tools. The second section of the book focuses on what I call the Together Tools, the components of which will help you capture incoming work and then prioritize and plan on a daily and weekly basis. I will share examples of longer-term lists, methods for handling the daily deluge, and effective ways to manage projects. Woven throughout this section is an exploration of a variety of tools – with both paper and digital options – for you to determine what suits your own preferences and work environment.

Put it All Together: Build Your Together System. In this brief section, we explore ways in which you will want to practically implement your Togetherness. Clipboard person? All digital? Move around all day between sites? I want your system to be airtight and trustworthy.

Section 3: Get the Team Together – Teammate Tricks to Move the Work Forward. The final section of the book focuses on practices of the most Together Teammates we have worked with over the years. It is a culmination of dozens of interviews, reviews of samples, and many stories and examples of how people in roles like yours have not only excelled but also felt balance, agency, and autonomy over their work. Focused on concepts like "systems spotting" and "outcomes ownership" of the work, I hope this section helps you feel empowered and ready to grow in your career.

Together Tours. I'm a realist, and I believe there are many ways to do Togetherness well. To illustrate this point, I've interviewed and included several Together Tours where individuals in teammate roles share their approach to Togetherness, how it has evolved over time, and how they have built tools to stay Together. My hope is that at least one of these will spark something for you and inspire you as you set up your own Together System.

Conclusion. In the final chapter of the book, you will find some options to reset when days go off the rails, take colleagues on a Together Tour, and stress test the entire thing. You will also figure out your personal method for implementing different sections of the book.

Additionally, because I know some folks will read this book through the lens of how they can support their teams, I have added **Manager Moments** to the end of most chapters. I recommend managers read each chapter in full first, and then use the Manager Moments to assist with implementation.

FAQ: Will this book help me if I have been in my job for a long time? Yes! I wrote this text to help all people in teammate roles – whether brand new, a few years in, or with dozens of years' experience in their role. If you are figuring out what the heck is even happening in year one or trying to change a culture two decades in, this book will give you tools to set up and sustain your systems – and even your organization's systems – for the long term.

Terminology Choices

Because this is a text that will be read by anyone from an executive assistant to a chief operating officer – and countless roles in between – I tried to use more generalized terminology throughout. Additionally, some readers may work in nonprofits, others in schools, and still others in hospitals and other mission-driven environments. There are a few terms I use interchangeably throughout, and I encourage you to substitute your own language as it fits.

- *Manager.* Some people use supervisor, or boss, or other terms. Generally, when I use the term "manager," I am considering the person you report to.
- *Colleagues.* I use this term to mean people with whom you work regularly and closely in your organization. Speaking of . . .
- *Organization.* I use this and it could be swapped for company, team, school, or another term that describes your entire entity.

With regard to pronouns, I will use contributor's first names and preferred gender pronouns when referring to direct quotes and artifacts. When using fictitious or generalized people, I will often use they/them pronouns.

HOW TO MAKE THE MOST OF THIS BOOK

I don't recommend inhaling this text in one sitting (unless you truly want to). In fact, I assume you all have some pretty strong Togetherness practices in place already – and you just came here for more. I assume you have some tools and habits that already work really well for you, and that's great – keep them in place. Consider this text a chance to polish up any rough parts, find any missing pieces, and generally enhance your Together Toolkit. I suggest you plan your overall path through the book over time, and grab the chapters that ring most strongly or where your Together Self-Assessment directed you.

There are a few features that could help make this text come alive for you:

- **Reader Reflections.** Sprinkled throughout each chapter, you will find questions to support your exploration of your own tools and habits. You can either print out the Reader Reflection at www.wiley.com/go/togetherteammate or use the downloadable electronic version from the same location. You are also welcome to take old-fashioned notes within the book, if you wish. The Reader Reflections are designed to push your thinking and also force a bit of decision-making as you consider how to take the principles I'm promoting and make them work for you in a tangible way.

- **FAQs.** Given my experience supporting many Together Teammates over time, I have tried to anticipate questions you, the reader, may have about various tools or routines. I am also keenly aware of how difficult Togetherness can be, and I try to offer concrete tips and stories throughout.

- **Turbo Togetherness.** The Turbo sections serve as chapter conclusions. They restate the key points of the chapter, and summarize the next steps to get you started right away.

- **The Together Group website.** To stay current on new technology, Together experiments, and other people's approaches to Togetherness, be sure to check out my blog and other resources on our website at www.thetogethergroup.com. You can also complete a contact form and reach me directly with any thoughts and questions.

- **Together templates and book samples.** We have created a set of downloadable, modifiable templates for you to use if you find any of them helpful, and to customize as you see fit. Additionally, you can also view many of the samples featured in this book up close and in full color at www.wiley.com/go/togetherteammate.

- **Social media.** For a bit of Togetherness fun and behind-the-scenes view of my own life and work, you can find me on Instagram, occasionally on Facebook, and on LinkedIn. You can also sign up for my monthly Together Tips newsletter at https://www.the togethergroup.com/contact/newsletter/.

You may also find yourself setting this text down for a while, digesting one particular chapter for a month, and then coming back to revisit later. Or you may feel perfectly Together *now*, but want to dust off your Togetherness skills for an upcoming job or life transition. The point is, use this book in the way that is most helpful to you in this moment!

LET'S GET THE TOGETHER PARTY STARTED!

This book is one of the most important texts I've written because I've come to believe *your* roles – the people magically, smoothly, and proactively moving things ahead – are what unleash the potential of an organization's mission. Yet sometimes your roles get left behind because there is so much focus on the program – whether that is the students, the young adults, the workforce – that the support systems can be forgotten. I've been privileged to work with many Together Teammates over the years, and I'm eager to finally have a text that empowers you in the unique aspects of your roles – as well as gives you the appreciation you deserve.

Ready? Let's do it! Now that you have started to consider the tools and approaches that will help you get it Together, let's begin with Roles, Priorities, and Year-at-a-Glance.

CHAPTER 2

Get Crystal Clear – Roles, Priorities, and Targets, Oh My!

I hope you are fired up and ready to go after reading the introduction to this book. But before we go all in on To-Do lists and calendars, it's time to get clear on your overall charge in your role. In any position, it's important to articulate the actual outcomes that spell out success for that particular role. Because this text is focused on people in service-oriented and often process-oriented roles, outcomes can be more challenging to identify. But if you don't get clear up front, you don't have a way to see and track your results. This matters because, well, we all want to know we are meeting the expectations of our roles – and it is gratifying and empowering to feel confident in your contribution to the overall mission of the organization.

In this chapter, you will:

■ Clarify the expected outcomes and possible inputs of your role

■ Propose or refine priorities and goals

■ Track progress toward these priorities for yourself and share out that progress

■ Create your Year-at-a-Glance to see how the pieces fit together

Because sometimes teammate roles have outcomes that are fuzzy, because it is easy to get lost in the small tasks of the day, and because it can feel like you sit far from the actual mission of your organization, having a cohesive vision of success in your role (and how it fits into the overall work of the organization) *and* a path to get there will help you be effective, proactive, and successful. It may take some work on the front end to define the outcomes of your role – especially if you are brand new to your organization or have been doing the work a long time – but being able to see how you contribute to the mission, where your work adds value, and how you define success will make your role far more satisfying. Convinced? Concerned? Come join me on a process to achieve role clarity and understand how these outcomes fit into the broader work of the organization. Let's start with what success in your role actually looks and feels like.

WHAT IS YOUR ACTUAL JOB? GET CLEAR ON THE OUTCOMES AND INPUTS

Admittedly, this was one of the hardest sections of the book to write. With positions that often have millions of small tasks, it can be hard to define big-picture outcomes with clarity. But if you don't, you won't be able to hold yourself accountable for outcomes, think beyond the basics of execution, and see how your work impacts the larger mission of your organization. There is a lot of literature around goal-setting, such as Jim Collins's BHAGs (Big Hairy Audacious Goals), or SMART goals (specific, measurable, achievable, relevant, and timebound), or OKRs (objective, key results). Given the abundance of tools and language that already exists, it's likely your organization may have its own in place already. We recommend you check what your organization uses and use that as your base. If there isn't a set list of outcomes for your role, ask about how success in your role will be evaluated.

FAQ: What if there are simply no outcomes to be found anywhere? This happens. Whether your role is brand new or your organization is a start-up or there is simply no language around setting clear outcomes, you may hit only dead ends when searching for appropriate goals for your role. In this case, this chapter is all the more important for you! I recommend working through this entire chapter – and at the very least – setting clear outcomes for yourself and to share with a manager. Even if your manager has never thought in this way before, this is a helpful process to name what you are working toward and how. It will assist in showcasing the value you add to the organization, and it will keep roles and responsibilities clear. A few concrete actions you could take are:

- Ask your manager: "What does success look like for someone in my position?"

- Review your original job description. Typically, the areas of responsibility are spelled out and you can start there.

- Look at other examples from your organization. Maybe there is a role that is similar enough to yours that you can have a starting point.

- Find your organization's mission statement and consider how your work fits into the goals.

- Read board reports, quarterly updates, newsletters, or anything else that communicates progress toward the organization's mission.

Before we jump into priorities and target setting for your role, I want to make sure you deeply understand what your job responsibilities actually are (I'll call them outcomes for simplicity's sake) and what actions to take to achieve them (let's call these inputs).

Let's say you were a recruiter for your organization, and you may generally understand your job as the following areas: **Source, Recruit, Select, Secure, and Onboard.**

To take that a bit further, you may have asked in the interview process, "What am I actually responsible for in this job?' and the job description may have laid out some sub-bullets to support those outcomes.

You could use something like the following chart to determine inputs, or what you are actually doing each day, for each of those outcomes.

Outcomes	Inputs
Source candidates for various network positions	Source online databases and websites Comb databases of local universities
Recruit candidates from a variety of locations	Attend virtual and IRL job fairs Speak at business school events
Select candidates using our recruitment models	Design new interview materials to test skills for network roles Roll out online interview process

Outcomes	Inputs
Secure talent to commit to organization	Create sell package tailored to each candidate Collaborate with hiring managers for Day-in-the-Life
Onboard candidates through their first week	Join HR team for onboarding events Give school tours to connect to the mission

FAQ: Do I need to think about this if I've been doing my job for years?
I think yes. The reason I believe this is that I see roles and responsibilities start to morph and blob and one cannot even recall what exactly one was hired to do! Some scope creep, some covering someone's parental leave and then never giving the responsibilities back, and boom, you are semi-responsible for everything! By rebreaking down your role, it can help give clarity to where you should spend your time, how to set your goals, and where you may need (polite) boundaries.

If it feels a little hard to do this, then that is sort of the point. The reason I want to force the outcomes to be articulated is that will likely connect to your priorities, your Year-at-a-Glance, and ultimately your calendars, lists, and other Together Tools. Give it a try.

Reader Reflection: What are the outcomes of your role? What inputs are required to get there?

Outcomes	Inputs

DEFINE SUCCESS IN YOUR TOGETHER TEAMMATE ROLE – SET THOSE PRIORITIES AND TARGETS

The challenge in many Together Teammate roles is that measuring the impact and effectiveness of your work can occasionally be murky. For example, how do you measure the smooth logistics of the group interview day? Or if you play a role in supporting a data team, how do you measure your contributions to the board report? See where I'm going here? Because of this unique challenge, while I believe very much in priorities (mostly because they help determine where to spend your time), sometimes you will want to set specific targets. This helps you, as a Together Teammate, both measure your own success in your work (and identify areas for continued growth), and also articulate for others the clear targets you are reaching through your efforts.

Brett's Priority Setting

Brett, a regional director of operations in southern California, had to get creative with establishing targets for his team. To accomplish this, Brett provided a menu of options and then helped schools set their own priorities and targets depending on their individual context.

As you can see in this model:

- **Priorities are organized by role and into buckets.** In the roles of School Business Operations Manager, Registrar, Receptionist, and Operations Coordinator, each has clear priority areas, such as "Compliance," or "Attendance," or "Enrollment." This helps keep everyone focused on their main things.

- **Targets are specific and measurable.** Starting with the priorities for the role, one of which may be "support family engagement," Brett made the goal measurable – 30 parents attend the meeting – and then the teammate can lay out actions to achieve them.

- **Timeline and excellence-oriented.** When priorities are slightly harder to measure, you can still make them geared toward success. For example, "Lunch tables are set up before lunch daily." The timeline is clear, and you may need to even develop a picture of what a great lunch table looks like. Boom! You measured – and hit – that target.

Seeing priorities and targets rolled up for an entire team like this is helpful for a few reasons:

- Each person can see how they are contributing to the bigger-picture priorities. It's very motivating to think about how your specific contributions are helping recruit students to a school.

#	School Business Operations Manager	ADSO initials
(1)	Day-to-Day Ops: 3+ average on quarterly snapshots	
(2)	Compliance: 93%+ on Compliance Dashboard	
(3)	Student Recruitment: Will be an average of 2 metrics, each weighted at 50%: - October: % Enrolled to Norm Day Target for whole school on Norm Day for the ending year (SY20-21) - June: % Enrolled to Start of School target for entry grade on June 1st of the new year. (SY21-22)	
#	**Registrar**	**ADSO initials**
(1)	**Student Recruitment: FY21 and FY22 New Student recruitment goals-** Student Recruitment: Will be an average of 2 metrics, each weighted at 50%	
(2)	Attendance: 96% overall students attending all day in live and independent	
(3)	Compliance: 93%+ on Compliance Dashboard	
(4)	TBD	
#	**Operations Coordinator (minimum of two goals)**	**ADSO initials**
(1)	Operations Compliance: Day-to-Day Ops: 3+ average on quarterly Health & Safety snapshots	
(2)	**Enrollment: Student Recruitment: FY21 and FY22 recruitment goals: Marketing /Communications**	
(3)	Family Engagment: At least 30 parents attend every parent meeting	
(4)	Day-to-Day Ops: 3+ average on quarterly snapshots: CEP 100% families submission	
#	**Receptionist (minimum of two goals, borrow from BOM goals where applicable, i.e TNTP, enrollment)**	**ADSO initials**
(1)	**Enrollment: Student Recruitment: FY21 and FY22 recruitment goals** Sub Goal: Present virtually at 2-3 community events, preschools, or city council meeting between October 6-Feb. 12	
(2)	Day-to-Day Ops: 3+ average on quarterly snapshots	
(3)	Family Engagment: Co-Lead 1 Parent Workshop between October - May 2021	

Figure 2.1   Brett's Priorities and Targets for His Team.

■ These priorities can help you communicate and align your time to work to meet them. "Hey team, I'm heads down preparing for this family workshop today!"

■ Gives the team a rallying point and an opportunity for celebration and appreciation. "Hey all, you rocked that – we reached our target of 30 parents in attendance!"

No one likes working without a purpose, so taking the time to spell out the priority and target up front will pay off in the long run. This allows you to see if you are meeting expectations, identify where you can strengthen your organization, and see your contribution to the mission. Sick of hearing me say that yet? Good, because I may repeat it in different forms at least 10 more times.

We just reviewed a model for setting priorities and targets across a team; now let's peek at a team still in the teammate realm, but in roles with more autonomy over their work and time.

Jenn's Team-Level Targets

In an education nonprofit, senior team members set targets around staffing summer trainings. Jenn, a leader at a national nonprofit, worked with her team on their priorities and targets for a summer teacher training institute. They did this based on past data and current needs. Similar to the previous examples, Jen worked to make the team's targets very measurable, sometimes in creative ways.

STAFFING

- Maintain 48 hour or less response time in Staff Inbox
- Develop report summarizing Staff Inbox trends and activities created to inform FY21 strategy
- 100% of all pre-service programs are staffed by first day of training week
- 90% of national staff members are hired in time to attend summer staffing training
- 60% of staff members identify as a person of color
- 40% of staff members, who disclose, identify as coming from a low income background
- Hiring team has a set of updated job descriptions for all national roles by October 1
- Retention campaigns are completed by November 27
- 100% of hiring teams feel the staffing process was clear and met their needs to staff their sites with high quality, diverse staff members in FY20
- 95% of offer letters – from staff retention through late staffing – are generated on the agreed upon timeline with Human Assets
- 90% of pre-service programs who accessed centralized staffing resources or other staffing supports agree that they were valuable and supported them with staffing their sites
- 90% of site directors and ops leads feel the staffing process was clear and met their needs to staff their sites with high quality, diverse staff members in FY20
- 80% of staffing leads feel they're a part of the supportive network of pre-service staffing leaders by the end of the season

---

Figure 2.2   Jen's Team-Level Targets.

As you can see, this team's priority as it relates to staffing falls in a few buckets to help make the targets measurable.

- **Deliverable-oriented.** For example, "Develop report summarizing institute inbox trends." The target is completion of an excellent report.

- **Customer-service perceptions.** In many customer service roles, no matter how senior, there may be targets around meeting particular timelines, such as "Maintain 48 hour or less response time on Institute Staff inbox," and "100% of people feel the staff process is clear." This is key because much of your work may have timeline implications in terms of how people feel about the work based on how quickly you can respond.

- **Process-related.** Process-related goals relate to designing, rolling out, and executing a process on your team. For example, "Retention campaigns are completed by November 27." This relies on this team to build a retention campaign. Yes, there may be an outcome attached to that, like 90% of staff retained, but this operations team may share this outcome with other members of the team.

This blend of targets represents the challenges and solutions to coming up with priorities and targets for Together Teammate roles – ultimately supporting the larger part of a mission through important functional work that helps drive the priorities.

 Reader Reflection: Do you need to refine any priorities to make them more measurable?

GET YOUR OWN PRIORITIES IN ORDER

I am deliberately *not* using the word "goals" in this chapter very often. The reason is that a lot of your organizations may have or not have language around this, all of which may vary. To try to simplify the equation I'll be calling them priorities (what matters most) and targets (how you know you achieved them). Whatever you call them, the most important thing is you *have* them, and in my experience, I frequently see them set for programmatic roles or more senior roles, but the operations and support roles are often left hanging to figure out on their own. So let's do this. Let's figure them out so you can celebrate your successes and see where you can continue growing.

CHECKLIST FOR PRIORITY/TARGET SETTING IN TOGETHER TEAMMATE ROLES

■ Is there any organizational guidance I can use as I set my priorities and targets?

■ Is there anything included in my performance evaluation?

■ Is there an appropriate number of priorities and targets? (Meaning don't have just two, but also not an epic spreadsheet either.)

■ Are my targets clearly measurable? On what intervals?

■ Will I be able to unambiguously and easily see if I have hit my targets?

■ Can I see how the priorities fit into the mission of the organization?

■ Have I communicated or sought input from my manager or colleagues for my priorities?

Typically, I see three ways to set targets to measure your priorities in teammate roles. Some may fall into several categories, and these buckets are meant to give you guidance to make things measurable.

■ **Deliverable-oriented.** These goals are often related to producing something needed for the team, such as a report or a grant proposal.

■ **Customer-service focused.** Stakeholder-focused goals are measured via surveys issued to people and their feedback. For example, if your stakeholders were regional executive directors rating the smooth conference operations on a survey at the end of the conference, that would be your data to measure your success.

■ **Process-related.** Process-related goals may be measured in several ways, but they are usually something like "Improvements to parent newsletter."

If you do not have any priorities or targets in place, and your organization doesn't have interest in setting them, set your own and propose them to your manager or colleagues. You want to focus your work on what matters and communicate your progress to others. Naming these targets is also a unique way to draw boundaries around your role. I'm *not* saying that you should do this in order to start saying no all the time, but rather when new work is assigned, you may say, "Let's see how this fits in with the other parts of my role we have established." If you find your work frequently outside the bounds of agreed-upon priorities, it may be time for a courageous conversation about a title change, a salary increase, or some other form of recognition for the additional work you are doing.

Now that you have your priorities in place, you will want to figure out the best way to track and communicate progress toward the targets.

TRACK FOR YOURSELF AND SHARE PROGRESS

Often you will have to be the person keeping your goals front and center. It can be easy to slide out of the spotlight in supporting roles, and this is okay. However, you want to keep your priorities front and center for yourself, to help focus your work. In this section, I will explore how to track your own progress, and sometimes use your targets with your manager(s) and colleagues to stay focused on existing and new work, define success, and discuss challenges.

Using your priorities and targets to update your manager on progress at some regularly scheduled interval does the following:

- Demonstrates your tangible contributions to the organization's overall mission

- Highlights need for help or capacity when working on priorities for others

- Celebrates success in targets reached and helps you and the organization take on new challenges

Let's peek at a few models of ways to both track and then share out your progress – for yourself and others.

Priscilla's RSVP Tracker

Priscilla, a director of operations for a start-up advocacy organization in Oakland, was responsible for recruiting and marketing to drive attendance at various voter candidate events around the city. She was in charge of multiple events at one time, and she had clear and measurable targets in place related to each event. Let's look at how she set up her chart to track RSVPs to direct her own work and then share with her manager.

	Goal	8/31/20	9/7/20	9/14/20	9/21/20	9/28/20	10/5/20
<u>Voting Power Pledge</u> - 11/3		37	37	37	37	51	52
D7 Candidate Forum Eventbrite RSVP - 8/24	202	202	202				
<u>D5 Candidate Forum Eventbrite RSVP</u> - 9/24	200	10	19	39	61	146	
<u>D3 Candidate Forum Eventbrite RSVP</u> - 10/1	200		0	9	18	31	62
<u>D1 Candidate Forum Eventbrite RSVP</u> - 9/30	200		0	27	35	49	94
<u>RSVP FIA Summit + Elections Kick Off</u> - 10/6	1000	9	12	25	29	36	50

Figure 2.3   Priscilla's Target Tracker for Candidate Forum RSVPs.

Priscilla worked with her manager to set targets per event, as well as ways to show progress in recruiting attendees. She set up a tracker in Microsoft Excel to record how RSVPs were looking against the overall target. This helped Priscilla – and her entire organization – in several ways.

■ **Communication and status check.** Priscilla tracks all incoming RSVPs all week and brings her tracker to her manager for their weekly meeting. This way she can give a written or verbal update on each event. This also taps into a few Together Try-Its all at once: Show Your Work and Forecast Forward.

■ **Ask for help.** If Priscilla noted that one event was lower in RSVPs than others, she could give data and context in a team meeting, discuss with her manager, and then the team could look as a whole on how to deploy resources to improve the outcome.

■ **Propose humans to help.** Often, as Together Teammates, by Being the Bird's-eye, you can determine and assist others with saying things like, "We have hit the goal for our 10/1 Candidate Forum RSVPs, but we are worried about the 10/6 event. I propose we move Martin's outreach to the 10/6 event."

Reader Reflection: How are you tracking progress for yourself? For others?

Shannon's Priority Tracker

Let's see how Shannon, a senior leader of operations, does this with her entire team. Shannon's team targets are listed by Priority Area, Goal, and Target. But most interesting is how she and the team track their progress.

Key Goal	Priority	SY20-21 Goal/Benchmark	Target	Owner	Current Status	Current Risk	Current Data	Links to Full Data
	Academics	% of Freshmen On Track	90%	HS PAL	On Track	Sunny	100%	
	Academics	% of grades 3-8 on track	80%	MS PAL	On Track	Sunny	73.57%	https://docs.google.com/spreadshe
	Student Agency	Average Daily Attendance	95%	DSOs	Missed	Typhoon	83.88%	https://docs.google.com/spreadshe
	Student Agency	% of students who have submitted at	100%	CC/CEO	Achieved	Sunny	100%	
5	Student Agency	% college acceptance (% of seniors	100%	CC/CEO	Achieved	Sunny	100%	75% of seniors have 2
	Student Agency	1-year dropout rate	3%	COO	Missed	Sunny	0.00%	In CPS dashboard
	Community	% of high school students on track to	90%	CC/HS				
10	Community	% of total staff (including 85% of key	75%	COO	Missed	Partly Sunny	81%	https://docs.google.com/spreadshe
7	Impact	Student return rate from Fall Count	15%	MCE	Missed	Stormy		https://docs.google.com/spreadshe
	Impact	% enrolled by First Day of School	100%	MCE	On Track	Partly Sunny	294 enrolled	- min of 321
	Impact	Days cash on hand in operating	30	COO	Missed	Partly Sunny	14 days	
	Impact	DQI (Data Quality Index) score 99%	99%	COO	Somewhat On	Partly Sunny	98.95%	Within CPS Dashboard

Figure 2.4 Shannon's Target Tracker.

As you can see, on a regular interval, Shannon and her senior team update the progress toward their targets with the following helpful categories in mind:

■ **List the priority.** This is useful so you can sort by the various areas of priority. In an ideal world, these are connected back to overall organizational priority areas.

■ **Spell out the target.** This is simply the exact thing you are shooting for. In Shannon's case, her team has set an exact percentage. Measurable! Clear!

■ **Name the owner.** Take the time to get clear on the actual owner of the target, the person ultimately responsible for ensuring the target is hit. This will become especially useful later in the book when I discuss Outcomes Ownership.

After that, Shannon and her team kept each other in the loop on progress by having sections for:

■ **Current status.** This is useful to see where things are at a given point in time. If you want to see the color-coded sample, peek over on the website at www.wiley.com/go/togetherteammate

■ **Current risk.** This category identifies where you are feeling confident or worried. Having this information can assist you in asking for help, managing expectations of others, and adjusting course. Shannon's team has descriptive risk categories from sunny to typhoon!

■ **Current data.** This forces you to measure progress toward certain targets at different periods of time.

Shannon says, "We revisited our goals weekly as a team because so much of our time can get swallowed by things that feel critically important but actually have nothing to do with our goals. Keeping our priorities front and center reminded us to prioritize the work that was actually most important to achieving them, and helped build ongoing accountability."

Whether for an individual or an entire team, the transparency of priorities and targets is helpful to give you insight into your work, help you Pivot Powerfully if things are off track, and focus your time and collaborate with others.

To be clear, regular updates on progress toward outcomes isn't unique to Together Teammate roles. However, priority-setting and progress-tracking are often overlooked in your roles because it is easy not to pay attention to the countless small details that ensure these tasks go flawlessly. Managers *want* all of these things to go well, but they are likely not attuned to the millions of steps it takes to actually make it happen. It could be easy not to notice how well a trip was planned, how smoothly credit card reconciliation went, or how flawlessly laptop distribution flowed this year. Remember in the introduction of this book when I mentioned a former colleague who said "operations are like air"? This is why it is helpful to track and share your successes in making things go smoothly.

 Reader Reflection: How will you keep your manager, your team, and yourself informed on progress toward priorities?

 FAQ: All of this data and numbers and targets and such is making me feel icky and micromanaged. Why do I have to do this again? Good question. It certainly doesn't mean you are a failure if you don't hit them, but more a sign that perhaps your tactics are not the right ones and you may need to change course on how you spend your time and assign your tasks. No one likes to feel like they are just a robotic set of numbers, and if the goals are used well, it should feel exciting and motivating.

QUESTIONS TO ASK YOURSELF AS YOU SET UP TARGET TRACKING

☐ How often and in what way do you need to check in with yourself about progress toward priorities? (Note there is an upcoming chapter on a Meeting with Yourself, which is a natural inflection point each week.)

☐ Who is the right person (or the right people) to share your progress with? Is it by email, within a meeting, or part of some more formal presentation?

☐ What are the right intervals to share progress? Is it a fast-paced project, like Priscilla's, or priorities and targets for the year, like Shannon's and Brett's?

☐ What data or self-reflection do you need to assess your progress?

☐ What is the most digestible format of progress tracking? A simple table? A slide?

☐ What do you want your action steps to be afterwards? How can you record them? The next section of this book introduces a few Together Tools, such as Long-Term Lists and Weekly Worksheets, that can support you taking action after reflecting on progress.

Now that you have a clear sense of the outcomes you are responsible for and how to share progress along the way, I think it can be helpful to take one final step and see how they fit into a full yearly cycle. This is what I call a Year-at-a-Glance. Let's consider this final step.

YEAR-AT-A-GLANCE – MAP IT ACROSS A CALENDAR

Almost all of the samples to follow show individuals or managers of behind-the-scenes roles thinking long-term over the course of the year. On one hand, you could operate in the mindset that every minute is a crisis or last-minute emergency. And that may be true a small percentage of the time, but for most of you, there is a predictable flow for the year, if you can Be the Bird's-eye and pick your head up to lay it out clearly. The goal here is to see the big picture, so that you can prioritize and make the right choices in the day-to-day.

Whether your role has existed for 20 years and been done successfully before or if your role is completely brand new in a start-up organization, you will want a sense of what is coming your way so you can ensure your workload actually achieves the goals from the first part of the chapter. In my experience, it is rare you will be handed an exact playbook for your particular role, or if you are, you will be handed something so complicated you will need to define it for yourself anyway. Enter what I call a Year-at-a-Glance.

Sometimes your head can get stuck in executing the project or event you are in, and before you know it, you take a breath and find yourself amidst the next one, already feeling behind again. This can result in never feeling like you have the space to do the prep needed on a timeline that will make it all feel manageable.

 Year-at-a-Glance: A bird's-eye view of your buckets of work and associated tasks laid out across a longer-term time frame. (Not necessarily a year, but go with me here! You'll want it to be at least a few months.)

SHELLY'S YEAR-AT-A-GLANCE

Shelly, a former program assistant in a university setting, created a Year-at-a-Glance for her role across various departmental initiatives. Her role included lots of day-to-day functions: reception duties (answering phone and greeting visitors), ongoing communications (weekly email newsletter, social media for the department), financial functions (expense reports, invoices, ordering supplies). With the combination of these recurring duties, but then other more seasonal items, it was helpful for Shelly to lay out her Year-at-a-Glance.

Civic Engagement Department Program Assistant Year-at-a-Glance												
Month	September	October	November	December	January	February	March	April	May	June	July	August
University Calendar	orientation & fall quarter starts	fall quarter	fall quarter	finals & winter break	winter quarter starts	winter quarter	finals & spring break	spring quarter starts	spring quarter	finals & graduation	summer	summer & fiscal year ends
Department Happenings	*Fellows training *Voter Registration Drive			*Launch summer application	*Applications incoming	*Applications incoming	*Applications incoming	*Launch Fellows application	*Fellows selection	*Summer program starts	*Summer program	*Summer program ends
My role	*training logistics *prep all voter reg forms *process completed forms	*process completed voter reg forms		*market launch of summer program	*process summer program applications	*process summer program applications	*process summer program applications	*process fellow applications *interview candidates	*interview candidates	*On-site summer program logistics *Honoraria for guest speakers	*Honoraria for guest speakers	*Logistics for closing celebration *Honoraria for guest speakers *start voter reg prep *fiscal year closeout

Figure 2.5   Shelly's Year-at-a-Glance.

Let's see what Shelly did here:

■ Laid out her specific Program Assistant responsibilities, such as processing applications, interviewing candidates, and training logistics.

■ Then she added the University Calendar and Department Happenings so she could see the other things going on that impacted her role. For example, in December the application is launched, and this has a big impact on Shelly's workload. It is helpful for Shelly to know and plan for that in advance.

■ Lastly, Shelly can then communicate to people around her and know when there is time to get ahead on other parts of her role based on what the department is doing at that time of year.

ERYN'S YEAR-AT-A-GLANCE

Eryn, an associate at a DC-based nonprofit, created a Year-at-a-Glance of her entire program year so that she could understand the impact of the organization's calendar on her workload through the course of a year.

	Business Development	SLC	TLC	KC	EdEx	Operations + Logistic	Team + Strategy	Sustainability
June		–Tuition due	–Applications due –Interviews	–Applications due –Interviews				Ongoing–grants cycles
July							Team Retreat	
August			–Commitment forms due	–Commitment forms due	–Launch recruitment	–Reach out to Allison at TNTP for Insight survey data and actions steps		Board meeting (audit review, ED + org goal setting)
September			–Tuition due (link on website?) –Cohort launch	–Tuition due (link on website?) –Cohort launch				
October	–Target LEA list –Files, folders, etc							
November	–LEA emails sent –Publicizing							Board meeting (strategic planning)
December	–LEA meetings scheduled –Publicizing	–Launch recruitment			–Launch cohort		–Team stepback	
January	–LEA meetings begin –Publicizing							

Figure 2.6 Eryn's Year-at-a-Glance.

Eryn chose an academic year down the left, and the main functions of her role horizontally. This tool allows Eryn to do a few things:

■ Identify both peaks and valleys in her workload, and figure out how to lean into that rhythm.

■ Plan ahead to be sure each of these work streams is receiving the time and attention it needs to keep her overall work moving smoothly.

This is an example of an overall zoom-out to see the bigger picture before getting into the details. It can be very easy to get into the weeds of planning a cohort event or executing a fundraiser, but pulling up lets you see all of the puzzle pieces and how they fit together – which ensures that you aren't neglecting any aspects of your overall role. This can be useful if you have multiple projects, multiple managers or particularly heavy times of year. It also helps you play a role Being the Bird's-eye and the person who sees how the many moving pieces fit together. Lastly, it is a great chance to check in against your role's outcomes and priorities to make sure they are all reflected in a year.

Assuming no one handed you an exact playbook for your role, you'll have to build your own picture of the year – often by piecing together various sources of information. But it can feel challenging to figure out where to even begin, so in the next section you will find a step-by-step plan to understand your role. Even if you've been in your role for a while, you may find it useful to actually put what you know about your calendar into one place like these Year-at-a-Glance samples.

The task at hand is to create a Year-at-a-Glance that gives a high-level overview of how your workload supports achieving your goals and the organization's work over several months or the full year. So pull out or print out your Year-at-a-Glance and let's get started building a full picture. Now that you have seen some samples of how other people do it, it's time to build your own!

BUILD YOUR YEAR-AT-A-GLANCE

■ **Review your job description and outcomes** and get clear on items you completely own and when each should be started.

  ■ For example, let's say you are in charge of the annual book fair and it typically happens in April. My guess is you would need to start the planning with the vendor in December.

  ■ Let's plop that in the December bucket.

THE TOGETHER TEAMMATE | **YEAR-AT-A-GLANCE**

Top Priorities:
- •
- •
- •

Area of Responsibility	January	February	March	April	May	June

Area of Responsibility	July	August	September	October	November	December

RESOURCES: template

Figure 2.7   Year-at-a-Glance Template.

- ■ **Look on the organizational calendar** and find out your role in each event, whether supporting or staffing.

  - ■ For example, let's say you looked ahead on the calendar and noticed there was a data day at your school.

  - ■ While there is nothing explicitly stated in your job description, you can ask your manager, "What role, if any, do I play in a successful data day?" If their response is that you have a role, be sure to add that in to your Year-at-a-Glance!

- ■ **Understand your manager's calendar** and if any events impact your time.

  - ■ Outside of the organizational calendar, there may be other events where you lend support.

  - ■ For example, let's say your manager does a presentation at a conference each May. You should ask, "What is my role in helping you prepare for this conference? I anticipate you will want me to proofread the presentation, look at the guest list for possible networking, and put the agenda items into your calendar. Is that correct? Is there anything else I can assist with?" The next question is what timeline they want these things to be completed, so that you know where to slot them in to your YAG.

At this point, you have a high-level Year-at-a-Glance that shows the big picture of your role. The purpose of doing this is to anticipate the work and have a deep understanding of your predictable and repeated annual cycle.

TURBO TOGETHERNESS

The purpose of this chapter is to make sure you are clear on what you are working to achieve and how you will determine if you are successful. You identify priorities and set targets, for yourself, with your team, or both, and then you check how you are doing to get there. It can be easy and tempting to just jump into the work when there is so much to do right this very minute, but I promise if you step back, articulate clear outcomes and your path to get there, then you will both feel and be more successful in your role.

Here are the quick and dirty steps for this chapter:

- ■ Set your priorities with a manager or colleagues. If no one is doing this with you, I suggest you do it yourself and then share a draft with people and ask for feedback.

- ■ Track how you are doing toward those targets and share out as appropriate to colleagues or your manager.

- ■ Get a sense of your workload over the course of the year and lay out a strategy to plan ahead appropriately.

MANAGER MOMENT

If you are in the position of managing a person in a support role, you may be wondering how to support this process. Good, I'm glad you are thinking this way. Or maybe you even manage people who manage people and you need to figure out how deep to go into the roles and priorities. You have a few possible next steps:

- Make sure your Together Teammate is clear on their overall outcomes and the inputs to support getting there.
- Read this chapter with the member of the support team and ask them to create a draft of their own priorities and targets.

Together Tour

Ashley
Project Manager
Charlotte-Mecklenburg Schools
Charlotte, North Carolina

Ashley Cotton

WHAT IS YOUR MOST USED TOGETHER TOOL TO KEEP *YOURSELF* TOGETHER?

Pause to Plan. In my professional life, most definitely my Outlook calendar! I put everything on it (even little tasks that will only take a few minutes). This helps me not overlook anything, and allows me to manage my time appropriately.

In my personal life, the Notes app on my iPhone. My husband and I have a shared list of all the things we need to do, organized by category (for example, grocery store, house projects) and we check them off as we go.

HOW DO YOU RE-TOGETHER YOURSELF WHEN UNEXPECTED THINGS POP UP?

Plan to expect the unexpected! I build "flexible time" into my Outlook calendar every day. If nothing pops up, I use that time to get ahead on items that I have scheduled for later in the week. If something does pop up (and it often does!) I can shift tasks that need to be rearranged due to the unexpected and still complete them later that day, because I've given myself that buffer.

WHEN IS A TIME YOU HAD TO ADJUST YOUR TOGETHERNESS PRACTICES AND WHY?

I had to make some adjustments when transitioning to a new role! Prior to joining Charlotte-Mecklenburg Schools, I had a really good system for staying on top of my work at the education nonprofit I worked for. But once I joined Charlotte-Mecklenburg Schools, my old system didn't work anymore because it simply wasn't relevant to my new role. This made me realize that there are so many systems out there that help with Togetherness, you just have to find the right one for yourself and your context!

HOW HAS TOGETHERNESS HELPED YOU COMMUNICATE AND WORK WITH OTHERS?

 Clear the Cobwebs. Togetherness has helped me better set clear expectations of myself and teammates! I try to always end meetings by outlining our "next steps" and who is responsible. This way we all know what we need to do next and it's clear who should do each part.

HOW DO YOU HANDLE WORKING WITH COLLEAGUES WHO ARE SLIGHTLY LESS THAN TOGETHER?

 Stand in the Shoes of Others. Patiently 😊. And with friendly reminders! I often find that colleagues who seem "slightly less-than-Together" aren't intending to be disorganized; they just have too much on their plate and/or don't have a good system for keeping track. I'm not afraid to follow up on emails with gentle reminders or send a text to ask where they are on something and find out how I can help them accomplish it.

WHY DOES TOGETHERNESS MATTER TO YOU AT WORK AND AT HOME?

Togetherness for me is a "way of life." It helps me feel less stressed or worried that I will forget something knowing I have it written down somewhere!

Together Teammate Self-Assessment: Consider Your Current Organizational Tools, Habits, and Routines

Welcome to the world of Togetherness! It's Maia here and now that we have been introduced, and had the chance to work through your Roles and Goals, I thought it might be time for you to reflect on your current Togetherness habits and practices. Take a quick spin through this self-assessment (also available as the first page of our Reader Reflection – downloadable from www.wiley.com/go/togetherteammate). While I think reading *The Together Teammate* start to finish is generally best, this self-assessment could assist you in focusing your reading direction, celebrating your existing strengths, and considering what you can add to your Togetherness Toolkit.

Evaluate the degree to which your current practice meets the descriptions.
5 = awesome, 4 = good, 3 = so-so, 2 = some gaps, 1 = big gaps.

Bucket	
Bucket 1. My organizational system is Comprehensive and Reflects my Priorities.	**Ratings:**
a. I understand my role, the goals of the job, and the priorities I need to accomplish.	
b. My view of predictable and routine work for the year is clear and written down.	
c. My calendar reflects my priorities.	
d. I have time blocked for proactive work. I am usually able to respect this time.	
e. My system is comprehensive. For example, all deadlines are in one calendar. All To-Dos are in one place.	
f. I have a place to record longer-term action items and I regularly refer back to them.	
Bucket 2. My system helps me manage my Energy and Attention.	**Ratings:**
a. I plan my work with an eye toward my energy levels (if my role allows me the flexibility to do so).	
b. I am able to focus for a sustained period of time during work blocks.	
c. I complete tasks efficiently with little procrastination.	
d. I can accurately predict how long my To-Dos will take to complete.	
Bucket 3. My system lets me Plan, Prioritize, and Pivot as needed.	**Ratings:**
a. I pause to regroup and look ahead on a daily, weekly, and monthly level for myself and my team.	
b. I articulate my work to my manager and team so they have an appropriate line of sight into my role.	
c. When I feel overwhelmed or buried, I have a method for getting back on track.	

Bucket	
d. When I pivot to deal with a crisis, I'm aware of the trade-off(s) I am making.	
e. When I am over or under capacity, I communicate clearly and often with my colleagues and manager.	
Bucket 4: My system is Consolidated, Synchronized, and Streamlined.	**Ratings:**
a. I have a place to note immediate To-Dos that pop up during the day.	
b. It is always possible to use my system. For example, if I track things digitally, I can always access these digital tools.	
c. My system is highly portable; if I leave my workspace, it is easy for me to carry my tools everywhere all the time.	
d. If I use digital tools, my system is synchronized across all devices.	
e. If I use paper-based tools, they are consolidated into one clear system.	
Bucket 5: I create Systems, propose solutions, and look ahead regularly.	**Ratings:**
a. When I see a pain point in my work or the work of those around me, I pause to consider if a larger-scale system could alleviate the stress.	
b. When I notice a problem, I feel empowered to list possible recommendations to solve the problem.	
c. My written communication is clear such that it is easy for the reader to have all the information needed and reply or take action efficiently.	
d. I look ahead on my calendar and the organization's calendar to plan backwards to meet deadlines.	
Overall Strengths?	
Overall Areas for Improvement?	

In my 20 years of traveling and teaching Togetherness, I will often meet folks who are extremely eager to jump in headfirst. I assure you, it will hurt and your habits may not stick. I offer you a few ways to possibly focus your learning.

- **If you are in the earliest stages of Togetherness** (and occasionally identify with the term "hot mess"), I recommend starting with building the Weekly Worksheet in Chapter 6 and completing that Meeting with Yourself from Chapter 7. This tool/routine combo will provide you with the most immediate sense of relief in your workload. Do this for 4–6 weeks, tweak as needed, and then expand into other Together Tools for yourself.

- **If you came to this book with your weeks generally under control,** please pay special attention to the long-term tools I offer, such as Goals, Long-Term List, and Comprehensive Calendar. They will push you out of the day-to-day and get you into that Forecast Forward kind of mood.

- **If you arrived here with your Together Tools in place, but feel as if you are operating in Total Task Mode,** lean into Section 1 to make sure your goals are completely clear and you can see how your tasks add up to the larger picture.

- **If your personal Together Tools are totally set,** focus on Section 3 around Getting the Team Together – consider how you can communicate to lead others to action, make the most of your meetings, and really put a lot of the Together Try-Its in place.

- **If you are teaching others Togetherness,** note that, as my experience has taught me, Togetherness is an incredibly personalized topic that can also bring up lots of feelings for people. Pride, shame, guilt – you name it, I've seen it. For those of you coaching or teaching others, take time to learn their habits and preferences, what has worked and what hasn't, and remember *your* way may not necessarily (in fact, likely won't) work for anyone else.

- **If you are supporting a Together Teammate,** please don't just hand over this book and say "read it." Read each chapter alongside your teammate, review the Manager Moments (when applicable), and take time to discuss and contextualize along the way.

 Reader Reflection: Where does it make sense for you to jump in? Why?

Get Yourself Together: Create Your Together Tools

CHAPTER 3

Look Far Forward – Create a Comprehensive Calendar

Now that you have a clear sense of your Role, Goals, and Year-at-a-Glance, it is time to enter the world of your first Together Tool – and hopefully the one you may have in place already – a Comprehensive Calendar. The purpose of having your long-term calendar – likely laid out digitally in whatever calendar technology your organization uses – is to get a Bird's-eye view of upcoming events, *deadlines*, and appointments – across your own work calendar and organization, and maybe even your personal life too!

In this chapter, you will:

■ Capture all upcoming deadlines, events, FYIs, and appointments for the next 6–18 months

■ Determine the one consistent calendar you will use for all items

■ Consolidate various calendars into one singular location

While much of your work can feel day-to-day, even minute-to-minute, it can be helpful to step back, take the long view, and backwards map against deadlines. Picture the feeling of looking ahead and spotting a deadline for a big grant due in a few months that your manager is writing with your support. Once you spot that deadline looming, you can snap into action and play a role in blocking time on people's calendars to support the grant writing work, scheduling meetings to review progress, and ensuring you have the space in your days and weeks for the support you'll be asked to provide. And, because I hope this book is useful for personal priorities as well, you may look ahead and see an important birthday of a friend or family member, and you can get ahead on ordering a personalized gift or message now. Calendars may be technical, but they can also be meaningful.

WHY INVEST IN A LONG-TERM CALENDAR?

Of all the Together Tools, this one should feel the most obvious and familiar – which is why I'm leading with it. A Comprehensive Calendar is exactly what it sounds like – a singular (yes, you heard me right, though as always, there is flexibility around this) long-term calendar that captures every single deadline, event, meeting, FYI, and priority in one location.

> **Comprehensive Calendar:** A macro, long-term view of your time aligned with your priorities through thoughtful time budgeting and deadline consolidation.

For a lot of you, deadlines and events come flying from a lot of directions each day. Perhaps some are sent as actual calendar invites directly to your digital calendar. Lucky you, those are the easy ones. They are there waiting for you. But what I also want you to be on the lookout for is the other items that *should* land in your calendar but that often lurk in other locations, such as:

■ A newsletter that is sent by your manager or another team member with bunches of deadlines and events (This is especially important if your organization does not have its own calendar where items are already entered.)

■ A Project Plan with a whole lot of rows with your name on them with clear deadlines (more on Project Plans, both owning and being part of them, in an upcoming chapter)

■ Quick deadlines shared verbally at a staff meeting that impact your workload

■ An email sent by a colleague asking for a certain report at a certain date and time

■ A calendar sent by your kid's school with half-days, dress-up days for spirit weeks, and more

■ A grad school syllabus with project deadlines and term paper due dates

You see where I'm going with this, right? Dates and deadlines – for the short and long term – fly at you fast and furious all day long. I want you to have one location (that is not a list) to catch them *all* so you can see them on the landscape of a calendar. If they exist in separate locations, as in the bullet points above, then you run the risk of missing a deadline, not seeing when due dates collide, or not noticing a week that you may be completely over-tapped. Let's peek at a few examples of how Together Teammates use their Comprehensive Calendars to catch the deadlines, Forecast Forward, and Be the Bird's-eye!

COMPREHENSIVE CALENDAR SAMPLES

In this section, we will explore various samples of Comprehensive Calendars from individuals in Together Teammate roles as varied as directors of data analysis to talent recruitment managers to regional directors of operations. What you will see in each sample is that each individual took the time to record every single deadline, consolidate all calendars into a singular location, and review ahead regularly (more on that in a chapter on Meeting with Yourself). In most cases, these folks chose to use digital calendars because that is what their organizations already used. We will review options for tool selection coming up. As you look at these samples, pay attention to what you already do well (and my guess is most of you have a good starting point for this one) and where you may want to add additional components to your calendar.

Dominique's Combined Google Calendar

Dominque, a director of data and technology for a network of schools in New Orleans, keeps a robust Google Calendar. Let's peek at what she captures and why – and as always, if you want the full-color version, pop on over to the book's website at www.wiley.com/go/togetherteammate.

Dominique is using her calendar to its fullest, and let's check out some of the components she chooses to include:

■ **Physical location.** Dominique moves around between various school sites, a network office, and a home office. To keep all of this straight, and to share her location with her colleagues, Dominique lists her locations as "All-Day Appointments" at the top of her calendar, so it is clear when she is "Home," versus "Height" – one of the schools.

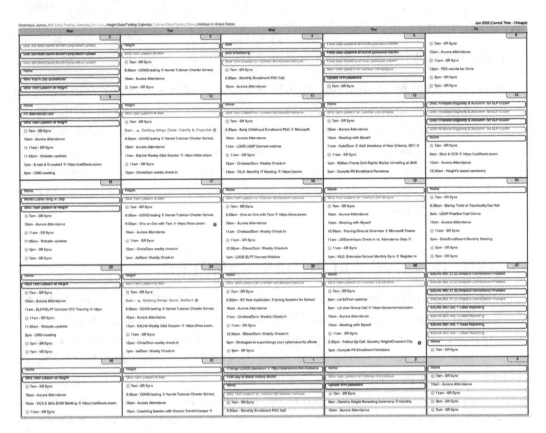

Figure 3.1 Dominique's Comprehensive Calendar in Google.

■ **Deadlines.** She records all deadlines in one single location, which allows a bird's-eye view of upcoming work. For example, on the 5th, the Food Data is due at noon. On the 12th, Eligibility for State Testing Accommodations are due. This is useful for a Together Teammate juggling multiple deadlines because it allows her to scan ahead and identify what is coming – and what she can get a head start on. Win-win.

■ **Combination of multiple calendars.** If you peek in the top left-hand corner, you can see that Dominique has added multiple calendars within her organization, such as the Data and Testing Calendars across all three school sites. This lets Dominique see what is happening in all the schools she supports. Google Calendar gives her the ability to view or not view particular calendars at any one time.

Reader Reflection: What are the sources of your multiple deadlines and due dates? List them here so you have them ready to go when you populate your calendar.

Figures 3.2A and 3.2B All-Day Calendar Appointments in Google and Outlook.

FAQ: Should I share my calendar with others in my organization? Of course, everything around here in the Together-verse is always understood as a matter of choice and preference. Most organizations I see with digital calendars do have some level of sharing happening, and permissions and viewability vary by organization. For example, some organizations allow everyone to see every detail of others' calendars and some places just show free/busy. In general, I view calendars as communication tools to Show your Work to others, signal your priorities and availability, and schedule meetings efficiently. If you are not sure of the norms within your organization, observe and ask!

Let's peek at another Together Teammate Comprehensive Calendar sample.

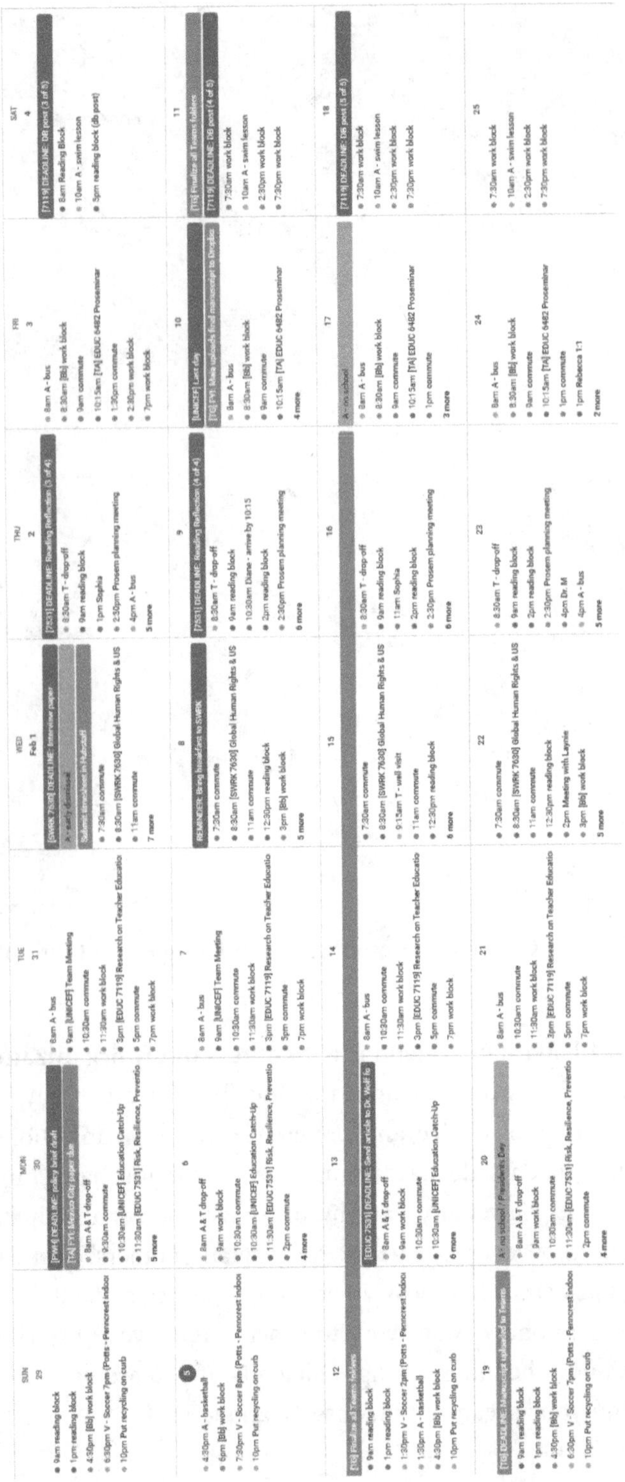

Figure 3.3 Maggie's Comprehensive Calendar in Google.

Maggie's Google Calendar

Maggie, a graduate student and member of the Together Team, uses Google Calendar to combine her graduate school life, her personal life as the mom of two small kids, and her work getting this very book in your hands. Let's see how she does this.

Similar to Dominique, Maggie gets the key components of a Comprehensive Calendar in place:

- **Key deadlines.** Maggie has varied sources of deadlines – even just for school, she has multiple classes, due dates, and exams! By taking items out of her course syllabi and loading them into her Google Calendar, she can see how all of her courses fit together. This also allows Maggie the time to plan ahead to meet those deadlines without the stress – we hope!

- **Put in the personal.** Maggie is also a working parent, and she pulls some important dates from her own kids' school calendars, such as noting there is no school on President's Day, and days with Early Dismissal. While many of you may balk at putting personal items on your Comprehensive Calendar, and I hear this, sometimes work and life deeply impact each other. Maggie needs to know when her son has a half-day because that impacts her work schedule.

- **Phases of work.** Of course, I should point out February 11–16, when Maggie inserted an all-day event over multiple days to get this very book in your hands prepared for the publisher. It helps to see the process span across multiple days because that lets Maggie pace out her work.

Reader Reflection: What personal items will you include on your Comprehensive Calendar?

FAQ: I don't want to share my personal stuff on my work calendar. What are my options? I hear you loud and clear. And some of you may work in organizations where it is just unacceptable – whether formally or informally – to have personal items in your calendar. That said, at some point you may have a dentist appointment in the middle of the workday and you need to make it clear you aren't available for meetings at this time. You do have some options here. The first is that you can simply mark the appointment as "private" and leave it at that. If that doesn't feel comfortable for you, you can also give your own appointments a

(Continued)

> secret code. For example, you could call your soccer game something like "planning work block." Or your last option is to utilize technology solutions and have separate calendars for work and home and set yourself up to view them both on all your devices so that at least all items are viewable in one digital home. As long as you can see all the calendars in one place to avoid Calendar Collisions, it's all good!

Let's peek at one more sample before I turn to summarizing the components and then ultimately walking you through crafting your own Comprehensive Calendar.

Stacia's Outlook Calendar

Stacia, a manager of talent recruitment for a network of schools in Nashville, uses an Outlook calendar to track all of her deadlines, for-your-informations (FYIs), and other key organization happenings. Let's look at the how and why of Stacia's approach in her Outlook-heavy work environment.

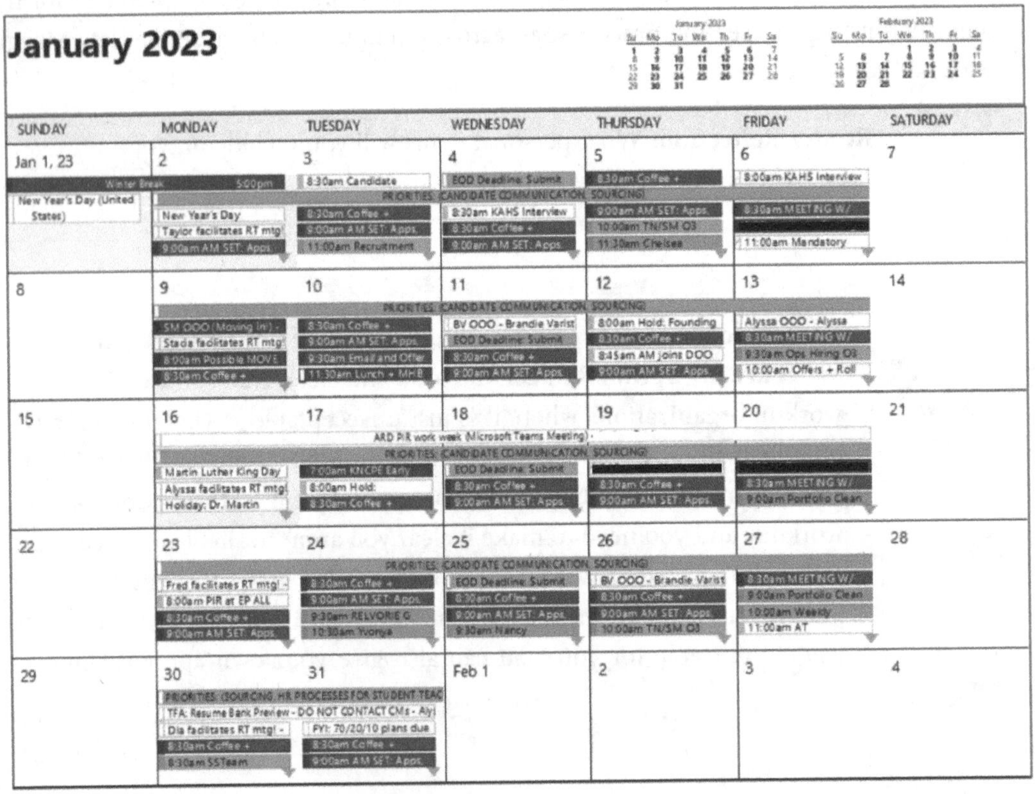

Figure 3.4 Stacia's Comprehensive Calendar in Outlook.

Similar to the previous examples, Stacia makes use of color-coding to delineate the components of her calendar. She makes a few other key moves to keep her calendar fully comprehensive. (You can see color versions on the book's website at www.wiley.com/go/togetherteammate).

■ **Strategic use of color-coding.** Color-coding can be a useful way to signal priorities, highlight deadlines, or otherwise visually delineate different kinds of projects.

■ **Lists priorities for the week.** This is a great use of the All-Day Appointment feature across several days to signal a phase. Stacia is able to boldly declare the priority of "Candidate Communication and Sourcing" and span it across the entire week (hint: might be time to reference your Year-at-a Glance!). This lets her check to see if she is spending her time on what matters during these days, and also communicate her priorities to others.

■ **Names colleagues out of office.** It is helpful for Stacia to know that on the 26th she has a colleague out of office. This kind of information lets her plan ahead, cancel or reschedule meetings, and otherwise be aware of what is happening around her organization.

 Reader Reflection: How would listing your priorities for the week in your calendar support your work?

 FAQ: What about the hourly portion of my Comprehensive Calendar? Should I use this too? Yes, you should! I will cover that more in the upcoming chapter on weekly planning. As you can see in Brett's example on the next page, Brett has all of the All-Day Appointments in full use to show his deadlines, due dates, and FYIs, and then he also goes in to add his meetings, personal obligations, and work time. Some of your jobs will allow you to block time on your calendars for items other than meetings, and some of you will need to leave that time open for incoming work – depending on the nature of your roles. But if you find yourself wanting to get ahead in this chapter, by all means, enter those recurring meetings, specific duties, and personal events too.

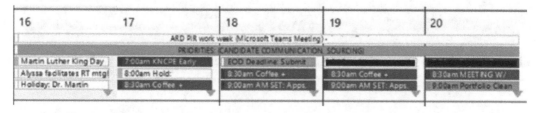

Figure 3.5   Up-Close All-Day Appointment Usage in Stacia's Outlook Calendar.

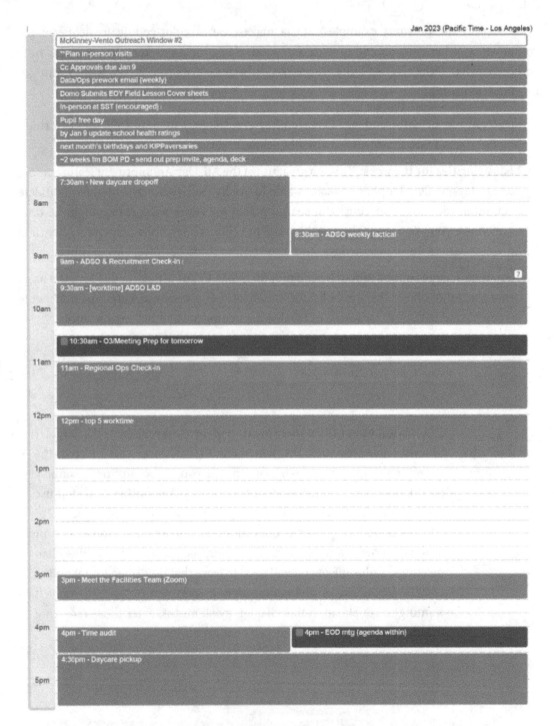

Figure 3.6   Brett's Comprehensive Calendar – with daily appointments added.

FAQ: Maia, I hate the monthly view of my digital calendar. Help! This comment deeply resonates with me. For those of you who also end up with many timed appointments and meetings in your workdays (more on that below), the monthly view of the digital calendar gets cluttered and clunky very fast. Consider it a view you flip to that allows you to plan ahead by scanning the All-Day Appointments, and a necessary evil. Occasionally, I find Together Teammates who prefer a wall or paper calendar, and I support this choice (and you will see more on this in the next sample). The challenge, of course, is so many of our meeting invites come in via our digital calendar invitations. If you choose to keep a paper-based calendar, you will have to do the extra work of taking everything out of the digital and writing it in your paper-based calendar.

Let's review one final Comprehensive Calendar version – a paper-based option.

Teresa's Paper-Based Calendar

Teresa, a senior manager of events and operations for a large charter school network, operates in an Outlook calendar environment, but sometimes finds the monthly view can get a bit cluttered. She keeps a visual paper-based calendar that shows her big events and travel only.

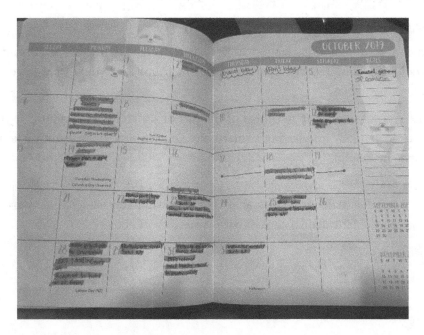

Figure 3.7 Teresa's Paper-Based Calendar Extraction.

As you can see, this kind of calendar is one that often brings great comfort and familiarity. It is portable and customizable – and perhaps, most importantly, lets you scan for the really big stuff without all the daily clutter. I refer to it as a Calendar Extraction. This is often a visual monthly calendar – perhaps on your desk, your wall (this is where I keep mine), or in a planner – that just highlights the big stuff. It isn't meant to keep everything (those details are over in digital-land), but lets you scan in a simpler way. Not everyone needs a Calendar Extraction, but if you find yourself drowning in details, it may be a great option to allow you to pick your head up into the bigger picture.

Now that we have reviewed several different models, identified essential components, and seen ways Together Teammates use their Comprehensive Calendars, let's select your tool and build your own!

SELECT A CALENDAR TOOL

Of all the Together Tools I discuss in this section of the book, this one may be the easiest to get started on because typically your organization chooses for you and it is likely Outlook, Google, or iCalendar. That said, if you need more portability or find it especially helpful to hand-write things or work on paper, you might go the direction Teresa has chosen. As you select your own personal Comprehensive Calendar tool, consider:

- How many different calendars do you have floating around? If you have more than four, my guess is you will want to consider a digital option.

- Do you personally prefer paper or digital calendars?

- How much does your organization utilize digital calendar invites? If all staff at your organization are expected to keep a digital calendar updated, you'll want to go with that digital tool.

- Are you in front of a computer most of the day or do you move around? If you move around a lot, you may find having a smartphone, tablet, or a printed-out version of your calendar to be helpful.

 Reader Reflection: Your answers above will likely lead you to your particular calendar tool. What is your tool of choice?

FAQ: How do I combine multiple calendars?

There are lots of instances of Calendar Babies, where you may find you have multiple digital calendars that you want to put in one singular location. For example, like Dominique, you may have multiple calendars connected to different sites you visit. Or like Brett, you may have different process calendars for things like testing or transportation. Fortunately, there are many technology solutions available, whether subscribing to one Google Calendar from another (check your calendar settings) or viewing your personal Google Calendar in the background of your Outlook calendar (the instructions change constantly for this, so internet your way into the instructions!).

BUILD YOUR OWN COMPREHENSIVE CALENDAR

All of this calendar excitement, right? Most likely you are at a good starting place for this process, but consider this moment a good Calendar Checkpoint for yourself. Pull out your chosen Comprehensive Calendar tool, get cozy for an hour or two, and let's get everything into one singular location. I'll take you through step by step to make it easy on you, I promise. Gather any and every calendar baby in front of you: Project Plans! School calendars! Conference calendars! Your kids' activity calendars! Grad school calendars! Tab them up or print them out and let's have at it.

Get Your All-Day Appointments in Order

- Add deadlines and due dates, both personal and professional, for items you both own and support. Make sure you consider one-off items and recurring items.

- Note key events, such as board meetings, galas, graduations, and other organizational happenings.

- Input FYIs, such as colleagues out of office, holidays, half-days, etc.

- Insert locations, if you move around or will be out of office.

- Plan your own Out of Office days . . . if you don't take them, they won't happen.

- Consider building in a Buffer Day if you will be out of the office at a conference or on vacation.

- Bonus points if you want to add a "start date" as an All-Day Appointment to help you get a good start on work well before the actual deadline.

At this point, I'm aware the All-Day Appointment feature will look very full. But at least you have one single source of truth and you can see what is coming for months ahead. How good does it feel to look down the road six months from now and be aware of every known deadline that is coming?!

Make Sure the Meetings Are in Place

This one's optional; it's meant for those who want to get ahead now. Remember that later there will be a time to build out the specifics of your day-to-day, but if you're feeling inspired, go ahead and do it now!

- Enter meeting times, locations, and preparation needed for any recurring or one-off meetings.

- Add any personal appointments that take place during work and nonwork hours.

Well, hey! Nice work. How did that feel? I did this process and just realized we have some spring break collisions in my family – for one and a half years from now! Well, at least Dr. Together and I can start thinking about our childcare situation well in advance – or at the very least, whether we can squeeze in a vacation with the Together Teens in a few years since all the school schedules line up for once!

HOW TO USE YOUR COMPREHENSIVE CALENDAR

Once your Comprehensive Calendar is up and running and full of all the things, my hope is this is an easy tool for you to maintain. A few tips to ensure your calendar is accurate, current, and comprehensive.

- **Portability.** Keep your Comprehensive Calendar with you at all times. Yes, that may sometimes look like your smartphone in your back pocket, ensuring your calendar is fully synched, or carrying your paper planner with you at all times. Deadlines and due dates pop up at the strangest of times, and it is easier to just load it in the calendar than write it somewhere else. If your role doesn't allow you to carry a smartphone or laptop, then keep a paper-based backup calendar to "catch" the deadlines and bring them to your digital calendar later.

- **Keep it really comprehensive.** Whether you merge into one calendar or subscribe from one to another, beware of deadlines that can be noted in separate locations. Your great-aunt's birthday *is* important, and I don't want it to get forgotten. Think of anything and everything that can land on this calendar (or at least in one viewable location) and get it entered.

■ **Look forward.** This will be a big topic of the Meeting with Myself chapter, but I want you to use your Comprehensive Calendar to Forecast Forward Frequently. The most Together Teammates are the ones who say, "Hey team, I was looking into May (yes, I know it is February right now) and I noticed that we have a team retreat without a location. I'm going to start the research for a venue now and bring it to our next meeting. Confirm or reject." I guarantee you will both be an office superhero and reduce any last-minute scrambles for yourself and the team.

The only way to make this calendar work for you is to ensure it is comprehensive and consistent. I assure you that you will feel a greater sense of control over your workload – and your life – when you can see all the deadlines, due dates, and events in a singular location.

TURBO TOGETHERNESS

Hopefully, this chapter helped you ramp up your calendar to be consistent, long-term, and comprehensive. While most of you likely already have some kind of calendar, the tricky part is ensuring that it includes everything so various parts of your jobs and lives don't have a Calendar Collision. To recap, let's be sure you:

■ Select one consistent calendar tool for work and enter all the FYIs, holidays, deadlines, and other important information for your organization.

■ If you select a paper-based calendar and work in a digital organization, please recognize that it will take some work to pull items off your digital calendar and into your paper tool. I support you!

■ Layer in all of the due dates related to your own role, both the recurring and the one-off.

■ Determine how you will record your personal items and appointments, whether as a separate digital calendar or on the same one.

■ Regularly look ahead to identify deadlines, events, due dates, and other items so that you can Forecast Forward for yourself and others.

CHAPTER 4

Build a Long-Term List – Yup, This Is Everything!

Now that you have your actual goals and a vision of what success looks like in your role and you can see how work is spread out over the course of a full year via your Year-at-a-Glance (YAG) and your Comprehensive Calendar, it is time to get into the practical weeds of what you are actually *doing* day-to-day to achieve these goals. The purpose of this chapter is to take you on a journey to create a Long-Term List that will capture all the To-Dos. Yes, you heard me correctly. This is the big, giant, comprehensive list of everything. Don't be scared! In fact, be excited. Having everything built into a singular location (like we just did with your calendar) ensures you can forecast your workload, break it into tiny steps, and ensure that nothing – not one thing! – slips through the cracks.

In this chapter, you will:

■ Assemble all To-Dos over a medium- to long-term time frame

■ Evaluate multiple Long-Term List approaches

■ Select the most effective tool for your own Long-Term List

■ Build your own Long-Term List

For some of you, having a Long-Term List will bring a sense of peace and relief, as in "Okay, I see it all laid out and I can figure out how to sequence it." For others, it may cause stress or worry, as in "Okay, I see it all laid out, and I'm not sure how it is possible." Or you may feel a little bit of both. That is okay. I've said it before, and I'll say it again – having everything in one location that you consistently add to, curate, and then activate will eventually become second nature (if it is not already) and ease any fears of forgotten items, help you see where and when you need to ask for assistance, and help you very strategically plan your days, weeks, and months. Convinced? With me? Let's talk more about why in the next section.

WHY KEEP A LONG-TERM LIST

On any given day, you could be stopped in the hallway, emailed, called, texted, Teamsed (yes, that is a verb), or Slacked (yes, that appears to be a verb now too) with a variety of To-Dos. This is on top of the proactive work you already know you are assigned, and those middle-of-the-night flashes of that thing you thought of last week but didn't record anywhere. Let's peek at some ways people in a variety of behind-the-scenes roles manage this onslaught of tasks. And if you are wondering, when, oh, when can I focus on an actual week, Maia? – that is coming soon, I promise. First it will be helpful to get clear on *all* the tasks that need to fit into your weeks. For our purposes, we are going to call this the Long-Term List – all of the things you need to do (well, at least the predictable ones) while leaving extra empty rows on the list to allow room for the unpredictable stuff – to add up to the role and outcomes from the previous chapters. Ultimately, having everything on one list will help your job feel both manageable and meaningful because you can effectively keep up with what is in front of you, while also seeing the contributions for the long term.

LONG-TERM LIST SAMPLES

Let's review a few samples so we can see various approaches. As with all the Together Tools introduced in this book, I remain uncommitted to a singular approach or format. I will typically try to share both digital and paper models, and it is up to you to know your preferences and proceed accordingly from the initial Self-Assessment at the beginning of the book. I encourage you to think about what you already do to plan your work, and try to take advantage of some things you may do already. You might even have a tool that you can build out into your Long-Term List.

Ana's Long-Term List

Ana, a school operations team member in LA, keeps her Long-Term List in a table. This allows her to add some categorization, such as "Bucket, Start Date, Due Date, and Status." Let's peek a little deeper.

Bucket	What	Who Could A. Ros Delegate To?	Start date	Due Date	Status
Finance	Alondra-Credit card-(30 mins) Due August 29 - forms were sent	ARs	8/23	8/26	in progress
Whole School System	Brainstorm swag options - KV update overview tab	ARs	8/29/22	9/13/22	complete
Health & Safety	All school ops team members complete onboarding steps 3-5 for Professional Antigen Testing Playbook	OPS: CR, CG, HC, JRz, ARS	8/29	9/16	in progress
Whole School System	Add to dos from Admin To Dos to AR list - [Fundraising, field trips, emergency cards	ARs	8/29	9/23	complete
Development	BOY Survey Stepback [Action Req'd]	ARs		9/23	Complete
	The Together Teammate Class 2: Homework Volunteers! [by 5:00 PM on Friday, September 23rd]			9/23	Complete
	November snapshot classroom feedback- November snapshot prep: School Environment (Welcoming, Safe & Healthy) - Monitor and adjust systems and procedures to build strong habits and collective responsibility amongst all team members. Utilize the PERC and Customer Experience Snapshots as guides.			9/23	complete

Figure 4.1   Ana's Long-Term List.

In Ana's Long-Term List (you can always look at the full-color version over on the website at www.wiley.com/go/togetherteammate), you can see she took time to:

■ **List her tasks by Bucket.** Ana lists her long-term work by Bucket, or category of work. In a role with many moving pieces, it can be helpful to view your job this way.

■ **Identify the Whats.** Her "Whats" are carefully detailed and even include hyperlinks and notes to get the tasks done. This way she has the references she needs right at hand when she starts the task.

■ **Clarify Start Date/Due Date.** She also includes a Start/Due Date, which helps her get ahead on bigger tasks. Having her "start line" in place helps her note on her calendar when she wants to begin a task, and then, of course, knowing the Due Date helps her stay on track to finish on time.

■ **Name the Status.** The status of the list is important when Ana sorts and filters to see what may be "in progress" or "complete." This is especially useful if she needs to sort and group or assign tasks to others.

At this point, you may be starting to consider where you want to "keep" your Long-Term List. We will get there shortly, but first let's review a few more samples. I want to take you over to Eryn's Long-Term List, which utilizes task-management software.

Eryn's Long-Term List

Eryn, a cohort coordinator of a leadership development program in Washington, DC, uses software called monday.com to track all of her To-Dos in a singular location – accessible through multiple methods – her laptop, phone, tablet, and such. Let's peek at how a program like this can be useful when juggling many tasks.

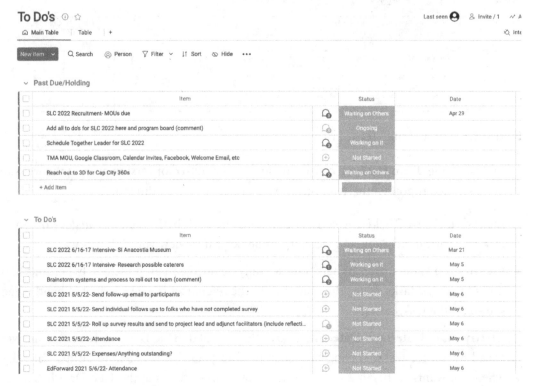

Figure 4.2   Eryn's Long-Term List in monday.com.

Eryn communicates with many team members – and also assigns tasks to her manager and colleagues – so having a shared software solution is useful for her small team to communicate.

While monday.com has the ability to sort in multiple ways, Eryn shares this view with us:

- **Past due/holding.** This section is helpful for any overdue items so Eryn can check on them and peek at status as well. She added the nifty status called "Waiting on Others." She can then sort by this status and send pleasant reminders to other people. Sound intimidating? Nah, Eryn is just Closing the Loops, an important Together Try-It practice. More on how to do that in an upcoming chapter.

- **Action item.** Eryn's action items are very bite-size and specific. For example, she doesn't just say, "Plan event," she says, "Research possible caterers." Making the tasks on the Long-Term List tiny makes them infinitely more doable. Additionally, if there are other "research" tasks, Eryn can consider "batching" them, otherwise known as grouping them and doing them all at one time. Eryn is also Showing the Work to her team by having items broken down in detail. This reassures people she is on it.

- **Due date.** This gives a constant view into the work coming down the conveyor belt and lets Eryn plan and communicate accordingly. She can easily say to her manager, "I will have survey results rolled up by May 6," thus exhibiting several Together Try-Its, such as Forecasting the Future and Being the Bird's-eye.

While this is all of Eryn's known work, she can also use monday.com to add tasks in quickly as they come up. Because of the sortability of the technology, the inevitable new To-Dos can quickly get tossed into the mix and then Eryn sorts them out later during her Meeting with Herself (more on that later).

Zipping back into Excel or Google Sheets for a moment, let's look at a Teammate with additional complexity in her role – and how her Long-Term List helps her manage the workload.

Liz's Long-Term List

Liz, a managing director of partnerships for a higher education institution in New England, keeps a detailed Long-Term List sliced and diced in multiple ways. For those of you managing a lot of people and complexity, you may need to filter your Long-Term list in various ways as Liz does. Let's dive into her sample.

Workstream/ Partner	Project	Task	Hrs	Priority	End date	Status	Next step/ notes	Help from
Grounding the team	Meeting matrix	XN/co-op	2	medium	21-Dec	not started		
Academic partners	Vision setting	Finalize academic partnership vision and determine next steps			21-Dec	in progress	Give to Elena	
Partnership ops	Sponsorship	Further flesh out sponsorship process and send to partners	1	high	21-Dec	in progress		
Partnership ops	Academics	FERPA policy and FAQ for partners	2	high	21-Dec	in progress		
JAX	Shared investment	Create proposal/strategy	1	medium	21-Dec	not started		
MaineHealth	Shared investment	Create proposal/strategy	1	medium	21-Dec	not started		
Partnership ops	Organization systems	Figure out how to track research/ entrep. Collabs and the role for partnership team			21-Dec	not started		
Grounding the team	Mission Vision Values	Get clear on next steps	0.5	medium	21-Dec	not started		
Partnership ops		Ask Ellen about NDA and MOU/ MCA	0.25	medium	21-Dec	not started		
Partnership ops		Get all MOUs/NDAs	0.5	medium	21-Dec	not started		
Other		Intro Kelly and Laura	0.25	medium	21-Dec	not started		
Partnership ops	Arc of the year - us/them	Draft this	1	high	21-Dec	in progress		

Partnership ops	Partner-by-partner roadmap	Update/finalize	2	high	21-Dec	not started	
MaineHealth	Virtual care	Evaluation plan for virtual care and how will we adjust based on feedback	1	high	21-Dec	in progress	
MaineHealth	Partnership management	Review info about MH strategic plan	0.5	medium	21-Dec	in progress	
Academic partners	Develop SOP for standing up 4+1	Develop SOP for standing up 4+1	2	medium	21-Dec	in progress	
Partnership ops	SOP for custom courses	Finalize this	2	medium	21-Dec	in progress	See Susan's note about textbooks
Stategic partnership work	TBD	Time for learning	1	high	21-Dec	not started	
Stategic partnership work	Product development	Need analysis across partners to inform product development	2	medium	21-Dec	not started	
Products	Product development	Running a section of data analytics/PJM		low	5-Jan	in progress	

Figure 4.3 Liz's Long-Term List.

Workstream/ Partner	Project	Task	Hrs	Priority	End date	Status	Next step/ notes	Help from
Academic partners	NU Flex and C.S. offerings for all of Maine (by Jan)		3	medium	TBD	not started		
Grounding the team	Update contracts sheet	Update and re-format contracts sheet and develop accompanying documents	1	medium	TBD	not started		
MaineHealth	Initiative development	Lab tech - set meeting with Alison - when?	1	medium	TBD	not started	Ask JO if we should discuss further	
Partnership ops	Systematizing offerings	Figure out badging - matrix of what is credit bearing, what is cert, what is badge	4	low	TBD	not started		
Partnership ops	Company profiles	Draft company profiles (1 hour/ profile)	8	medium	TBD	not started	Have Chloe/ Emma do this	
Partnership ops	Partner menu		2	medium	TBD	not started		
Partnership ops	Enrollment tracker	Draft this	2	high	TBD	not started		

Figure 4.3 (*Continued*)

Partnership ops	Budgeting for custom course dev	Financial planning for 1-off engagements, see JO's spreadsheet (June 17)	2	medium	TBD	not started	
Partnership ops	Employer recruitment strategy	Draft this	4	medium	TBD	not started	
Partnership ops	Organization systems	Get meeting scheduled with program directors for high demand programs to be able to speak to best courses to offer	0.5	low	TBD	not started	
Products	New products	Residency/apprentice model - write up for MA	4	medium	TBD	not started	
Products	Course development	Can we use Power B.I. in analytics courses?		low	TBD	not started	
Products	New products	Alignment with google cert	4	low	TBD	not started	
PTC	Custom course	Sketch out roadmap for engagement	1	medium	TBD	not started	

Figure 4.3 (*Continued*)

Liz uses Microsoft Excel to ensure her list is sortable and can filter in different ways. I was struck by a few things when she shared this model:

- **Workstream/partner.** It is often hard to brainstorm a total list of tasks when starting with a blank sheet of paper. Having headers such as "Academic Partners" or "Partnership Ops" helps Liz spell out her tasks related to each item. This can also help with batching tasks.

- **Projects.** Within each of Liz's workstreams are individual projects (some of which require Project Plans – more on that in a coming chapter). Being able to sort by project allows her to check in on all tasks related to a specific project when it's time to update that Project Plan.

- **Hours.** Although predicting the length of time of each task may be an imperfect science, it is very helpful when connecting it to your actual calendar (that chapter is coming too), to align on times with those around you (as in "Thanks for passing this task my way. I anticipate it will take me an hour. Does that sound right to you?"), and to be able to make decisions about what to pluck off this Long-Term List as your next task.

Liz also has the ability, like Eryn and Ana, to add things in as they come up. By simply creating extra rows and cells, Liz can enter proactive items that come up as she looks ahead or reactive small things that others assign to her. At the end of each week, Liz can filter for the following week and narrow in on what she wants to get done for just next week alone – assembling the basis of what we call a Weekly Worksheet (Chapter 6). I'm essentially trying to help you manage your workload by encouraging you to have a Long-Term List (this tool) and a shorter list for each week (which we will tackle shortly).

 Reader Reflection: What headers would be helpful on your Long-Term List?

Let's consider a different way to visualize a Long-Term List. So far we have looked at Lists that are organized as a long list of tasks (with columns to add additional information), but let's now look at another way to categorize your To-Dos, in a table that plots them out over time.

Fiama's "Shorter-Term" List

Fiama, a team member in a university setting, used a Shorter-Term List to handle a busy period in her work overall. Fiama created this summer projects tracker to ensure she was moving forward, both on her core job responsibilities and also on what her manager identified as "not urgent but important" projects. These are the things that it would be easy to leave undone forever but really should be accomplished to move her team's work forward. And slower times (like the summer for Fiama) are great opportunities to tackle such items. Similar to the other models, Fiama lays out all of her tasks, but she does so with time frames attached.

Green = Completed	5/23-5/27	5/31-6/3	6/6-6/10	6/13-6/17	6/20-6/24	6/27-7/1	7/4-7/13	7/14-7/15	7/18-7/22	7/25-7/29
Summer Events		Orientation 5/31-6/1 Team Meeting 6/2	Strategic Planning Kick-off 6/9	DAC Meeting (FR to present) 6/15		Mid-Summer Research Retreat 6/29	Fiama Vacation			Student Research Forum Week 7/29 (all week if virtual)
Miscellaneous	formatting/printing/assembly for Orientation items	Orientation support 5/31-6/1	DAC presentation prep		Mid-Summer Retreat prep support	Mid-Summer Retreat Support 6/29			Research Forum Prep Support	Research Forum Prep Support
Website	Draft "Resources" page	Draft "Resources" page	Edit "Research Opportunities" section	Edit "Research Opportunities" section	Edit "Resources" section	Update "Awards" section (AOA & DERA)		Start planning/proposing changes to "Home" page	Draft changes to "home" page	Gather Team feedback for "Home" page updates
ERAS Applications (goal: 40/week)				apps 1-40	apps 41-80	apps 81-100		apps 101-120	apps 120-150	CO 2022 FRCT Metrics Report
FRCT Funding Opportunities				Work on first draft	Work on first draft	Work on second draft			Makes edits based on Team Feedback	Makes edits based on Team Feedback

Figure 4.4 Fiama's Shorter-Term List.

Let's take apart why this could be helpful:

- **Break apart the blobby work.** You all likely have some important work that can, shall we say, linger on a list. I know I do. Breaking apart some of the blobbier (yes, that is a real word) kind of tasks is helpful to see what is actually required and how much time is needed to do it. For example, instead of just having "update the website" on a list (which might feel so overwhelming that it would never even get started, let alone finished), Fiama broke it down into sections that each needed to be edited.

- **Schedule the seasonal.** Summer – and many other times of year – can be wacky, with people out of office, our own vacations, and many other out-of-the-ordinary happenings occurring. For example, Fiama noted the organization's summer events like a Strategic Planning Kick-Off and a Mid-Summer Research Retreat. Slotting in these events first, at the top, and in bold, allowed Fiama to plan out her work around these key events. For example, the week before the DAC meeting, she included DAC presentation prep on her list.

- **Plan out the important work.** We all have important – but not urgent – work to drive ahead. All credit goes to Stephen Covey for this language of urgency and importance when thinking about our work. Fiama spread it out across the summer and ensured there was a plan to make it happen.

Fiama notes, "I needed an added bit of accountability, so with this chart I was able to determine what deliverables I could commit to each week, at my own pace, given other events going on each week. If I'm not perfectly on track, we can tweak it, but it gives me the motivation to work on items that aren't screaming for my attention and gives me the structure to know what to work on."

 Reader Reflection: Are there any times when your regular work is lighter and you could create a Shorter-Term List to push forward some important but not urgent tasks?

Now that you have reviewed multiple samples, let's dive in to figuring out where you want to house your Long-Term List.

SELECT YOUR LONG-TERM LIST TOOL

This tool will be used to create a comprehensive To-Do list for the year, and it will also be used to catch items that come up during the course of the workday, just the friendly hallway ambush, maybe a last-minute request, and maybe even meeting notes. The point here is you want to create *one* singular home for *all* of your To-Dos – both to codify the proactive work and to catch the reactive work, much as in the previous examples.

What you will want to avoid is:

■ Having any task live in your brain (it goes downhill fast, trust me!)

■ Having tasks live in multiple places. The most common challenge we hear in our trainings is not that people don't have systems; they have too many and that's not serving them well.

In terms of selecting a home for and designing your Long-Term List, you will want to think about:

■ Are you more likely to capture things and reference your List digitally or on paper? Think about when you are at your desk, in your office, wandering down a hall, at a conference, and so on.

■ Do you need any kind of sorting capabilities, by deadline, by priority, by week, and so on?

■ Do you need to be able to share your List with other people?

■ Do you want it to be snazzy with colors and images, or do you prefer an austere tool that focuses on function?

YOUR LONG-TERM LIST OPTIONS MIGHT INCLUDE:

■ **Straight-up paper and pencil kind of person?** You could select a notebook with columns, and carry it with you at all times. You could even make a page or two for each month or use large Post-its per month. This may work if you love your notebook, or are a bullet journaler or a Post-it person.

■ **Love to sort, filter, and color-code?** You might find yourself drawn to Google Sheets or Microsoft Excel. This gives you the flexibility to add your own columns and headers, and then go wild with the sorting or filtering as needed.

■ **Already use a digital notebook?** If you already use any kind of digital notebook, such as Microsoft OneNote or Evernote, then it's easy to add your Long-Term List into one of those tools. You lose the ability to sort and filter, but if you are already in the Microsoft universe, this keeps it simple.

■ **Need to share with others or assign tasks?** You may dabble in (or live in) software such as monday.com, Trello, Asana, or Smartsheet. My word of caution here is that you should only take this option if your entire team or organization is already committed to using the software. Otherwise you may end up tossing tasks into the ether with no reply!

Regardless of which tool you choose, the most important aspect is that you are consistent, and that the tool is portable and accessible (because, as you know, these To-Dos are popping up every second). Your overall goal is to have one Long-Term List that reflects the entirety of your workload as you know it.

 Reader Reflection: Where will you keep your Long-Term List and why?

Now that you have made this selection, let's talk about how to actually build and use the Long-Term List.

BUILD YOUR LONG-TERM LIST

It certainly might feel intimidating to build a Long-Term List all at once, so let's break the process into bite-size pieces (very meta, since the point of a Long-Term List is to break your work down into bite-size pieces). This may take a few hours, but I assure you, it will be worth it when you finish and have a sense that your work is manageable and meaningful. If it helps to have a starter template, feel free to download some of our modifiable forms at: www .wiley.com/go/togetherteammate. You may even want to print it and have it beside you to take notes as we walk through the steps or have it in soft copy to type in as we go.

■ Start by identifying all the daily or recurring tasks that are part of your role. For example, you might be tasked with creating a profits spreadsheet once per month. This goes in as a recurring task in the Long-Term List. If your role includes updating a candidate tracker weekly and sending the update to your manager, you would put this in your Long-Term List as well.

■ Take out the Year-at-a-Glance from the previous chapter. What are any To-Dos you can see? Break them down as small as possible.

■ Look at the organization's or team's calendar. Are there any events, meetings, retreats, or conferences where you can foresee being pulled in? If you are not sure, ask.

■ How about any Project Plans, either ones you are leading or ones others are leading? Where do you see your name? Take those tasks and plop them in your Long-Term List as well.

Consider the Right Time Frame

This will depend on your organization and its environment. For some of you, it may be a fiscal quarter. For some of you, it may be an academic trimester. Whatever you choose, I'd encourage you to try and keep it within the 6- to 12-month range. We have found this is far enough into the future where you can reap the benefits of foresight, but not so far ahead where planning feels amorphous and impossible.

FAQ: Do I always need a Long-Term List in place? After more than two decades of teaching Togetherness, I would argue that yes, a Long-Term List is always essential to see a road map of where you are going – and is often the way to actualize your goals. It can take big fuzzy goals and help translate them into something more manageable to execute over time.

Reader Reflection: What is the right time frame for your Long-Term List? Why?

Build out Your Column Headers

There are several ways to set up your column headers, as we saw in the previous samples. Think about the different ways you may want to sort and filter your Long-Term List. Here are some ideas:

- Deadline or due date for each task. This is useful if you have fast-paced work and need to sort quickly for coming due dates.

- Amount of time you predict a task will take. I find this helpful if you eventually place these To-Dos on your calendar.

- Level of priority for the To-Do. If you have a lot of different projects, it is helpful to see which are most important.

- Various projects or processes you lead. I love this one if you want to see all of your tasks grouped together by the different projects you lead or join.

Think about how you will use your Long-Term List on a regular basis and use this to guide which buckets to choose. And remember, this Tool can shift over time as your responsibilities shift, or as you start using it and realize a different categorization system might be more effective.

Reader Reflection: Which headers do you need on your Long-Term List? Why?

FAQ: Can I put personal items on my Long-Term List? By all means, *yes*. For many of us, the personal items too often are neglected or forgotten. If you feel comfortable, then certainly you can add personal items to your Long-Term List. Getting your car registered, the dentist scheduled, and your closet cleaned out (well, maybe not that last one) are important, take time, and require planning. Log them in that Long-Term List and trust that you will get them taken care of.

And if your workload feels impossible to predict, you can use a blank version of this tool to get after it by asking your manager things like, "I'm planning ahead and I realize I have no idea what May looks like in these three work areas. Can you help fill in the blanks for me?"

ROUTINES TO MAKE USE OF YOUR LONG-TERM LIST

You created a Long-Term List to keep yourself on track for hitting goals and to pace out your work. Now how do you use it to guide yourself as you work to stay focused on what matters? Getting dusty on a shelf or getting stuck in your hard drive won't help, so let's make sure it stays actionable and on track.

- Share it with a manager and/or colleagues to test for alignment.
- Review it at the end of the workday to see what you can cross off that was done that day and what to add for the following day (or month).
- Walk through it and update during your Meeting with Yourself (check Chapter 7 for more info).
- Make tasks even more bite-size in your Weekly Worksheet or Project Plans around the same topic (more on these two tools in upcoming chapters).
- Anticipate upcoming asks or tasks for other people to get on their radar in advance.
- Identify what information or feedback you may need to gather before you can accomplish the To-Dos.

What could this look like in actual practice? Let's review a few real scenarios and see how your Long-Term List could come into play. Read the following scenes and test your understanding.

Reader Reflection: Long-Term List Enactment Scenes

Scene 1:

You are in the middle of a very busy student enrollment season, and your manager comes to you with an excellent idea that they would like to see happen next month. Rather than say yes or no immediately, you could . . .

Scene 2:

You just spent a full workday playing whack-a-mole with vendor emails all day long; it doesn't feel like you advanced anything more meaningful ahead. Yet you can't get the upcoming staff holiday party out of your head (only four months away!). You could . . .

Scene 3:

You have a packed schedule in the lead-up to a long-awaited vacation. It feels impossible to get everything done. You could . . .

In each of the scenarios listed previously, you can see how a Long-Term List could allow you to Pause to Plan: pick your head up, do a double-check on what matters, and communicate accordingly. The absence of a Long-Term List could result in Checking-the-Box Mode (otherwise known as false Togetherness), Turtle Time (where you just tuck your head in and hope for the best), or People-Pleasing Disease.

FAQ: How is a Long-Term List different from a Project Plan? Great question. I like to think about your Long-Term List as a tool for just *you*, used to drive your work overall. Only you need to look at it! (You may use it to align with your manager on priorities and workload, but it's a tool to manage your own work.) Whereas a Project Plan is often a shared tool (more on that in Chapter 5) that allows you to drive a specific timebound collaborative project forward with others. In a Project Plan, often all parties need to be in the document adjusting and adding items and making updates, whereas your Long-Term List is a living document just for you.

TURBO TOGETHERNESS

While it can be easy to spend your days just knocking out To-Dos without an overall plan, I firmly believe that having a Long-Term List will help you capture every single task that comes your way, delay some items when necessary by sorting and filtering, and help you hack off the right stuff for the week ahead (our next chapter). The Long-Term List can also help you catch and place good ideas for later without feeling like you have to tackle them *right now*. Most of your work is mission-driven, thus you often feel the urgency on a daily basis to get it all done right now.

This chapter focused on long-term planning, often through the lens of prioritizing, tracking your work, and preparing yourself for the next few months. To get a jump-start here, you can:

- **List out your To-Dos** for the long-term, using your job description and any other goals or priorities in place (start with a brain dump if you like to think more free-form).

- **Consider where you want to "keep"** the long-term To-Dos, depending on how you want to organize them and if you are more paper-based or digital or if your organization already has task management software.

- **Review your Long-Term List** each week to see what you can activate this week (more on that coming, don't worry).

MANAGER MOMENT

With a million things a minute flying toward your Together Teammate, let's make sure you equip your folks with the tools they need to be successful.

- Determine if a particular tool is suggested in your organization or on your team. For example, in some cases, entire teams get on board with using one Long-Term List tool, such as Asana. If this is the case, please invest time and training into using it.

- Consider helping brainstorm the right columns for your teammate's Long-Term List. You may think the amount of time could be helpful; say that and check for alignment.

- Make sure meetings allow time for your direct report to capture and record next steps, and encourage these to land on the Long-Term List whenever possible.

- Whenever you can, encourage your colleague to Forecast Forward to anticipate items coming up several months down the road and periodically review with them.

Together Tour

Kevin Pesantez
Director of Operations
Coney Island Prep
Brooklyn, New York

Kevin Pesantez

WHAT IS YOUR MOST USED TOGETHER TOOL TO KEEP *YOURSELF* TOGETHER?

I utilize the GoodNotes app on my iPad. I have a notebook for note taking and my learning, a notebook for Thought Catchers for people I meet with, and a notebook for all things Kevin-related. I am new to a leadership role so I utilize my different notebooks in my planner to allow me to capture my learning and chunk it that way.

Keep It One-Click. Everything in my planner is hyperlinked so it is very easy to use and keeps me on the go. I also keep all of my work-related G-Suite tools on my iPad as well. This is my version of my Trapper Keeper! I have found my iPad to be an amazing tool to help organize my work life.

HOW DO YOU RE-TOGETHER YOURSELF WHEN UNEXPECTED THINGS POP UP?

When something unexpected happens, I try to stop and be sure to write it down in my Thought Catcher. Since these things usually are coming fast and furious, I jot the thought down when it comes my way, and then later transition it to the specific person's Thought Catcher I have for them so I am sure to cover it during our next meeting.

WHEN IS A TIME YOU HAD TO ADJUST YOUR TOGETHERNESS PRACTICES AND WHY?

This year was the most challenging year I've had to date when it comes to my Togetherness. I created my own system and use my iPad very religiously in my day-to-day life in my new role as Director of Operations. I've had to balance my newfound love for my iPad while also getting back to my roots with my Google Calendar.

Pause to Plan. I've had to marry both so I can build out my work week and truly gauge when I have the time to do the actionable things I capture in my Thought Catcher and/or short term/long term planning I need to do.

HOW HAS TOGETHERNESS HELPED YOU COMMUNICATE AND WORK WITH OTHERS?

My Togetherness has helped me communicate with others because it allows me to be realistic with my time and "pin things" as they come up and revisit them later. That is the secret to my sauce – finding a way to capture things as they come in, and know that I won't lose them but will deal with them at the appropriate time. The system that works for me is not for everyone but I have homed in on what works best for me and really made it a well-oiled machine for myself.

Togetherness allows me to lean into supporting people and what they need in the moment. When I'm in the grip, sometimes I can fall into this hole of "everything is urgent" but sometimes other people have things going on and I can't approach them with my full steam ahead. I have to pause and see if they are in a space to receive information or answer my questions.

Clear the Cobwebs. Sometimes I need to pause and capture it in my Thought Catcher so I can think through all the things I may need; input from them, feedback on something, decision, question, and/or action.

HOW DO YOU BALANCE THE PROACTIVE FOCUSED PART OF YOUR JOB WITH THE REACTIVE TASKS THAT POP UP?

Pivot Powerfully. It really is a balancing act! On my Google Calendar I place my arrival, departure, and work blocks. I feed my weekly To-Dos into my weekly plan. If something unexpected happens I revisit my To-Do list and shuffle it to another day of the week. This keeps me on top of my game and allows me to take in things as they come while staying on top of the things that will allow me to define success for myself in a day. And sometimes that looks like delegating work to others, if needed.

HOW DO YOU HANDLE WORKING WITH COLLEAGUES WHO ARE SLIGHTLY LESS THAN TOGETHER?

I had to learn a lot about self-awareness and understand that this area of time and task management is a work in process. I have really worked hard over the past six years in finding "that thing" that works for me, but I acknowledge that it may not work for others.

Stand in the Shoes of Others. I have to meet people where they are and I have to understand my learning style and acknowledge other people's. I have tried countless different systems, but I have come to a place where I took a little from all of these to make what I have today. With that being said, I needed to also allow others to find the thing that works for them. Only through this process can they find the things that make these amazing ideas in Togetherness "sticky" for them.

WHY DOES TOGETHERNESS MATTER TO YOU AT WORK AND AT HOME?

Togetherness matters to me a lot because it allows me to leave work at school and truly focus on my personal life when I walk out of the school building. It will always be a work in progress but I stay Together so I can take care of myself and so I can show up better the next day and continue my work to do everything in my power to ensure our scholars have the best school experience possible.

CHAPTER 5

Break Down the Big Stuff – Project Planning

While literally hundreds of books have been written about project planning – including our own micro-book, *The Together Project Manager* – I didn't feel we could skip it here and still have a book for you, dear Together Teammate. While other sections of this book cover tracking tasks for others, assigning work to your colleagues, or Clearing Cobwebs of murky tasks, I want to spend this chapter focused on what is an actual project, why build a Project Plan, and how to use a Project Plan with the rest of your Together Tools. Different than your Long-Term List in the previous chapter – which is a tool used just for you – your Project and Event Plans may involve other people in your Plans, thus changing how you may want to think about formatting and explaining your thinking. Project Plans are *also* how you lead yourself through epic multi-stage processes, support others, and Be the Bird's-eye to achieve the outcomes of your project.

In this chapter, you will learn to:

■ Design Project Summaries to invest and align people in your project

■ Determine the best way to structure your Project Plans

■ Build a Project Plan

■ Decide how to share Project Plans with others in the most effective form

■ Rally and invest others in your project's outcomes

■ Anticipate problems and plan for the unexpected

One of the key ways you can distinguish yourself as a Together Teammate is the ability to break down a large-scale outcome into manageable bite-size pieces, shepherd yourself and others to complete the work, and then ultimately achieve the desired results. Anyone can have an idea for a fundraising gala, but not everyone can take that vision and then break it down into steps laid out over time that involve coordinating multiple people. That is where *you,* my friends, step in as the MVPs of your team. Let's read along and learn some tricks to make the magic happen.

DETERMINE WHAT NEEDS A PROJECT PLAN – AND WHAT DOESN'T

Each of your organizations likely has different approaches to planning. Some of you may work in environments where a standardized Project Plan template is required for each project, and some of you may be employed by places where the vibe is "Project Plan?! Who has time for it? Who needs it?" Whether you are at one of these extremes or, more likely, somewhere in the middle, you will want to adapt to the environment you are in, or possibly advocate for a stronger culture of planning.

 Project Plan: Articulates the goals, tasks, owners, and resources to accomplish the outcomes of a particular project. It clearly defines all work related to the project and who is in charge of various project pieces.

Once you get started down a planning path, it can be tempting to whip out Google Sheets for everything. Temper yourselves, my friends, and ask what truly warrants a Project Plan – and what doesn't.

A Project Plan is likely needed for:

■ An event with multiple contributors, such as a donor gala or a curriculum night

■ A process, such as a website redesign or new employee handbook

■ A season, such as voter registration drives or new teacher training

■ Something new and complex you have not yet executed

For example, if you are asked to plan a voter registration drive that involves your entire staff and an army of volunteers, then yes, this needs a specific Project Plan that others can view and check in on because it involves multiple people, requires lots of materials, and is on a clear timeline. If you are asked to determine a new math curriculum for your school district that mainly involves you doing layers of research and presenting recommendations, then you may not need such an involved Plan – but you may want to sketch out something rough to guide you. If you are asked to schedule several complex meetings, you likely do not need a Project Plan, as this is more of just a list of tasks. In some cases, your Long-Term List (from the previous chapter) may suffice, but in other cases, you may need a specific and separate Plan focused only on your project. Before you go down the path for Project Planning, it may even be worth asterisking the work from your Year-at-a-Glance that you believe requires a more detailed Plan – whether to guide you or others – and then align with your manager or colleagues to gain agreement and investment.

Think collaborative, complex, and time-bound. Of course, there are no hard-and-fast rules in the world of Togetherness, so you will likely need to do some experimentation to see what would benefit from a specific Project Plan. Sometimes, you may even find yourself several steps down the Project Road and at that point realize you need to map out the path forward more clearly. It never hurts to stop and create the Project Plan at whatever point you realize it would be helpful to get your head around the whole thing start to finish.

A Project Plan is likely *not* needed for things like:

■ Your daily workflows and tasks

■ Standard operating procedures, such as running payroll (this may need deadlines in your Comprehensive Calendar, but not a detailed plan)

Keep in mind that a Project Plan often serves two purposes. First of all, it is a tool to help you organize and guide your own thoughts toward implementing complex projects because it will help you sequence in the right order, see dependencies, and possibly identify steps you may have missed. The Project Plan tool should *also* be something that helps others see the work (Show Your Work!) and supports you in assigning work to others in the project – helping them see the big picture as well as where they fit in to the details.

In all of the forthcoming examples, your brain may start to think, "Why bother to document or write all of this down since I'm the one doing most of the executing and I could perhaps do this in my sleep?" Well, a few reasons I would like to give a gentle nudge here.

■ **Your brain is not failsafe.** Trust me. One of my favorite books is Atul Gawande's *The Checklist Manifesto*, the premise being that many of our brains need the checklist as a double check. Even when we have been doing this thing for many years and have it down pat, a checklist is still a valuable tool. No one wants a "Shoot, this one time I forgot to order the coffee?!" moment. (As a vulnerable aside, my team and I will never quite forget the moment where we shipped all of our materials to Newark for a training, and one very, very important item was missing, resulting in a massive scramble and visit to approximately four Staples stores to gather this certain supply. #mortified. If I had referenced my packing checklist before my train to Newark, I could have saved a lot of people a lot of hassle.)

■ **You want to take advantage of small pockets of time.** Your days are likely super busy with a million *other* projects unrelated to this one. By looking at your overall steps in bite-size pieces, it may be easier to find 15 minutes to make a phone call to secure a particular facility rather than wait for a larger chunk of time to emerge.

■ **You want to be able to assign tasks to others.** Even if there are only a few other pieces that other people are responsible for, it is helpful to identify them in advance, help others see where their parts connect to the bigger picture, and in some cases apply gentle pressure for them to see how one delay impacts the entire system.

■ **You want to reuse in the future.** If you have a similar event or project coming up again, think of how lovely it will be not to have to start from scratch and to have a base to start from. Or if you are training another person to take your spot, it is helpful to have the steps laid out for them. (Imagine how good you would have felt if someone had handed you a set of Project Plans already made when you started your role!)

 Reader Reflection: What projects in your world may warrant a Project Plan? Why?

Now that you have an idea about which projects may need a Project Plan, let's pick our heads up and create what I call a Project Summary – an overview of the project – created before you even begin. Project Summaries are prime examples of Showing the Work, and a great opportunity to align with others on the outcomes.

CREATE A PROJECT SUMMARY

Before you get super excited and jump into the details of creating a Project Plan (#guilty), it helps to step back and do some Project Preplanning, so to speak. Remember in college how much easier it was to write the term paper if you first created the outline, perhaps spoke to a professor or roommate about your vision, and *then* started writing? Well, enter the Project Summary. In this section, I will take you on a tour of a few Project Summaries. As always, keep in mind these examples are meant as inspiration, not a set of rules. It is up to you, dear reader, to adapt and modify as you see fit.

Fiama's Research Awards Project Summary

Fiama, a teammate in higher education, was in charge of the Dean's Excellence in Research Awards for her department. Before she jumped in to the project in full force, Fiama took the time to lay out an overview of the project. Let's take apart what she did and why.

University of Maryland
SCHOOL OF MEDICINE

Office of Student Research

Project Name: Dean's Excellence in Research Awards

Project Definition: Select and award two MS4 students with the DERA award at the Awards Ceremony (typically day before Commencement Ceremony).

Project Team Members & Roles

- **Fiama** – manage process; order/create deliverables
- **Greg** – select awardees; approve all deliverables
- **Rick/Miriam/OSA** – provide input on awardee selection

Key Project Deliverables

- Award description/instructions PDF & invitation email
- Online application
- Results/submission tracker and tally system
- Communications: Accept letters, not-accept letters, general announcement (in newsletter)
- Student checks
- Student plaques
- Plates for OSR perpetual plaque

Project Budget

- $500 per award = $1,000 total
- $250 for plaques and plates

Main Project Phases

Project Bucket	Person Responsible	Timeline
Create student application	Fiama	January
Promote award and request responses	Fiama	Mid-February through Mid-March
Organize submission data (tally by points)	Fiama	Mid-March
Select student awardees	Greg (Miriam, Rick, OSA input)	Names to Office of Development by 1st Friday in April
Communications: Accept letters, not-accept letters, general announcement (in newsletter)	Fiama	April
Process checks, plaques, and plates	Fiama	In hand by May 1

Figure 5.1   Fiama's Project Summary.

Fiama rose up out of the project details, and she took the time to get clear about:

- **Project team members and roles.** Have you ever taken part in a project where you actually had no idea who else was involved and what role they were playing? Well, this cleans that up in one swoop. When sharing your Project Statement (more on that later in the chapter), Fiama is listing who exactly is on her project team (Fiama, Greg, Rick, Miriam, etc.) so they know in advance.

- **Key project deliverables.** This is a great way to align with your manager or the person who assigned you this project on what key deliverables (or in laypeople's terms, products) are part of the project. For example, in Fiama's case, the online application was a big part of the research awards project. By naming this clearly, she can also ask her boss how much they want to be involved with each deliverable.

- **Project phases.** Project Phases help clarify the large parts of the project along a general timeline. This is useful when planning around other organizational events and when thinking about your own and others' capacity. For example, Greg needs to "select student awardees," a key part of the project, and he has a hard deadline of April 1. If Fiama lets him know this timeline through sharing this Project Summary, he can ensure he has time blocked on his calendar for this task.

Fiama says these tools help her because, "They allow me to self-manage with minimal supervision from my manager (who works across several departments and technically is only part-time in my office). These tools are meant to give me the responsibility of setting my own pace and ensure I am accountable to myself – and my manager." In fact, this is the case with many Together Tools. Likely no one is telling you, "Please submit your Comprehensive Calendar and Project Plans on X date."

I would be remiss not to mention that taking the time to write up the Project Summary gives you the chance to flex your Together Try-It practices with and for your colleagues. It demonstrates you Forecasting Forward, Clearing the Cobwebs, Being the Bird's-eye, and Owning the Outcome. It isn't that those around you cannot do it; it is that this is the heart of what you – as a Together Teammate – can do for your organization to help advance its mission and outcomes.

 Reader Reflection: Consider a current or upcoming project on your plate. How would a Project Summary help advance the outcomes of your project?

Let's peek at a slightly different model, showing a New Teacher Orientation Project Summary at a network of schools in Atlanta.

Colleen's New Teacher Orientation Project Summary

Colleen was placed in charge of overseeing New Teacher Orientation for her school, and she needed to rally everyone around the same goal. Let's peek at how she did this in the following sample.

As you can see, there are several helpful sections to effectively summarize the project.

■ **Executive summary.** Can you state the goals and purpose of your project in two or three simple sentences? This is a great way to get folks on board with what you hope to accomplish. In Colleen's case, she cites the need to acquaint folks with norms and "excite and awaken their teaching genius." I'm fired up and I'm not even on the project!

The **Kindezi** Schools

Project Proposal Plan

New Teacher Orientation SY 22-23

Executive Summary
New teacher orientation is a week-long training event which provides an opportunity for new teachers to become acquainted with Kindezi norms and protocols, develop their pedagogical skills and curricular understanding, and excite and awaken their own genius.

Goals
1. New teachers will understand and be able to articulate Kindezi's core values, norms and professional expectations
2. New teachers will understand and be able to articulate the academic visions and navigate and use all pertinent curricular resources
3. New teachers will feel like they are part of the Kindezi family and will leave excited and eager for the upcoming school year

Vision
New teachers will have an experience that embodies Kindezi, one that is full of urgency, rigor, high expectations, love and joy! New teachers will attend high-quality training and professional development sessions, learn about and bond with new team members, and leave feeling excited and prepared for the upcoming school year.

Nonnegotiables
Please remember our organization's commitments to effective planning and facilitation. Namely, you should build in time for modeling and practice.

Timeline (Include any practice sessions)

Project Timeline		
Milestone	Description	Delivery Date
Logistics	Determine date, location	March
Outline content schedule	Outline the sessions and content to be covered	April
Confirm dates for facilitators	Send calendar invites to all session facilitators to hold for summer	April

Figure 5.2   Colleen's New Teacher Orientation Project Summary.

- **Crystal-clear goals.** We all want to know if we have been successful with our project efforts. Colleen very clearly lists the goals or outcomes. For example, "new teachers will be able to articulate the academic vision" and so on.

- **Sequential timeline.** Each planning step builds on the other steps, and this lays out the idea that logistics, content, and facilitation preparation need to happen in a certain order.

Having this Project Summary at hand ensures you can align on expectations, solicit input, and ultimately confirm the path forward on your project. This can prevent you from going too far down a project path and having to backtrack once you realize that where you are headed isn't where your manager intended, or that you don't have the resources necessary to proceed as you had envisioned.

 Reader Reflection: Practice writing a two- or three-sentence executive summary for a current project. How would you explain the purpose quickly in a meeting with your manager?

PROJECT PLAN SAMPLES

As mentioned earlier, there can be multiple approaches to actually mapping out the tasks that need to be done. As you review these models, you will want to note which Project Plan tool each teammate selected, how they broke down a larger objective into bite-size tasks, how they listed out a clear human responsible for each step – unless it was almost entirely self-led by them – and how they sequenced things in an easy-to-follow order. Ultimately, each of the deadlines should pop back over to your Comprehensive Calendar, and some of the work time may land on your Weekly Worksheet (more on that soon).

Let's visit a simple self-led and executed model, Clara's graduation Plan.

Clara's Graduation Project Plan

Clara, a former director of operations of a teacher training program, was in charge of the graduation of the residents at their Boston-based program. Clara executed most of the project tasks herself, so other people didn't necessarily need to see all the details of the overall Plan. Only Clara had to step back and brainstorm all the tiny tasks needed to pull off graduation. The next image shows a snippet of Clara's thinking. As always, for full examples, please pop over to www.wiley.com/go/togetherteammate.

Graduation To-Dos

Month(s) before:
- ❑ ~~Okay date with CP in Big Hall?~~
- ❑ ~~Email grads date and details~~
- ❑ ~~Send grads survey of gown size + names on diplomas~~
- ❑ ~~CHECK GOWNS, CAPS, HOODS AND ORDER EXTRA -- at least 2 months in advance!!~~
- ❑ ~~ORDER DIPLOMAS~~

Week before:
- ❑ ~~Finalize program (+ 2 speakers)~~
    - ❑ ~~Send program to printers~~
- ❑ Email out final details to MET grads
- ❑ Get video of MET grad students
- ❑ Get CSPO6 volunteers to help w/ reception
- ❑ ~~Double check with insurance for reception~~
- ❑ MAKE VIDEO
- ❑ Iron graduation gowns (pressed dry cleaners)
- ❑ Iron tablecloths (3) (pressed dry cleaners)
- ❑ ~~Get notary stickers for dipomas + envelops for diplomas (Staples)~~
- ❑ ~~Make sure we have enough serving trays (currently at Milk St.) -- if not, Amazon order.~~
- ❑ Sign diplomas

Friday before:
- ❑ Balloons
- ❑ Food (grapes, cheese, crackers, ham, sparkling water, champagne)
- ❑ Utensils (plates, cups, napkins, platters)
- ❑ ~~safety pins~~

DAY OF:
- ❑ Set up chairs + podium
- ❑ Set up speakers / projector / make sure tech is all set
- ❑ Move planters
- ❑ Set up balloons
- ❑ Set up tables in lobby
- ❑ Set up food on tables (cut cheese, wash grapes, etc.)
- ❑ Store everything else in room / extra chairs
- ❑ Tell CSPO6 volunteers what to do
- ❑ Turn off elevators
- ❑ 3:30pm - arrival deadline for MET grads
- ❑ Diplomas in alpha order; on podium
- ❑ Line up order + processional
- ❑ Safety pins for hoods (to hook to gowns)
- ❑ 4:00 - practice processional
- ❑ 4:20 - picture on the stairs
- ❑ CHECK OUT procedure: (CSPO for check out?)
    - ❑ Fold your gown + put in this pile
    - ❑ Fold your hood + put in this pile
    - ❑ Put your cap here
    - ❑ Envelope for checks/cash
- ❑ CLEAN UP!
    - ❑ Trash in dumpsters
    - ❑ Big Hall back to lunch set up

Figure 5.3 Clara's Graduation Project Plan.

In this case, Clara selected a simple Word document, and completed and generated most of the next steps herself. Yet she still writes them down and puts them in a checklist. Why?

- **Make the tasks tiny.** The checklist encouraged her to make all of these tasks tiny, which enabled her to fit them in her calendar. She didn't just list "program"; instead she listed "Send program to printers." The more bite-size, the better. This will also help you if your project calls for you to assign tasks to others.

- **Backwards mapped before the event.** She can sort the checklist by timeline for the tasks. Clara noted what is Week Before, Days Before, and so on. This also allows the Project Plan to be recycled year over year.

- **Delegation planned in advance.** Clara noted when she needs to pull in others, such as "Get Stig/Scott to sign diplomas." This is a case where she needed others to execute part of the project, but they didn't necessarily need to be involved with the details of the Project Plan. Clara could simply give them a heads up that they needed to block out time for the signatures.

It may feel like a waste of time to write them all out, especially if you are personally leading most of the Project Tasks, but trust me, it's better than forgetting one tiny detail and then finding yourself ironing graduation gowns yourself the morning of a graduation. Or realizing at the very last minute you needed your manager's signature on the diplomas, but they are not available. As with all of my planning tools, the overall goal is to manage ourselves, but also to Forecast Forward for asks of others. If you feel stuck brainstorming all the steps to make something happen, start by envisioning the end product, the people involved, and then use some sticky notes to brainstorm how to get there.

Emily's School Name Change Project Plan

Emily, a special assistant in Brooklyn, was responsible for overseeing the process to change the name of a school in their network – no small task! Emily created her Project Plan in Microsoft Excel, and she also chose to add a calendar view to the left-hand side. This is very helpful when thinking about weekends, holidays, and other conflicts with the timeline.

Planning Calendar

April 2022

M	T	W	Th	F	Item	Owner	Key Partners	Dependencies	Key Dates	Notes	Key Events	Date
				1	Develop and finalize communications plan	Emily	Nadine, Bernard			Current & prospective staff letters (FACS, EFACS, All staff) Current & prospective family letters (FACS, EFACS)ACS & AL Board communications Public-facing blog post for FACS and Ascend websites		
4	5	6	7	8	Draft staff, family, board, and public communications	Emily	Nadine, Bernard, Wintanna, NDOs, Jordan, Beth					
4	5	6	7	8	Outreach to Refined Sight (external signage design/install vendor)	Emily	Morgan, Nadine, Bernard					
11	12	13	14	15								
18	19	20	21	22								
25	26	27	28	29								

May 2022

M	T	W	Th	F	Item	Owner	Key Partners	Dependencies	Key Dates	Notes	Key Events	Date
2	3	4	5	6	Cost review and approval	Emily	Exec Team					
2	3	4	5	6	Finalize written communications	Emily	Nadine, Bernard, Wintanna, NDOs, Jordan, Beth					
9	10	11	12	13	Communications translations	Emily						
16	17	18	19	20	Roll out staff and family communications	Emily	Nadine, Bernard, Wintanna, NDOs, Jordan, Beth					
23	24	25	26	27	Begin FACS digital assets and external signage design	Emily	Sophie, Tech, Nadine, Bernard, Wintanna, NDOs, Jordan			Mascot Letterhead Email signatures		
30	31											

22 Quarter 4

Figure 5.4 Emily's School Name Change Project Plan.

Planning Calendar

June 2022

M	T	W	Th	F
		1	2	3
6	7	8	9	10
13	14	15	16	17
20	21	22	23	24
27	28	29	30	

22 Quarter 4

Item	Owner	Key Partners	Dependencies	Key Dates	Notes	Key Events	Date
Complete FACS digital asset design	Morgan	Emily, Nadine, Bernard, Wintanna, NDOs				K-8 last day of school	6/10
Conduct contract review for FY23	Charlise	Finance, GC			Ensure school name is changed as contracts renew for FY23	Staggered Ops summer vacation	6/13 - 7/1
Change school name in Infinite-Campus	Danny	Amy, James				Leader summer vacation	6/27 - 7/15
Change school name in Ceridian	Marjorie						
Ascend website updates	Janisha	Emily, Nadine, Bernard			Universal name changeUpdate school landing page and link to blog post		
FACS website updates	Bernard	Emily, Nadine					
Install new external signage	Bernard	Refined Sight, Nadine, Emily, NDOs, Morgan					
Update staff and student laptop names	Travis	Tech					
Update school sharefile name	Travis	Tech					
Update school listservs	Travis	Tech					
Update school name in cost center	Travis	Tech					
Update ringcentral greetings	Travis	Tech					
Update talent marketing & recruitment materials							
Update school name in ACS/AL Board materials	Emily	Finance					

= Schools and AL closed
= Schools closed

Figure 5.4 (*Continued*)

Let's highlight a few aspects of Emily's sample:

- **Tasks start with verbs.** Similar to Clara, Emily made the tasks (or "items") as small as possible. For example, "Change school name in Infinite Campus," or "Install new external signage." This allows her to give other people bite-size tasks to work on and not make it overwhelming, and also allows her to fit her bite-size tasks into her busy days and manage herself to complete the work.

- **Ability to sort and filter.** At any time, Emily can sort by who the "Owner" of the item is or by key dates. This is very helpful as she assigns tasks to others and keeps track of items assigned out.

- **Room for notes.** Emily has left room for notes, where she can capture additional details related to the action item.

- **Dependencies are called out.** Emily left room for dependencies, or in other words, noting when one of the tasks is dependent on the others. This can help her better assign due dates and she can also name the sequence of events for people so they can understand the ramifications of the timeline. For example, Emily could say, "The name change must be confirmed by the board before we can announce it on websites."

 Reader Reflection: Does each of your Project Tasks have a clear owner? If not, how could you get there?

Inspired? Excited? I am! Let's review one final model before we think about how to apply this knowledge to your own projects.

Eryn's Recruitment Project Plan

Eryn, an operations team member at a DC-based nonprofit providing leadership development, oversees gatherings for the various leadership cohorts. In contrast to Clara's previous example, Eryn's work is ongoing over the course of the year with leading several cohort events (versus Clara's one-time graduation event) and involves gathering and packaging content from a number of people. Let's look at how Eryn juggles planning multiple events at once. If your project is complex and you are juggling multiple projects, it may make sense to select some kind of project management software. In Eryn's case, she uses monday.com.

Eryn chose to use monday.com, project management software that is customizable and accessible to multiple people on multiple devices. This is because of the complexity required to gather all the items for cohort gatherings and communications. Eryn says,

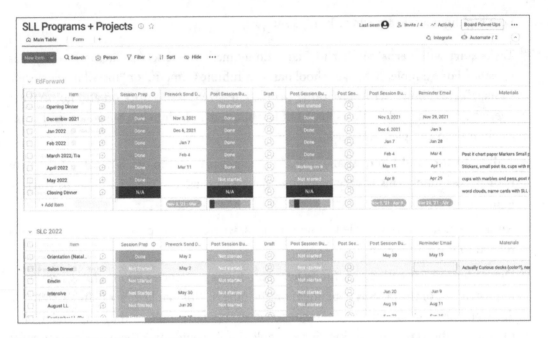

Figure 5.5   Eryn's Project Plan.

"The automation of monday.com helps make sure reminders go out to the various people involved in my project, and I can also repopulate for each event without having to rewrite out each task." Good old classic Systems Spotting. Specifically, Eryn did a few Together Teammate tricks worth pointing out:

■ **Use of similar steps within each cohort gathering.** Eryn listed each cohort gathering along the Y axis, and because each gathering has similar steps, she listed the steps across the X axis. She noted when prework will be sent, when content will be drafted, and when reminder emails will be sent. This is also helpful to see the bigger picture of the year.

■ **Room for status checks.** A benefit of using some kind of project management software is often the ability to capture status. In this case, Eryn can easily see what is "done," versus "not started" versus "working on it." Eryn can then quickly scan or even sort to check on project progress.

■ **Clear owners.** If you click more deeply into monday.com, you can see who is responsible for each step. This allows Eryn to preview and delegate out the work more easily (more on that in a coming section). Using monday.com, or similar software such as Asana, Smart-Sheet, or Trello, also allows your colleagues to more easily access your Project Plans. This is useful if they are entering or updating their own tasks along the way.

Reader Reflection: Do you have any recurring projects where it would make sense to put them all into one Project Plan?

BUILD YOUR PROJECT PLAN

Now that you have viewed a few Project Plans (from the very simple to the very complex), and likely have built or seen lots more over the course of your careers, let's prepare to build your own Project Plan. It may be useful to have an actual project in mind so you can get some real work done right here while reading. In this section, you will make decisions on which tool to use per project (spoiler alert: it should change depending on the project).

Decide Which Tool to Use for Your Project Plan

As you can see from the examples above, a Project Plan can take many forms. Before you jump headfirst into your favorite spreadsheet, I recommend you consider what you actually need. Let's look at how the previous teammates selected which tool to use when for their projects:

- Clara was responsible for most of the design and execution of the graduation event, so she chose a basic checklist in a Google Doc because she was mostly managing herself on this event. Clara used this list to work on the graduation project during her calendared work time and during her check-ins with her manager.

- Emily, charged with the school name change, needed to involve multiple layers of people with many opinions. She also needed to show people how the steps of the project connect with the calendar; she chose to use Microsoft Excel so she could customize the columns and lines for her particular project. Since there is a lot of collaboration with others, sorting quickly by person or status was helpful to keep her project on track.

- Eryn's project was managing the recruitment of leaders for a new cohort – and her organization uses monday.com as a shared tool. This project involved directing multiple people to play a role in the selection process. Therefore Eryn used monday.com because the whole team is already in it on a daily basis. Additionally, it gives others a level of transparency into the progress of the project. It becomes very easy for others to see what is assigned to them.

The main takeaway here is that you don't want to use a one-size-fits-all project planning approach for every project that comes your way. You want to be intentional with your choice, which tool your project needs, and what will best guide your work. Ideally you are armed with different possibilities in your toolkit, and ready to activate the right option for your particular project.

Think of a specific project you have on your plate currently. Ask yourself:

- How simple or complex is my project?

- Am I the sole author of the Project Plan or are other people involved in drafting the Project Plan?

- Am I using the Project Plan to direct others' work or just my own?

- Do I want to assign other people tasks directly from the Project Plan, or do I want them to jump in and grab their own tasks?

- Do I want to be able to print my Project Plan?

- Do I want to be able to view it both online and offline?

- How do I want and need to sort and filter?

- Will I use my Project Plan to provide updates or will I communicate out in other ways?

- Is this a project that will be repeated and I might want to use this Project Plan again in the future?

Once you know the answers to these questions for the project at hand, you may decide that a simple Word or Google Doc will suffice for your more straightforward projects. But your complex projects may require some sort of sortable project management software, such as Asana, monday.com, or Smartsheet. As mentioned previously, if your organization already utilizes a certain project management tool or system, you will want to jump on board with what exists rather than introduce something new. If you have completely free rein in selection of Project Planning tools, take a spin through my blog at www.thetogethergroup.com to learn about different and ever-changing options.

FAQ: What if I love a type of project management software that other people don't know how to use?

I would not recommend expecting people to use brand new software and execute Project Tasks all at once. You will want buy-in for any software implementation before diving in. That said, if the Project Plan you are working on is mostly for your own use, have at it!

Reader Reflection: Consider some upcoming projects. What project management tools will you use and why?

Now that you have chosen which tool to use – remembering that I want you to flex your planning muscles and have lots of tools in your toolkit – it's finally time to do the planning. The next section will take us deep into the details of actually creating the Project Plan. Can't wait, right? Me neither. Let's go!

Break Projects into Smaller Steps

Now that we have reviewed a few completed Project Plans, you may be wondering how on earth you actually populate one. There are a few different options, most of which require you to sit by yourself – or with a colleague – and conduct some deep thinking.

- **Brain dump.** You could simply start with a blank slate and consider all of the steps it would take to execute your particular project. You can type them or write them, but the goal is to empty your brain and not worry about sequencing or owners or dependencies yet. Just get them out of your head. Once you have your brain dump, you can organize the steps into the second option, buckets.

- **Bucket.** You could think about the larger buckets of your project. For example, if you are planning a recruitment event, there may be buckets of work related to "Materials," "Interview Scheduling," "Sourcing," and more. After you identify the buckets, you can think about small steps to achieve each bucket. Again, don't worry about owners or timelines yet; your goal is to get all the content on paper.

- **Calendar.** Some folks like to jump right to this step by plotting each small task on a calendar and assigning the timeline from the outset. If you are a visual thinker, you may find sticky notes and a wall calendar to be helpful. Others may prefer to create the timeline digitally in an online calendar.

However you choose to get to these smaller steps, make sure each one starts with a verb and that if you were assigned to do it, you could create a clear spot on your calendar to make it happen. This is the difference between saying "Recruitment VIP email" versus breaking it down into "Draft Recruitment VIP email," "Load Recruitment email into Mailchimp and test with three people," "Send recruitment email to five recruiters in other organizations." The reason it is important to do this is that every single task takes time, and I want to make sure you have a method for creating the time to make the project happen!

 Reader Reflection: What is your personal approach to project planning? Why does this work for you? What does or could change by project?

With your project up and running, you will find that you need to proactively communicate with people along the way, both to provide updates and to assign tasks. Let's explore how to do this in the next section.

COMMUNICATE ABOUT THE PROJECT WITH OTHERS

Once your Project Plan is ready, it is time to involve others. You may want to introduce it with a specific big-picture launch, an email kickoff, or simply by assigning tasks to others. Some of this will depend on whether the project is new, controversial, or complex.

There are a variety of ways you could introduce your colleagues or managers to your project:

- **Just assign people (or yourself) tasks and go about your business.** Clara's managers may not even need to get an official project introduction about their role in signing the diplomas because Clara has led resident graduation for multiple years.

- **Piece out larger portions of the Project Plans, as needed.** In Emily's case, she may decide to assign all marketing tasks related to the school name change all at once.

- **Host a co-planning or kickoff meeting.** In some cases, like Eryn's leadership cohorts, you may want to pull the group together and review the project deadlines, owners, and decision-makers.

Once the project is underway, you will likely find you need to update people on the status of your project, request people to take on additional tasks (or remind them about what you've already assigned them), and get input from folks about various topics. While it can be hard to stop and communicate when you are in the midst of so much project *doing*, it will be essential for you to keep people in the loop, previewing challenges and anticipating decisions. Because likely only you know *all* the details of the project, everyone is counting on you to Be the Bird's-eye. There are a few ways you could communicate about your project throughout.

- **Share status updates during a check-in meeting with your manager.** Hopefully, you have regular meetings with your manager, and you can share status updates at that time.

- **Share project updates and assignments in Project Team meetings.** If you convene a group of people related to your project, you could give updates during the actual meeting and request the same of others.

- **Send some sort of regular project communication in writing** to the Project Team, highlighting successes, challenges, and any off-track moments.

Molly's Project Update

Molly, an operations team member in St. Louis, shares a Project Update with her entire team about the high school graduation process in the following sample.

Hi, all.

To say this week has been challenging is a significant understatement. I hope you all find time to take care of yourselves this weekend, however that may look.

I wanted to provide an update of where we are and the next steps regarding the Graduation Progress Project; I've already previewed all of this with Lauren W, who has agreed to help facilitate with seniors.

Updates:

1) Tonda, Lauren C and I have spent the last week combing through senior credits to correct for errors. A huge shout out goes to Tonda and Lauren C for managing the PowerSchool issues—there were many.
2) Each senior has a **Graduation Status Report** that details which credits they have earned and which they still need towards high school graduation. **These are attached.**
3) I created a deck that Lauren will present to seniors to remind them of the graduation requirements and some other key messages.
4) If (likely, *when*) seniors and/or parents have questions or concerns, they can complete this form. This will be the fastest way for students and parents to get a response right now. We acknowledge this isn't the best long-term solution for addressing student/parent concerns, but at present with everything else going on, its likely the best option. **If students or parents contact you, encourage them to complete this form.**
5) HERE is a draft of an email Lauren will send out to seniors and their parents. The email will provide the link to the dock and form, too.

Next Steps:

1) Lauren W will present the deck above and provide seniors with their Graduation Status Progress forms during a senior class meeting, ideally as soon as possible, but I acknowledge there is a lot going on.
2) Lauren W will send an email to students and parents after she presents this information so parents are aware their students have these reports and they will also have access to the form if they have concerns.
3) We (Tonda, Lauren C and I) will soon get started on the audit of juniors so we can provide this same information to them.
4) I am going to work with Lauren C and Tonda to determine students for whom we have more concerns related to on-time graduation, and we will make a plan to reach out to those families directly.

Tonda or Lauren, feel free to chime in, here.

Thanks, everyone. Please let me know if you have any questions or concerns!

Molly

Figure 5.6   Molly's Project Update.

A few things pop out to me in Molly's update. It does the following:

■ **Updates others on the project.** Molly takes the time to "anchor" her team in what has been going on in the background. Given that many people working on the graduation project have a million other things they are juggling, this ensures people are up to speed on the latest key information.

■ **Provides all necessary resources.** Molly has thoughtfully hyperlinked items, such as the deck needed to review with seniors and a draft email to review. If you want others to help, you have to make it easy on them, or what I call "One-Clickable."

■ **Gives actionable next steps.** Really, isn't this what everyone always wants to know anyway? What do *I* actually have to do next? Molly outlines that very clearly for folks.

Maggie's Book Launch Daily Email

The most recent book I released was my micro-book *The Together Project Manager*. It's 123 pages of this chapter's themes, so if you're enjoying this chapter, you may want to seek out the book for a deeper dive. But I digress . . .

In the leadup to our release date, my amazing book production manager Maggie started a practice of sending a daily email to all the people involved, including our graphic designer, our webmaster, and other members of the Together Team.

Things to note:

■ **Quick Reminders for All.** Maggie listed updates for the entire team at the top of the email, contextualizing where we were at collectively in the process.

■ **Specific Tasks Per Person.** Chad could scan for his role, Manuel for his tasks, and so on. We each knew what the other people were doing.

■ **Keep It One Click.** Maggie included the hyperlinks needed for Manuel, so he could easily execute his task.

And of course, that fun, encouraging tone is amazing as well.

Reader Reflection: Questions to ask yourself about project communications:

■ Who needs to be in the loop on my project?

■ Of those people, what information do they need to know? Just results? Challenges? Deadlines?

■ How does the person/people like to receive information? Verbally? In writing? Visually?

■ What is the right frequency and cadence to keep them updated?

From: Maggie
Sent: Thursday, October 14, 2021 9:26 AM
To: Maia, Chad, Manuel
Cc: Kendra, Heidi
Subject: TPM daily update: October 14th!

Hi TPM team! (FYI Kendra + Heidi)

Quick reminders:

- **Upload to Amazon:** By Saturday, 10/16
- **Updated Together Press website goes live:** By end of day Tuesday, 10/19
- **Book live on Amazon** (+ pre-orders delivered!!): Wednesday, 10/20

Here are everyone's next steps:

Maggie

- Confirm Together Talk details!

Maia

- Behind the scenes blog post
- Design back-and-forth with Chad aka group texts that bring Maggie joy

Chad

- Book anchoring chart: on existing image, add dotted lines
- Individual files for website – please email to me when ready:
  - Table of Contents
  - Reader Reflection Guide
- Reminder – social media post

Manuel

- Website updates!
  - Landing page text (here)
  - Downloadable files for readers
  - Reminder: will send you the files from Chad separately (everything else is in Dropbox)

Let me know of any questions!

Maggie

Figure 5.7   Maggie's Daily Book Publishing Project Email.

As you consider your own project participants, you will likely see some variation in how they like to stay informed on your project. While it does take more time, be open to differentiating your communications. Your overall goal as a Together Teammate is to keep multiple pieces moving forward, while doing the essential communication along the way. Yes, a little bit of personalized project communication may take some time, but it is better than working on a project all alone and hitting roadblocks, or getting asked annoying questions about a delay you deemed reasonable, or getting no help on tasks that could easily be shared.

 Reader Reflection: Think of a few projects you have coming up. How could your project benefit from a deliberate communication plan?

POSITIVE PESSIMISM: PLAN FOR THE WORST, HOPE FOR THE BEST

My old boss used to say that I was the most positively pessimistic person she had ever met. At first I wasn't sure that was a compliment, but I came to realize that it was! What she meant was that I was often making backups for backups. Will it rain? Will the internet go down? Will a bus be late? Now, I'm in total agreement with the school of thought that, as author Oliver Burkeman says, we are all at the mercy of "your total vulnerability to events." Indeed, we are all vulnerable to things out of our control. At the same time, there is likely a predictable series of "things that might possibly go wrong" in our work. My thinking is let's plan for the more typical ones, and then leave headspace for the truly unpredictable. So what do I mean by typical things that could go wrong? I mean, some of the very basics, such as internet outages, sick days, transportation emergencies, and the like. On any given day, any of these things can happen. Toss in some special events and even more humans, and things are even more likely to get bumpy.

PLAN FOR THE UNEXPECTED BECAUSE IT ALWAYS HAPPENS – TRUST ME

This is always a fun exercise, right? Let's think about everything that could go wrong with a classic example: a staff gathering, something we all know and understand. It could be a retreat, or a party, or a meeting, but something where you are bringing together a group of people.

I like to break down possible unexpected situations into categories:

- **What are human things that could go wrong?** Well, people could show up to the wrong location, they may forget to bring their printed prework, or forget to pack a charger. So: We could think about really proactive communication with directions to the venue, and also have a "Need Help?" box with extra power cords, copies of prework, and other items people may need. Lesson Learned: Have extras on hand.

- **What are venue things that could go wrong?** The door might be locked, the room might not be set up properly, the sound system that they promised would be flawless might not be working. So: We could arrive extra early and bring our own sound system. Lesson Learned: Pack your own speakers. Just kidding, sort of.

- **What are weather things that could go wrong?** The outdoor teambuilding part of the retreat could get rained out. So: We could start checking the weather a week in advance, and a pick a "decide by" time so we are not scrambling to communicate the morning of the event. Lesson Learned: Pick back-up days and times or a back-up location.

- **What are food things that could go wrong?** We could run short on picnic lunches for after the outdoor event. The vegetarian options might not show up. So: We could increase the order size. We could identify a back-up vendor. Lesson learned: Overorder.

- **What are transportation things that could go wrong?** Well, the laser tag vendor could have a flat tire and break down. That would really be a bummer at the end of field day. So: We could find out if they can deliver the day before so that there is a bit of a cushion. Lesson learned: Add time buffers.

Once you have considered how you will plan in advance for potential hiccups, you will want to document and communicate that to others.

INTEGRATE WITH YOUR TOGETHER TOOLS

Now that you have added at least one Project Plan to your Together Toolkit, you will want to integrate it into preparing for your week. We will cover this in more detail in a future chapter when I describe Meeting with Yourself and Weekly Worksheet.

When you review the Project Plans, you may want to:

- Sort and filter your tasks for the upcoming week and add them to your weekly plan.

- Sort and filter tasks for other people and send them assignments, reminders, or offers to co-work.

- Forecast Forward and look for possible trouble spots in the upcoming plan and identify how you will adjust.

TURBO TOGETHERNESS

Project Plans are an integral part of Togetherness, and they are a fantastic way to spread your Togetherness wings and practice your Together Try-Its. Often, one of the most unique skillsets you can offer in your role is the ability to clearly and efficiently manage multiple players through steps to lead to outcomes. People get busy and things get lost in the shuffle; having someone keep things on track is vital to achieve the goals you want. In order to get started, here is a quick checklist of action items.

- ◼ Determine what actually needs a Project Plan

- ◼ Create Project Summaries, as needed

- ◼ Decide which tool or format you will use to house your Project Plan

- ◼ Map out the tasks to complete the actual project

- ◼ Keep people in the project loop through regular updates and status checks

- ◼ Integrate with your overall Together Tools

If you are excited to dive deeper into Project Management, check out my micro-book *The Together Project Manager*.

MANAGER MOMENT

If you manage or lead Together Teammates toward various projects, then you will likely want a method to check on progress toward the outcome of the overall product – without getting buried in the weeds of multiple Project Plans. Let's say you have six direct reports running two to three projects each. Well, you get the picture. That is a lot of Project Plans to review regularly. So, how can you stay involved enough with your team's projects, without wading way, way into the weeds of the Google Sheets?! Here are a few strategies:

- Develop organizational common language on roles and responsibilities within projects. For example, who are the Deciders? The Recommenders? I personally like using the MOCHA framework from the Management Center.

- Be clear what level (shallow or deep) you are leaning in on each project and articulate that to your team members.

- Request Project Summaries for each project and review them regularly during one-on-one meetings.

- Set specific checkpoints or deadlines where you would like to hear updates and celebrates.

- Keep your eyes focused on the outcomes or goals of the project and pull up to review the bigger picture. Ask questions around the results.

- Be prepared to look and listen for roadblocks to help your teammate get to the outcomes without interference.

- Support in creating protected time for your colleague to focus on projects without interruption.

- Highlight progress being made (because your teammate may not have time to notice).

Managing people who are leading their own projects can be a great learning experience for all parties *if* you set it up for success on the front end. What doesn't work well is you, as the leader, constantly asking questions because of an absence of information or a lack of initial communication. Set up the systems to align on Project Summaries, get regular updates on the Project Plan, and be prepared to pitch in!

CHAPTER 6

Fill with Staples, Make Room for Snacks – Build a Weekly Worksheet

You are a Together Tool building machine! You have knocked out your Goals, your Year-at-a-Glance, the Comprehensive Calendar, and Long-Term List. (PS, nice work, y'all!) Now it's time to double down on an actual week. In work like yours, it can often feel like "Why bother to plan out my week? I'm just going to be responding to people all day long anyway," but most teammates truly do have more to their roles than the customer service or reactive portion. The reason you want to plan each week carefully – even though things *will* end up changing – is so that you can be clear on what matters most, support others as needed, leave room for last-minute items, and build in your own life too. The Weekly Worksheet is one of the most helpful tools in your Together arsenal to Pivot Powerfully. As a wise woman (oh wait, that's me!) often says, "The more planned you are, the more flexible you can be!"

In this chapter, you will:

- Articulate the purpose of planning ahead
- Review other teammates' Weekly Worksheets for ideas and inspirations

■ Determine a format for your Weekly Worksheet based on preferences and environment

■ Design your own Weekly Worksheet

Not planning ahead for the week leaves you potentially scrambling last-minute to complete things, possibly with unnecessary stress, and unable to effectively request help from others. And don't you want that wonderful and effective feeling of being proactive in your work – not simply reacting to things that come your way all day long? Sold yet? I hope so, because we see weekly planning make the biggest difference in people's lives when it comes to Togetherness. There's a reason why Pause to Plan is such an important Together Try-It. In fact, I even spend the entire next chapter walking you through how to make a checklist for this weekly planning. Let's reiterate the purpose of a Weekly Worksheet, and then we'll dive headfirst (in a good way) into various examples.

THE PURPOSE OF PLANNING FOR A WEEK

Your overall goal in planning your weeks with a decent level of detail is to have a clear sense of your priorities, and to position yourself to be ready to communicate to others and be flexible as things come up. Let's take a common analogy of grocery shopping. What happens if you just jump into the market without a list? I don't know about you, but that experience can leave me aimlessly wandering, blowing my budget, susceptible to purchasing snacks I don't need, and perhaps leaving without ingredients for complete meals. Now, translate this concept into how you prepare to enter your work weeks. If you don't have a strong plan around the proactive priorities (aka your work "staples"), you can easily spend the full week just grabbing work "snacks." By snacks, I mean the text, the email, the colleague who needs assistance right this minute – leaving the actual priorities of your work unattended to or without substantive progress. This is not to say you can't have a little room for snacks (M&Ms, anyone?), but you don't want them to squeeze out everything else.

 Weekly Worksheet: An hour-by-hour view of your time and To-Dos for the week ahead.

COMPONENTS OF A WEEKLY WORKSHEET

Before we jump into various examples, let's look at the anatomy of a Weekly Worksheet. Whatever form your Weekly Worksheet takes, there are some baseline components you'll want to have in place. As always, with any Together Tools, I welcome and encourage you to make it your own.

THE TOGETHER TEAMMATE® | **WEEKLY WORKSHEET**

_____'s Weekly Worksheet, Week of _____

PRIORITIES

Priority 1	Priority 2	Priority 3

SHAPE OF THE WEEK

	M	T	W	R	F	Weekend
Appts						
Deadlines						

Big Work	Emails/Calls (TMTs)	Meeting Notes

Errands/Home/Personal	To Read	Next Week

RESOURCES: template

© 2013 The Together Group, LLC

Figure 6.1   Weekly Worksheet Template.

■ **Priorities are named clearly.** This will be your Professional Priorities, hopefully distilled after working through Chapter 2 on your role and the goals/outcomes for your work. And yes, you can list your Personal Priorities too. It's helpful to list what is most important for the week.

■ **Clear view of deadlines.** The goal here is to make sure your deadlines are in one location for the week. For some of you digital folks out there, this will just be a slice out of your Comprehensive Calendar where they live as All-Day Appointments.

■ **Hourly schedule in place.** Whether you handwrite, or more likely, pull your weekly view of your digital calendar, I want you to place in your hard edges, such as appointments and meetings.

■ **Categorized view of your To-Dos.** Some of you may put your To-Dos directly into your calendar, and some of you may opt to put these in a separate list, or even (bonus points!) sort your Long-Term List into just the tasks for the particular week. Sometimes I like to call this the Little List.

■ **Room for the unexpected.** It's important to leave room for the work snacks that come in – both the welcome and the unwelcome ones. This may look like flexible time in your calendar, or open space to capture incoming To-Dos.

Now that you have a sense of the components of a Weekly Worksheet (Priorities + Schedule + Tasks + Extra Room), let's see how a variety of individuals build their own. Oh, yeah, and if you're worried about how much time it will take to create this on a weekly basis, I've got a whole chapter on this coming up. But the answer is . . . about 60 minutes once per week, and likely 10–15 minutes a day to keep this maintained as a relevant tool. It will be worth it, trust me! But I have a quick quiz for you first. I promise this quiz will help you see how you best want to build your Weekly Worksheet.

Pop Quiz: Are You A What-er Or A When-er?

First of all, there are no wrong answers, so don't be scared. This question is designed to elicit a quick reaction.

Quick Quiz: When you receive a new task due in a few weeks, do you prefer to

A. Add it to a list

B. Give it time on your calendar

C. None of the above

If you answered:

A. You are likely a What-er.

- You can often be heard saying things like, "Yes, I'll add that to my list!"

- You capture all tasks – big and small.

- You can be prone to . . . over-commitment.

If you answered:

B. You are likely more of a When-er.

- You may often say, "Sure, I can fit that in . . . next Tuesday."

- You often link tasks to specific times when you plan to complete the task.

- You can occasionally be perceived as . . . inflexible.

And if you answered C, just follow along for the ride and it will become clear.

The reason I began with this quick quiz is that some of you will realize that you may like to lead with a list for your week, and just use your schedule for meetings (What-ers). And on the flip side, some of you will find comfort in placing tasks for the week (taken from that Long-Term List) directly into specific time slots (When-ers). A lot of you will find a happy medium between What-ness and When-ness, which is my hope for you. And some of you will have to bend to your environment or role. What I mean by this is that if you work in an organization that is somewhat, shall we say, last-minute, then you may *have* to be a What-er to survive in that context because you will need the flexibility. If you work in a tightly scheduled meeting environment where events go back-to-back, then you may need to exercise some When-ness. The point here is selecting how you plan a week is going to be a combination of your preferences and your environment – sometimes they match, and sometimes there is tension. Making sense? If not, hang on for the ride as we review some samples of actual people, all of whom are somewhere on that What/When scale.

WEEKLY WORKSHEET SAMPLES

Most of us don't actually start a week with no plan and just react as things come up. More likely we have a sense of some things that happen regularly (let's call them our work "staples"), such as items that have recurring deadlines. And then we all have some items that come up on the fly or that pop up unpredictably (our work "snacks"). Our goal is to build in the staples and leave room for the snacks. Most Weekly Worksheets have a combination of staples, and much like a grocery list, you will likely scrawl or type additional To-Dos as they pop up all day long.

Let's see a few different methods that span across What-ness and When-ness, and across paper and digital. These are meant to give examples of ways Together Teammates plan their week, and you may find that you see something that works perfectly for you. But, more likely, you will decide you want to create your own. There are many forms it could take, but let's peek at a few popular options.

Jazmin's Weekly Worksheet: Google Calendar + Google Doc

Jazmin, a manager of school support and incubation at a nonprofit in Indianapolis, plans her week with the To-Dos first (as a What-er), followed by the schedule in her Google Calendar. Let's peek at how she planned out her week. As you review these samples, keep in mind you can always check the full-color versions at www.wiley.com/go/togetherteammate and part of the beauty is how individuals personalize their planning to their particular roles.

As you can tell, Jazmin wears many hats in her role, and it can be helpful to sort your To-Dos by the type of work you need to do. Think about it like this. If you wander into the grocery store with one huge list, it can feel hard to focus, it might take longer than you want it to, and you may become easily distracted. (Don't say it's just me!) So how do you push against this and strive for focus? Let's follow Jazmin's lead and learn from her approach. Here are some features of her Weekly Worksheet:

- **Categorized by type of task.** For example, Scheduling Work tasks may be very different than Meeting Preparation tasks. This can be helpful when Jazmin thinks about where she is physically during the day (because that impacts which materials she has available).

- **Strategic places for other information.** Jazmin also uses her Weekly Worksheet to grab other thoughts or ideas that pop up during the day, such as Newsletter Topics or Questions/Notes. While these are not exactly To-Dos, they are important items that need to be captured so she can return to them later. In the Together-verse, I often call these Thought Catchers.

- **Hard calendar edges in place.** Jazmin has space marked in her calendar for key meetings and events, as well as items for the weekend, such as the Mayor's Latino Heritage Celebration. This is pulled right over from her Comprehensive Calendar.

Weekly What to Do's

Week of 9/19-9/23

Calls/Emails	Projects	Scheduling	Meetings

☐ Respond to all RSVPs
☐ Walkthrough schedules
☐ Reach out to High Schools with College GO info
☑ ~~Email schools who have mail at the office~~
☑ ~~Send College GO info to high schools~~
	☐ Enrollment/Data Collection -using FormAssembly
	   ☐ Enrollment/data current and at scale
	   ☐ Deadline to have form sent out (ask Kelli)
	☐ School Website Information
		☑ ~~Connect Tata & Kelli~~
		☐ Edge21 Follow Up
		☐ Connect SM/LL & JJ
		   ☐ Tuesday 10-11am
			9/19
			  ☐ All Staff 9am
			  ☐ JS & JC Check In 1pm
			  ☐ JS & LL Check In 3pm
			9/20
			  ☐ Reschedule Dr. GL for October w/LL
			  ☐ P30 Set Up 11-2pm
			  ☐ Together Teammate 3-4:30pm
			  ☐ Quarterly Recruitment 6-7:30pm
			9/21
			  ☐ Edge21 Follow Up 11:30am
			9/22
			  ☐ Team Meeting 10am

Newsletter Topics	**Deadlines/Important Dates**	**Follow Up**	**Questions/Notes**
☐ New announcement (Rebuilding stronger plan) ☐ College GO ☐ Waiving college app fees (September 26-30th) ☐ Fellowship App Open ☐ Hispanic Heritage Month	☐ Count day(September 16th) ☐ Waiving app fees(September 26-30th) ☐ Data/Enrollment Collection (	☐ Deadline for enrollment/data form to be sent... ☐ Ask KM about LK-DoS position(next steps)	☐ What grade level each school plans to serve? ☐ Qualifications for DoS ☐ LK and JJ

Figures 6.2. Jazmin's Weekly Worksheet.

If we take my grocery store analogy a bit further, it's almost as if Jazmin created a set of categories like "Dairy, Produce, Frozen, Pantry," allowing her to get in and out of the store as efficiently as possible. Jazmin says, "My Weekly Worksheet helps me because I can prioritize my tasks by projects but also importance. It allows me to keep a weekly snapshot on one sheet, which makes it easier for me to manage and adapt to daily changes." Pivoting Powerfully, at its finest.

FAQ: How does Jazmin use this throughout the week? Can I see it in action? Jazmin's role also allows her to remain mostly digital, so she can keep this Google Doc + Google Calendar combination on her screens and devices all day – no need for paper here!

Jazmin starts the week with her plan, but then has room to add, delete, and move things around as priorities emerge or last-minute requests pop up throughout the week. This lets her be both proactive and flexible. Check out her active strike-throughs in this image as she completes tasks.

So you can see that your Weekly Worksheet helps you plan ahead *and* actively accomplish each of those tasks coming your way.

Weekly What to Do's

Calls/Emails	Projects	Scheduling	Meetings

☐ Set meetings with KM
☑ ~~TMT & OEI~~
☑ ~~Screenings for fellowship~~
☐ School Visits
  ☐ 5 more confirmations
	☑ ~~Enrollment/Data Collection using google docs~~
	  ☑ ~~Enrollment/data current and at scale~~
	  ☐ Need more enrollment form portfolio schools(listed in doc) Send to LL & JC for follow up
	
	☑ ~~School Website Information~~
	☐ ISLL info
	☐ POCs for schools
	☑ ~~Tutoring Program Powerpoint~~
	☑ ~~International Schools Trip (postponed until Fall)~~
	☐ BHM books for schools(in progress)
	☐ School Communication request form ?
	☑ ~~Intern tasks~~
		☑ ~~Ed Champions~~
		☑ ~~Fellowship Candidate Performance tasks~~
		☐ Fellowship formal interviews
		☐ Connections/check ins for KM
			2/6
			  ☑ ~~TMT/Gambier~~
			  ☑ ~~ISLL Planning~~
			2/7
			  ☑ ~~Lavinia training~~
			  ☑ ~~Update on Y22~~
			  ☑ ~~CLass~~
			2/8
			  ☑ ~~ISLL Planning~~
			  ☑ ~~ISLL Comms~~
			  ☑ ~~ISLL Internal~~
			2/9
			  ☑ ~~Team Meeting~~
			  ☑ ~~TMT/Lavinia~~
			  ☐ Teacher Mentoring Informational
			  ☐ Class
			
			2/10
			  ☐ Interns onsite
			  ☐ Team Lunch with potential candidate
			  ☐ Check in with PG

Figure 6.3   Jazmin's End-of-Week Weekly Worksheet.

Reader Reflection: What buckets might you need as you plan your week? Think about the categories of work you may need to do in a given week. And consider what new things are often coming up throughout the week that you'd like to jot down in a Thought Catcher right there on your Weekly Worksheet.

Eliana's Weekly Worksheet: A Together Template

Eliana, an operations team member at a school in the Bronx, preps for her week by blocking off time for her meetings, events, and work time, and she also leaves space for incoming tasks that she didn't know about before the week started. She is more of a When-er than Jazmin (above). What I mean by this is that more things are entered into her calendar. Let's go deeper and explore her approach. And if you like Eliana's approach, you can download a similar version on this book's website at www.wiley.com/go/togetherteammate.

Some of the blocks in Eliana's calendar are for meetings with other people. Many of the blocks are her own plan for how she will spend that chunk of time. Eliana is often on the move all day, so in her case it makes sense that she prints and carries around her Weekly Worksheet. She prefills some of her To-Dos, but leaves space to record new work as it arrives.

What stands out to me is:

- **Time blocked off for meeting preparation.** You *know* you have certain meetings that require various types of preparation, so it makes sense to block time to get ready.

- **Time allocated to attendance changes.** Student attendance is a big part of Eliana's role so time – at a certain time of day – is blocked off to do this work.

- **Beast Mode time.** Did you catch that Beast Mode time? This is where Eliana proactively blocks off time to focus on her priorities. And yes, I know you get interrupted all the time. Some strategies for that are coming up in the chapter on the Daily Deluge.

- **Strategic bucketing of To-Dos.** Lastly, Eliana created her tasks for the week by bucketing them with Big To-Dos (usually correlated to the calendar), Small To-Dos (these are often incoming during the day), Emails/Phone Calls that she needs to do from her workspace, and of course, Life To-Dos – because she is one person with one week that has to contain both work and life. Connecting back to our last chapter, Eliana can pull her To-Dos for the week from her Long-Term List. Think about it like hacking off a bit of the big list and creating your own Little List for the week ahead.

Reader Reflection: What stands out to you as you reviewed Eliana's Weekly Worksheet? What sections might you need for your Weekly Worksheet?

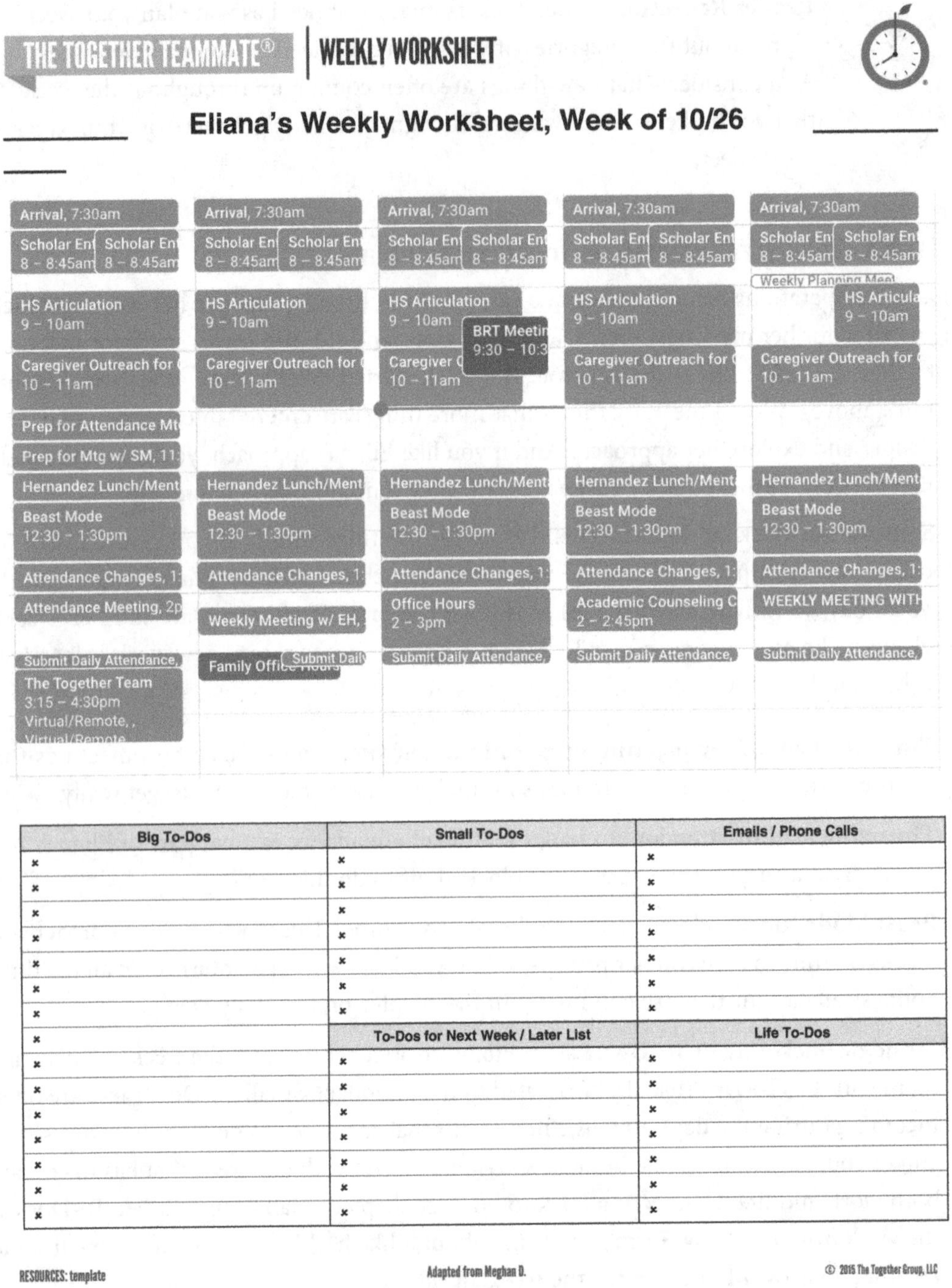

THE TOGETHER TEAMMATE® | WEEKLY WORKSHEET

Eliana's Weekly Worksheet, Week of 10/26

Arrival, 7:30am	Arrival, 7:30am	Arrival, 7:30am	Arrival, 7:30am	Arrival, 7:30am
Scholar Ent 8 – 8:45am	Scholar Ent 8 – 8:45am	Scholar Ent 8 – 8:45am	Scholar Ent 8 – 8:45am	Scholar Ent 8 – 8:45am	Scholar Ent 8 – 8:45am	Scholar Ent 8 – 8:45am	Scholar Ent 8 – 8:45am	Scholar Ent 8 – 8:45am	Scholar Ent 8 – 8:45am

Weekday columns content:

- **Monday:** Arrival, 7:30am | Scholar Ent 8 – 8:45am | Scholar Ent 8 – 8:45am | HS Articulation 9 – 10am | Caregiver Outreach for 10 – 11am | Prep for Attendance Mt | Prep for Mtg w/ SM, 11: | Hernandez Lunch/Ment | Beast Mode 12:30 – 1:30pm | Attendance Changes, 1: | Attendance Meeting, 2p | Submit Daily Attendance, | The Together Team 3:15 – 4:30pm Virtual/Remote, , Virtual/Remote

- **Tuesday:** Arrival, 7:30am | Scholar Ent 8 – 8:45am | Scholar Ent 8 – 8:45am | HS Articulation 9 – 10am | Caregiver Outreach for 10 – 11am | Hernandez Lunch/Ment | Beast Mode 12:30 – 1:30pm | Attendance Changes, 1: | Weekly Meeting w/ EH, | Family Office Hours | Submit Dail

- **Wednesday:** Arrival, 7:30am | Scholar Ent 8 – 8:45am | Scholar Ent 8 – 8:45am | HS Articulation 9 – 10am | BRT Meetin 9:30 – 10:3 | Caregiver C 10 – 11am | Hernandez Lunch/Ment | Beast Mode 12:30 – 1:30pm | Attendance Changes, 1 | Office Hours 2 – 3pm | Submit Daily Attendance,

- **Thursday:** Arrival, 7:30am | Scholar Ent 8 – 8:45am | Scholar Ent 8 – 8:45am | HS Articulation 9 – 10am | Caregiver Outreach for 10 – 11am | Hernandez Lunch/Ment | Beast Mode 12:30 – 1:30pm | Attendance Changes, 1: | Academic Counseling C 2 – 2:45pm | Submit Daily Attendance,

- **Friday:** Arrival, 7:30am | Scholar Ent 8 – 8:45am | Scholar Ent 8 – 8:45am | Weekly Planning Meet | HS Articula 9 – 10am | Caregiver Outreach for 10 – 11am | Hernandez Lunch/Ment | Beast Mode 12:30 – 1:30pm | Attendance Changes, 1: | WEEKLY MEETING WITH | Submit Daily Attendance,

Big To-Dos	Small To-Dos	Emails / Phone Calls
✗	✗	✗
✗	✗	✗
✗	✗	✗
✗	✗	✗
✗	✗	✗
✗	✗	✗
✗	✗	✗
✗	**To-Dos for Next Week / Later List**	**Life To-Dos**
✗	✗	✗
✗	✗	✗
✗	✗	✗
✗	✗	✗
✗	✗	✗
✗	✗	✗
✗	✗	✗

Figure 6.4   Eliana's Weekly Worksheet.

Similar to Jazmin, Eliana also used her Weekly Worksheet to actively move through her week, though, as noted, Eliana prints hers so that she has a paper version handy as her "live" document throughout the week. In fact, let's peer into an end-of-week image. She is even noting quick additions to her calendar that come up throughout the day as she moves around her school building. If your role is on-the-go, this is a great Togetherness practice.

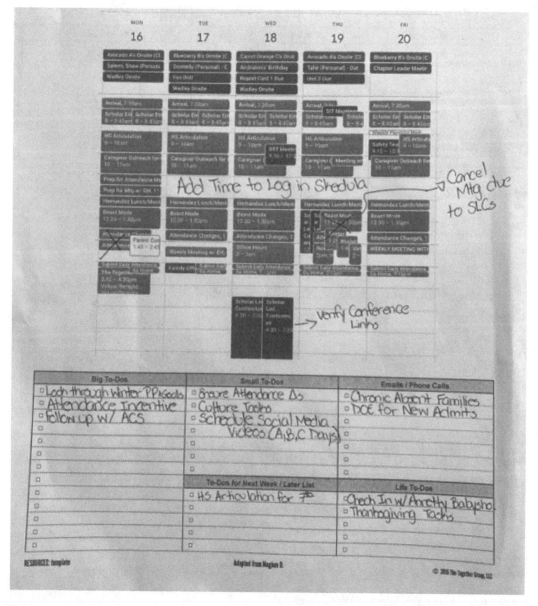

Figure 6.5   Eliana's End-of-Week Weekly Worksheet.

THE TOGETHER TEAMMATE® | WEEKLY WORKSHEET

Professional Goals		Personal Goals
1. Turn started applications into completed ones!		1. Complete tasks related to my new home and upcoming wedding.
2. To work on party planning for our big event for our new Cohort.		2. To take some time to do something for myself- other than work, eat, sleep, and plan my wedding.

Priorities/Work Time 1	Priorities/Work Time 2	Home/Personal
Email/ text students regarding their apps.	Meet with colleagues to strategize/ plan for the party.	Go to the formalwear place for my fiance's measurements and to pick out formalwear for groom and groomsmen.
Strategize with colleagues on new ways to get students to finish their apps.	Create an organized task list with tasks delineated to different colleagues.	Submit menus for rehearsal dinner and reception.
Visit schools with acceptance packages and acceptance awards for their senior banquets.	Start my first tasks from the spreadsheet.	Procure home insurance.
Communicate with school leaders to get their students to finish apps.	Meet with my manager and create a list of all items needed to purchase for the party.	Take a bath and get on my peloton!

Deadlines & Dates
Impromptu school visit at NHH on 5/4
Impromptu school visit to Mcmain on 5/5
Deliver acceptance packages and certificates by 5/6
Meetings with supervisor on 5/3 and 5/5
Party planning meeting on 5/5
Together team member homework due 5/4
Meeting with Jackie 5/4
SNAP docx due 5/4
Attend school check ins on 5/2 and 5/5

(Weekly calendar schedule block with entries including: TES Time, YouthForce Sta, Work block, NOAH May Sch 12pm, New Harmony 1pm, The Together Team Member (Class 1) 2:15 – 4:15pm Zoom link to come via email; In Person LAUNCH Success Training 9am–12pm, 1:1 EF & HC 1pm, Edna Karr Awar 6:30pm Edna K; Update Applicant, YouthForce NOI, SNAP E&T 1–2pm, SNAP monthly m, Send reminder t; LAUNCH Mixer/Welco 9–10:30am Circle, Douglas/ JFK 12pm, Enter applica 1–2pm, Hannah/Emily T; Update Applicant, In Person LAUNCH Fut ure 9am 310, Deliver T-shirts 1pm Livingston)

Follow Up	Next Week/Later	Thought Catcher	Thought Catcher
Check party planning sheet daily.	Send SNAP civil rights training list to Steph		
Follow up with students and schools re applications.	Check items on the move checklist		
	Attend 5 school check ins.		

Figure 6.6   Hannah's Weekly Worksheet.

Let's peek at another Weekly Worksheet model. This one leads with the priorities, adds the schedule, and then follows up with strategically grouped To-Dos.

Hannah's Weekly Worksheet: A Together Template

Hannah, a team member at a New Orleans workforce development nonprofit, sets up her Weekly Worksheet with a few distinct categories. While there are similarities with the previous models, each one has its own flavor and flair. Like Eliana, Hannah also uses a Together Template.

Hannah pulls elements slightly differently than the first two models. Let's dig in to what we can learn from this example.

- **Priorities are loud and clear.** Hannah is planning a big event for a cohort event and she's also planning her own wedding. Both are given equal weight at the top of her Weekly Worksheet. They are then given weight in her calendar.

- **Deadlines are shouted out!** Hannah keeps a list of her upcoming deadlines on the right-hand side of her Weekly Worksheet so she can keep them front and center.

- **Personal tasks and goals.** Because Hannah is in the midst of wedding planning, she builds those tasks right into her Weekly Worksheet as well. Hooray for balance!

- **Next Week/Later.** This is helpful because as Hannah moves through her week, she will inevitably have thoughts to jot for later. This space allows her to capture them for – you got it – later!

 Reader Reflection: How can you incorporate the personal side into your Weekly Worksheet?

 FAQ: What if I want to be a When-er and schedule in those work blocks, but I don't know how long something will take?

Ahh, this is an age-old and excellent question. It's often hard to know how long an assignment will take, especially if you are new in your role. You have a few options:

- **Determine level of priority.** Tier it if you have to, and then see how much time you can give it. For example, if planning the holiday party is one of my main priorities this semester and I have never created

(Continued)

an invitation before, I may want to just go ahead and give myself an hour or so to do this, giving it lots of room on my Weekly Worksheet. I can pay attention to how long it actually takes and remember for next time.

■ **Ask others who have done it before.** How long should it take to process all reimbursements? How long does it take to order lunch for this event?

■ **Figure out what tasks take you longer, for various reasons.** I'm a procrastinator when it comes to lesson design. I know this about myself and I have mechanisms in place to manage it. I imagine you may have a set of things that don't bring you energy and therefore may take you longer. Think about how to motivate yourself and remember that where you place it in your day will matter.

Let's move into the world of a Together Teammate who is a blend of paper and digital, as well as a combo of What-er and When-er.

Ashley's Weekly Worksheet: Outlook Calendar

Let's take a look at Ashley's Weekly Worksheet, housed in her Outlook calendar. As context, Ashley is a project manager in a large school district with requests flying in all kinds of directions each day. Ashley is oriented toward her digital When-er identity, but her system incorporates a bit of paper and a bit of What-er-ness.

You can see how she calendars in To-Dos. Of course, you may be thinking (or even, frankly worried) that packing your calendar too full will leave no room for responding to requests or proactively helping others. This is a case where buffering your calendar strategically can help. Let's peek in a bit more detail.

Ashley does a few things that help make her Weekly Worksheet a useful and practical tool:

■ **Blocks time for routine work at specific times of day.** Ashley receives a lot of requests that come up over email. In spite of books telling us "not to check email in the morning," most of your roles need to have a handle on email and work that comes in from the evening and early morning – especially items related to scheduling and events. Ashley blocks off time for these email checks in the morning and she also leaves extra empty work time at the back end of the week as emails and requests may start to build up.

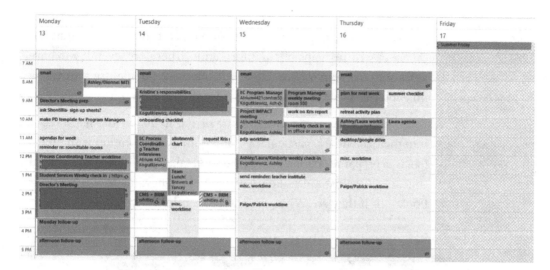

Figure 6.7 Ashley's Weekly Worksheet.

■ **Calendars out work blocks.** Ashley tries to calendar out all items for the week, including actual work blocks to work on various checklists, such as the summer checklist and the onboarding checklist. She also leaves miscellaneous work time for other items that may come up.

What about those items that just pop up during the day? Most very digital When-ers, like Ashley, may need something to "catch" additional tasks tossed at them. For this, Ashley uses a paper-based To-Do list throughout the day to capture new tasks that come up via email or text or hallway ambush, then she returns to her desk to either do it (and cross it directly off the list), if quick, or calendar it (back to Outlook), if it is longer.

FAQ: What if I want to keep a digital calendar, but use a paper-based or combo Weekly Worksheet?

You can do this! I call this a combo approach, and this is very typical for several reasons:

■ Most organizations use digital calendars to schedule meetings with each other and as communication tools for when you are and are not available. And many people carry phones where they can see this calendar.

■ A lot of you are on the move all day long, and paper can be an easier place to capture things on the fly, modify, and adjust manually – as

(Continued)

you saw in some of the previous examples. Not to mention the physical act of writing helps retain information. Therefore, even if you have a primary list somewhere digitally, I often see people use a traveling notebook or piece of paper to catch things as they come in.

■ I also see many people assign some of the items on the list directly into their calendars, particularly if it requires collaboration with others (such as preparation for a board meeting), takes long periods of focused time, or is against a deadline – like me blocking time to work on this book – or if they are When-ers and more calendar-oriented by nature.

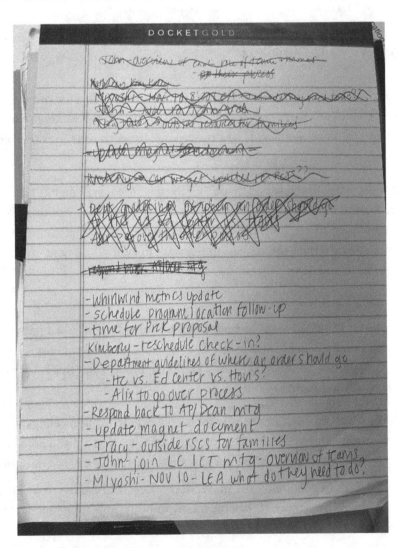

Figure 6.8   Ashley's Notebook to Catch New Work.

As you looked at each of these Weekly Worksheet samples, you probably noticed a few common themes:

- Each person considered the various inputs they generated or received.

- Consideration was given to their own physical environment and materials.

- Individuals varied between What-ers and When-ers and paper and digital choices.

- The level of detail varied depending on the role.

What everyone has in common is one centralized location for capturing their To-Dos and Calendar items and for the week – both proactively and reactively. What I have seen repeatedly is that Pausing to make a Plan for the week ahead – in whatever form that takes for you (I will introduce a systematic approach in the next chapter) – reaps benefits by giving you a clear sense of what matters the most, confidence in your plan for the week, and a strategy for capturing new work. Your Weekly Worksheet will help you feel a sense of control and empowerment – and hopefully enjoyment – in your role.

PERSONALIZE YOUR WEEKLY WORKSHEET TOOL(S)

The good news is that you have many, many options for a tool to help plan out your week. For many of you, your organizations already exist in some kind of digital calendar platform, and that is going to present the least amount of work for you to make a plan for your week. If you happen to be more paper-based or more of a What-er, that's okay too, of course. For most of you, your Weekly Worksheet will be some combination of your Weekly Calendar plus a set of lists for the week, most likely pulling some items from your Long-Term List and Comprehensive Calendar. Building it (which you only need to do once and then you'll have the template to use on a weekly basis) is about selecting the right planning tool that fits you, your organization, your work, and your life.

One frequent challenge with selecting a Weekly Worksheet tool is that there are so many choices out there. Rarely – and hopefully never – is this choice mandated by your employer. This will often be a personal choice, and whether you modify a Together Template, rely solely on the weekly view of your digital calendar, or construct your own, it is dependent on:

- Your own personal preferences. Do you prefer to write or type items?

- Your own appetite for various pieces of technology or paper. Are you more of a digital or paper calendar person?

■ Whether your job is mobile or stationary. For those of you who are often on the move, you may find that you want to print out your Weekly Worksheet and carry it, or perhaps view it on a tablet to update items as they keep coming in.

■ Your level of personalization needed. Do you need a section to capture questions for your manager? Do you want several lists of To-Dos for the week, organized in a certain way – such as type of task like Jazmin and Eliana, or by length of time it would take?

While this is not meant to be prescriptive and I think it is truly a bit of a Together Trial and Error to find your best fit, I have typically seen:

■ When-ers will likely find ways to include as many things as possible into their actual calendars for the week – even priorities.

■ What-ers will feel more peace with a more open calendar and tons of room for proactive and reactive lists.

These things matter because they impact your design of your Weekly Worksheet!

If you're still feeling stuck about what tool, recall that you just took a spin through a few samples to see this idea in action for others. We have lots of blank templates available at www.wiley.com/go/togetherteammate and you are very welcome to borrow from those for a plug-and-play experience. Or if none of the templates quite fit the bill, or if you crave some more color, flair, or just making it your own with specific categories or sections, you are encouraged to personalize your Weekly Worksheet template. Which of the previous samples were most resonant with you?

Reader Reflection: What form will your own Weekly Worksheet take? Why is this the best choice for you? Feel free even to sketch one out with sections you may need.

FAQ: Should I include a personal section in my Weekly Worksheet?
If your Weekly Worksheet is an Outlook or Google Calendar that can be viewed by other members of your organization, this is an important question to consider. From a practical standpoint, if you have a passport appointment in the middle of the workday or need to make a phone call about the DJ for your wedding, it is likely helpful to have that appointment (and travel time) in your calendar or that task on your list. The rest is a matter of your organization's culture and your personal preference.

Some of you may work for organizations where "bringing your whole self to work" is encouraged and you feel personally comfortable with this. Others of you may wish to put the "after 5 p.m." items somewhere else entirely – a personal refrigerator calendar or a planner. Some of this decision-making may also depend on how flexible your work is, if it blends into evenings or is a hard stop. If there's a chance you'd be asked to stay late to work on something, it might be important to block off when you have evening commitments in your personal life, to be clear about which evenings you aren't available to work late. If you have personal To-Dos that must be handled in the workday, by all means, toss them on your Weekly Worksheet.

PRACTICE BUILDING YOUR FIRST WEEKLY WORKSHEET

Now it is time to build your own! Yes, like grocery lists, your Weekly Worksheet will likely look different than those of your colleagues, and that is okay.

What we want to consider is how to "structure" yours so it best works for you.

- **Plan the priorities.** What matters the most this coming week? What actions can you take?

- **Plop in the recurring To-Dos.** Hopefully, those recurring deadlines are listed in your Comprehensive Calendar. Let's plop that on your schedule for the week. Consider what energy level the tasks take and what physical location is easiest to complete the work. Plot that in too.

- **Check the meetings.** Do you have any meetings coming up? What kind of preparation is needed? What kind of follow up can you anticipate? Go ahead and block that time out as well.

- **Block out customer-service time.** Are there any times of day or week when you know will be heavy on requests? People lining up to ask you questions? If so, let's put that on your calendar too.

- **Plot the personal.** Any personal events happening? Or ones you want to happen? Go ahead and map this out. It's important, so get it in there.

The purpose here is to make sure you have considered each item that could impact your week overall. Keep in mind that your Weekly Worksheet equals your Calendar plus Set of

Little Lists for the week. Depending on your predilection for What-ness or When-ness, you may have a fuller calendar and smaller or *no* Little List (hey When-ers!) or a bigger Little List and a less full-looking calendar (What-ers!). Regardless of where you place the To-Dos, you also want to mine for other places To-Dos could emerge (hint, hint: Long-Term List) so you can get ahead on planning for them.

■ Are there any newsletters or staff memos that determine action items?

■ Are there any organization-wide trackers or calendars that result in To-Dos for you?

■ Do any project plans exist where you are tagged with To-Dos or are leading for others?

■ Are there any meetings or events coming up where you assist or lead preparation?

■ What other information might you want to capture during the week? Think of Jazmin gathering newsletter ideas or another person summarizing thoughts for their manager.

All of these questions have led you to build your own Weekly Worksheet that reflects priorities, meetings, events, and To-Dos for the week ahead. Now that you have built it, it will only work if you actually use it. The final section of this chapter will be how to bring your Weekly Worksheet to life throughout your week.

PUT YOUR WEEKLY WORKSHEET INTO ACTION

Of course, all of this weekly planning won't be useful at all if the Weekly Worksheet gets created and then set aside. To make this tool work for you, it needs to be a living document integrated completely into your workday. This will help you respond to new requests with ease, shift priorities as needed, and/or stay the course when necessary. Let's talk about the how (and why) of keeping your Weekly Worksheet humming.

■ **Share your Weekly Worksheet with your manager for alignment and accountability.** Likely you have planned out your upcoming week by Friday (don't worry, I aim to convince you of the necessity of this in the next chapter). At this point, it usually makes sense to share your plan for the week with your manager(s). This serves the purpose of proactively communicating your planned tasks, flagging capacity issues as too full or have room, and if your manager is, let's gently say, Less Than Together (LTT), you can assist them in forecasting items for the future. This could look like emailing it to them, sharing it in a one-on-one meeting, or posting it on some kind of shared organizational software.

■ **Keep your Weekly Worksheet accessible.** Whether your tool is paper-based or digital or a combo of both, I want you to keep your Weekly Worksheet with you at all times – whether in your pocket on your phone or printed out and on a clipboard in your backpack. This is important so you can regularly refer to it, and catch items as they are tossed your way. We are going for a one-stop shop here, the *one* place you look each week.

■ **Pay attention to your notations.** Your Weekly Worksheet may look messy by the end of the week, especially if you are more paper-based. This is okay. It simply means you're using your Weekly Worksheet wisely and capturing everything that comes your way. For example, you may find yourself jotting notes throughout the week about what to share in the staff newsletter. Well, pay attention to that because maybe your Weekly Worksheet needs a staff newsletter section.

You will likely make edits to your approach over time. This is a good thing. I've been weekly planning for decades, and I am never afraid to change things up as circumstances dictate. There was a period of time I personally needed to become a more paper-based What-er, and then another period of time when I had to be super "When-ish." My goal here is that you can plan in a way that meets your particular needs at the time. In a way, the process of getting very clear about the week ahead is more helpful than the product itself. One common misconception for people is that if they don't follow their Weekly Worksheet to the letter exactly, they are failures. Exactly incorrect! The goal is to have a map for the week created by Pausing to Plan – and then feel confident in making adjustments when they inevitably become necessary – which is Pivoting Powerfully.

Reader Reflection: How will you hold your Weekly Worksheet close throughout the week?

TURBO TOGETHERNESS

The Weekly Worksheet is really a cover sheet of all of your Together Tools mushed up together for the week. Consider yourself pulling from your various sources (Comprehensive Calendar, Long-Term List, Project Plans) and creating a very detailed plan for the coming week. The key takeaways from this chapter are to have you feeling both "I can and will plan ahead for the week!" as well as "Things change throughout the week; my Weekly Worksheet will help make choices and Pivot Powerfully!" While I know many things come at you fast and furious all week, my hope is the Weekly Worksheet will ground and guide you to be both focused and flexible for the week or weeks ahead. To get started on your Weekly Worksheet, here are the steps:

- Determine your preferred Weekly Worksheet method based on your What-ness or When-ness and preference for digital versus paper.

- Determine the personalized categories needed to fill in for each week.

- Create your Weekly Worksheet and use it throughout the week.

- Rely on that Weekly Worksheet when things "come up" (and we know they will) and use it to evaluate and make trade-offs between your To-Dos.

CHAPTER 7

Host a Meeting with Yourself – and Prep for the Week Ahead

Now that you have all of your Together Tools in place, the next step is to create a routine for using them, keeping them current and useful. A Meeting with Yourself is where you pause, clean up the week behind you, and prepare for the week – and possibly months – ahead!

In this chapter, you will:

■ Determine which specific Clean Up tasks and Prepare tasks to conduct weekly

■ Build your Meeting with Myself checklist

■ Identify the best time and location to hold your weekly Meeting with Yourself

■ Plan how to communicate your weekly ritual to your team and others

■ Communicate adjustments needed or questions that arise as you plan

While it may feel like the stuff of daydreams to be able to stop and plan for the week ahead (I mean, great idea, Maia, but who has the time, in the midst of the workday, no less?!), this weekly ritual is imperative to ensure you reflect on what you accomplished, clean up the week behind you (deal with those sticky notes, perhaps?), pause to plan ahead, and perhaps even communicate with others and align on your workload for the week ahead.

Meeting with Myself: A systematic weekly meeting with yourself where you look back and look ahead to create your Weekly Worksheet.

MEETING WITH YOURSELF: THE WHY

In our almost 20 years of Together-ing with thousands of amazing people across the country, we have officially landed on the number one rule of Togetherness: Pause to Plan each week. This is when you will take a breath, clean up the week behind you, and get ready for the week ahead. Here is what you will accomplish by doing this:

- Clean up and process the inevitable backlog that emerges from the course of the week

- Celebrate your wins for the week and show gratitude to others

- Look ahead for the next week to specifically to see what is coming, and what requires preparation or delegation

- Plan out your actual work by stating your priorities, figuring out your Whats and Whens, and leaving room for things that come up

- Make sure you have enough professional and personal time buffers

- Communicate to others accordingly regarding priorities and tasks for the coming few weeks

So what specifically does this Meeting with Yourself entail, anyway? On a very practical level, it is a time once per week when you pause to plan the week ahead by reviewing all of your Together Tools to "clean up" the week behind you and then "prepare" for the week ahead. This is when you will go through each of your Together Tools and check in on your Priorities, review the Year-at-a-Glance, look ahead on your Comprehensive Calendar, and pick things off your Long-Term List. Additionally, you will check the status of your Project Plans and ultimately build your Weekly Worksheet.

 Reader Reflection: How could Pausing to Plan each week help you professionally and personally?

Think about it like this. Have any of you ever worked in retail or food service in your careers? [author raises hand for McDonald's and the Gap in high school]. And did you ever work the closing shift? [raises hand again]. Likely, there was some sort of store closing checklist that cleaned up the messy workplace: tally the register/cash, refold piles and piles of T-shirts that customers left in a mess, and tidy up the dressing rooms. And then you probably had a set of tasks to ensure opening the next day would be a prepared and fresh start (tasks such as refilling the walk-in refrigerator with burger condiments, restocking the frozen fry bin under the fryers, and checking the schedule of who's working tomorrow). Even if you never worked in retail or food service, you get the picture.

Sometimes these kinds of routines feel obvious, but when we are tired or depleted, it can be easy to skip them or forget them, only to have it be harder on us the next day. So, my goal in pushing documentation of your Meeting with Myself checklist is that having it written helps ensure it will actually happen, and a bonus is that it makes it easier to communicate to colleagues what you are doing and why. I don't know about you, but if I just enter "planning time" in my calendar, it sure can be easy to fall in an internet rabbit hole during that time instead of actually doing the planning.

What do I mean by checklist, anyway? At the most basic level, it is a written routine you use to clean up the week behind you and prepare for the week ahead.

THE TOGETHER TEAMMATE® | **MEETING WITH MYSELF**

Clean Up	Prepare
•	•
•	•
•	•
•	•
•	•
•	•
•	•

Figure 7.1 Meeting with Myself Checklist Template.

So, why a checklist or a "plan to plan?" Very simply, it is remarkably easy to skip a Meeting with Yourself. (See above re: internet rabbit hole.) It's not something that anyone else will be expecting of you, and amidst all your many priorities, it's a tempting thing to delete from your calendar. Whether it feels like you simply have too much to do to Pause to Plan or Forecast Forward, whether you are too tired to pick your head up and take a moment to Be the Bird's-eye, or whether you worry it may look to others like you are not actually doing the work you are paid to do (though I would strongly argue planning is the most important thing you can do for your organization), every force in the world will push back against you taking this 30–60 minutes once per week. Having a supportive checklist makes it much easier to ensure you actually do it. (And you might even want to build in some structural incentives – ask me about my apple fritter habit!)

Let's start with reviewing some of my favorite samples to see this in action.

MEETING WITH MYSELF CHECKLIST SAMPLES

Let's peek at a few personalized checklists from others. As you look at these examples, consider the actions you need to take each week during this time. You'll want to consider what format or tool is best to house this checklist. You might also start thinking about when and where you will Meet with Yourself. The purpose of reviewing these samples is to see different ways in which people Meet with Themselves to prepare for the week ahead – ultimately building their Weekly Worksheets.

Stacia's Meeting with Myself Checklist

Stacia, a recruiter for a group of schools in Nashville, keeps her Meeting with Myself checklist in her Outlook calendar as a recurring weekly appointment. She carefully divides her meeting into Clean-Up Items; this is a list of the items to take care of to put the previous week to rest, tidy up loose ends, and Close the Loops (another Together Try-It). She then pivots to Looking Ahead, and completes some key tasks to make sure she has a strong plan to enter the week.

As you can see, Stacia designed her checklist very specifically for her role. There are a few things I'm excited to point out:

■ She updates the recruitment tracker, a spreadsheet she uses to track all candidates currently in play.

■ She builds in time to send gratitude emails and messages. How lovely is that?

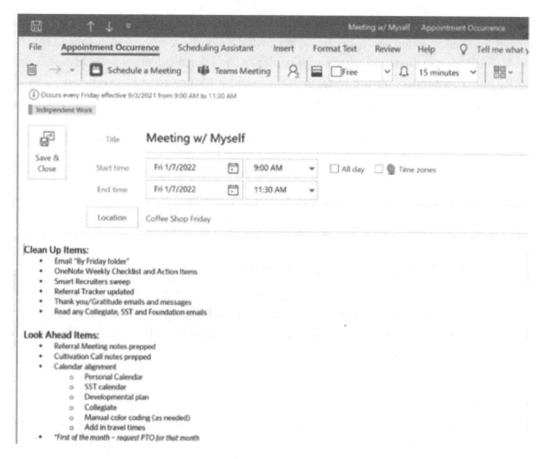

Figure 7.2   Stacia's Meeting with Myself Checklist.

■ In her email, there is a "By Friday" folder. This is where Stacia slides messages she receives throughout the week that need to be addressed by the end of the week. During her Meeting with Herself, she clears this folder. Yes, this *is* doing some of the work (rather than defining it), but Stacia blocks enough time to make sure it can happen without derailing her whole meeting.

■ Stacia then takes the time to align her various calendars (Personal, SST, etc.) for the following week with personal and travel times included.

Stacia describes the impact of her weekly planning process: "My Meeting with Myself helps me prepare for the week to come because in the world of recruitment, no week looks the same as the last. There are *many* stakeholders (potential candidates, active candidates, principals, hiring managers, current teachers, and other leaders) who I'm in contact with weekly – lots of moving parts. My dedicated time with myself helps me take time to clean up any loose ends, while also focusing on my own development and planning ahead for the week to come; it realigns me with my priorities. After I finish Meeting with Myself, I feel clarity and a rootedness for the week to come because I know what's to come and how to best build in work time as well as mental health time!"

 Reader Reflection: How could a Meeting with Yourself help *you*?

Let's look at another example of someone else's closing out a week and preparation for the next.

Dominique's Meeting with Myself Checklist

Dominique, a director of data and technology for a large charter network in New Orleans, set up her Meeting with Myself checklist as a series, with the option to check off each step of each week's meeting over time. Gotta love a data director! Let's dive in a bit more to Dominique's organized approach.

Dom's Meeting with Myself SY 22.23

Looking Back	09/29/2022	10/06/2022	10/13/2022	10/20/2022	10/27/2022	11/03/2022	11/10/2022	11/17/2022	12/01/2022	12/08/2022	12/15/2022
Review Chris/Dom meeting notes for action items	☐	☐	☐	☐	☐	☐	☐	☐	☐	☐	☐
Review CCS/Striz meeting notes for action items	☐	☐	☐	☐	☐	☐	☐	☐	☐	☐	☐
Review Data Manager meeting notes (Height, Akili, Tubman) for action items	☐	☐	☐	☐	☐	☐	☐	☐	☐	☐	☐
Review Team Data meeting notes for action items	☐	☐	☐	☐	☐	☐	☐	☐	☐	☐	☐
Clean up desktop	☐	☐	☐	☐	☐	☐	☐	☐	☐	☐	☐
Clean up Inbox	☐	☐	☐	☐	☐	☐	☐	☐	☐	☐	☐
Review & Reflect on Weekly worksheet "What did I accomplish? "What happened? "How does it make me feel? "What do I need to do next?	☐	☐	☐	☐	☐	☐	☐	☐	☐	☐	☐
Looking Ahead	09/29/2022	10/06/2022	10/13/2022	10/20/2022	10/27/2022	11/03/2022	11/10/2022	11/17/2022	12/01/2022	12/08/2022	12/15/2022
Update Weekly Worksheet "What are my priorities and goals? "What needs to come off the Later List in Keep?	☐	☐	☐	☐	☐	☐	☐	☐	☐	☐	☐
Update calendar with work times for tasks	☐	☐	☐	☐	☐	☐	☐	☐	☐	☐	☐
Update Later Lists	☐	☐	☐	☐	☐	☐	☐	☐	☐	☐	☐
Start agendas for next week's Check-Ins	☐	☐	☐	☐	☐	☐	☐	☐	☐	☐	☐

Figure 7.3 Dominique's Meeting with Myself Checklist.

Similar to Stacia, Dominique bucketed her Meeting with Myself Checklist into two categories: Looking Back and Looking Ahead. Dominique was incredibly purposeful and detailed as she built this checklist, and if you reference the version on this book's website at www.wiley.com/go/togetherteammate, you will even find she hyperlinked to various items she needed. Here are some of my favorite highlights of this model:

- **Meeting notes review.** Dominique has specified which of her various meetings have notes to review. For example, you will see Dominque link to her meeting notes with her manager (Chris), Data Manager meetings, and Team Data meetings. Certainly, many of you take notes in your meetings, but finding a systematic time to review those notes can feel impossible. (For more details on meeting notes, don't worry, that's coming in Section 3.)

- **Clean up the physical and digital spaces.** Dominique reserved some time to clean up the digital and physical spaces. You know, files that accumulate in Google Drive and papers that can quickly pile on desks or in bags. (And yes, you guessed it, we have a chapter coming up on organizing digital spaces as well.)

- **Look ahead to build the Weekly Worksheet.** Keeping it very true to form, Dominique then notes that the Looking Ahead section is all about the building of the Weekly Worksheet – with adding work times to the calendar for tasks. Dominique notes that she can look at her Priorities, Later Lists (equivalent to the Long-Term List), and Project Plans to pull out items for the week.

Ultimately, when Dominique completes her Meeting with Myself, she then feels prepared to tackle the week ahead. She says, "I've found it tremendously helpful to have a Meeting with Myself . . . it's valuable time to review what's happened and what I need to look toward. It's so useful to have time dedicated solely to organizing my thoughts and actions for the upcoming week. It helps me feel more prepared, and in turn that raises the confidence and trust of those I support and work alongside."

 Reader Reflection: Jot down a few Clean-Up and Prepare items for your own Meeting with Yourself. They don't have to be the same as Dominique's, but think about your own role and the tasks that would help you clean up and prepare each week. If it helps, go ahead and download one of our free Together (modifiable) templates and create a recurring digital appointment on your calendar.

Lauren's Meeting with Myself Checklists

Lauren, a manager of special projects for a large nonprofit organization, creates a recurring appointment in her Outlook calendar – in a table form. This image shows how she wisely uses this time.

Similar to the other examples, Lauren has strong Clean-Up and Prepare sections. She also adds some more of her own flavor to personalize her process:

- **Set the stage.** Lauren realizes that entering into the "planning zone" may take a few steps, so she lights a candle, grabs a beverage, and puts on some mood music.

- **Make it multiple choice.** Lauren gives herself a bit of "multiple choice" as she cleans up. For example, it doesn't just say "clear inbox," but rather "forward, respond, sort, or delete." By making her choices clear, she doesn't let herself get stuck staring at those emails lingering in her inbox.

- **Reflect.** The Prepare portion starts with a bit of reflection with "roses and thorns for the week." Like many of you, Lauren is moving quickly to execute all of the work, so she dedicates this time to considering her successes and areas of growth.

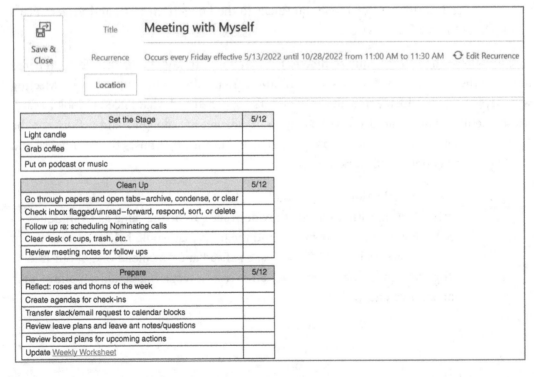

Figure 7.4   Lauren's Meeting with Myself Checklist.

■ **Move Whats to Whens.** Lauren takes the last step in building her Weekly Worksheet by transferring Slack or email requests to actual calendar blocks, thus "When-ing" up her "Whats." (If you skipped the Weekly Worksheet chapter, I'm not mad, but you might want to go back and take the When-er or What-er Quiz so you know what I'm talking about here!)

 Reader Reflection: What could you do to Set the Stage for your own Meeting with Yourself? Do you need some music, a snack, or a couple minutes of meditation?

 FAQ: Is Meeting with Myself actually doing the work or just planning the work? This is a question I've grappled with for years! The best analogy – credit given to a member of my team – is to think of a Meeting with Yourself like meal planning, not like meal prepping. For example, when you're meal planning, you are likely digging around in the refrigerator to see which items you have to use up, looking at the calendar for the week ahead to see where you need to have a meal prepared for a late night getting home, and then paging or scrolling through some recipes to see what you want to actually cook. What you are likely *not* doing with this time is the actual shopping, chopping, and cooking. Of course, if you see a few quick items in the fridge to chop up before they go bad, go for it. This is the equivalent of getting out a few quick emails (like Stacia blocking time for her Friday email folder), but you are not deep cleaning the fridge or getting to the bottom of your inbox during your Meeting with Yourself.

Let's peek at one more model.

Brett's Meeting with Myself Checklist

Brett, an operations manager for a network of schools and a manager himself, uses OneNote (a wonderful digital notebook with sections, tabs, and labels) to lay out his weekly planning checklist. Brett breaks his checklist into thoughtful sections. Let's take a look at how he structures his Meeting with Myself checklist.

Weekly planning checklist

PURPOSE - USE PRINTOUT
1. This time is to DEFINE the work, NOT DO the work.
2. Complete all self-meeting checklist items
3. Map out calendar for next week
4. Complete and print Weekly Worksheet & Later List

1. PREWORK
1. Have a short term task list in place to write on to not work-snipe yourself
2. Turn on music - *I won't back down*
3. Pause inbox

2. GROUND YOURSELF
1. Goals for the year / progress to goals - FY20 Annual Planning sheet
2. Reflect on purpose and impact of your work (Read Gratitude folder in email)

3. GET CLEAR (My "inbox" is in the following spots): 15 minutes
1. Capture any notes/stray papers
2. Process *Desktop*
3. (Optional: Review Mindfulness key pointers)
4. (Optional: Review/purge/organize Reference folder)
5. (Optional: Clean up bookmarks)

4. GET CURRENT (Do, delegate, or defer)
1. Plot time for reimbursements in Certify (including Mileage!)
2. Plot time for Bonusly! Gratitudes
3. Email
   1. Email Inbox + *Action* box
   2. **WAITING FOR folder
4. Review SL/BOM Meetings for common agenda items - put in All DSO tab
5. Outlook calendar - past week **30 minutes**
   1. Review any meeting notes
   2. Defer any items
6. Outlook calendar - next week
   1. SCHEDULE ANY O3 SHADOWING --> MAP OUT SCHEDULE (CHOOSE 1 ADSO SHADOW DAY - ROTATES TUES/WED/THURS)
7. *Outlook calendar - including SL calendar*
   1. *2-3 weeks*
   2. *Plan trips to San Diego (monthly 2 days) -*
   3. *3 month scan - USING THE WORD CALENDAR PRINTOUT*
   4. Check <u>Uconn</u> calendar
8. Review Project List _Notes Onenote
   1. Anything to activate for next week?
9. Review / Update PRIORITY PLAN in Google (2 months)
   1. Anything to activate for next week?
   2. BOM PRIORITIES / PRIORITIES PLAYBOOK LOOKAHEAD (these should really be part of the Priority Plan meeting - happens monthly)
10. OPTIONAL: Review/update Someday/Maybe list section in
    1. Anything to add for next week?
11. Finalize <u>weekly worksheet</u> (<u>covid version</u>)
    1. Actions associated with priorities
12. Print weekly worksheet

5. OPTIONAL: GET CREATIVE
1. Review areas of focus
2. Watch any of my recorded coaching meetings

Figure 7.5   Brett's Meeting with Myself Checklist.

Let's dive into Brett's sections a bit more.

■ **Pre-work.** Brett begins with getting his head and heart in a good place. He has music on and he has paused his inbox. For more on how to make that happen for yourself, check the Daily Deluge chapter.

■ **Ground yourself.** Most of you reading this book are in some kind of mission-driven environments. I love how Brett pauses and reads his gratitude folder, and checks his annual goals to keep his work rooted in its purpose.

■ **Get clear.** This is an idea borrowed from David Allen's *Getting Things Done*. Brett is going through each of his "inboxes," and processing any incoming work.

■ **Get current.** This is Brett catching up on any tedious tasks, such as mileage, and giving himself some room for bonus work, such as gratitude notes as well.

After all of these steps are done, Brett is ready to set up the coming week by referencing his other Together Tools:

■ Project Plans

■ Priority Plans

■ Upcoming Events – plotting work trips and checking the UConn calendar. (Gotta get the personal stuff in there too!)

At this point, Brett is ready to make sure his Outlook calendar is set up for the coming week (his Weekly Worksheet), his tasks and meetings are aligned to his priorities, and he is ready to go for the week ahead.

What I love about Brett's model is it carefully takes him on a Together Tour of all of his Tools, in service of aligning his time with his priorities. I asked Brett what weekly planning like this does for him, and he told me, "My Meeting with Myself helps me prepare for the week because I'm able to follow a systematic checklist that helps me get clear and organize my work. I find that it's my most important meeting of the week. By getting myself organized on a Friday, I'm much less likely to worry about work over the weekend and I feel confident heading into Monday. The checklist/agenda for the meeting is key because it allows me to go on autopilot and follow the steps."

BUILD YOUR OWN MEETING WITH MYSELF CHECKLIST

As you build out your Meeting with Myself checklist – with sections to first set the stage for your meeting and then (1) Clean Up the Week Behind and (2) Prepare for the Week Ahead – what should hit your list? Let's systematically explore this together.

- **How will you Set the Stage?** Do you need some music? A snack? A locked office? Some deep breaths? Consider how you will get into the headspace of Pause to Plan. I like an apple fritter to help me along.

- **What do you need to do to Clean Up the week behind you in your own role?** And if you need to add some personal items, absolutely feel free to do so. For example, I have a lot of personal paperwork that accumulates over the course of a week (stuff the kids bring home from school, mail to go through, etc.). Please use the previous examples as inspiration for your own Meeting with Yourself.

- **What would help you Prepare for the Week Ahead?** Do you need to review any memos or newsletters that come your way? Block out the Focus Time on your calendar with what you will specifically tackle? Shorten or rearrange any meetings? Get clear on what tasks you'll be doing during certain work blocks or add to your list for the week? Create time to prepare reports or agendas? And same story as my above comment: please get the personal preparation in here too. This could be meal planning based on your work schedule; it could be adding body movement into your Weekly Worksheet; it could be looking at your kids' activities and making sure those are noted. You can bet when I see a Monday night that has Girl Scouts, soccer, and I'm teaching an evening class, I will have planned to pop something in the crockpot that morning (#oldschool).

 FAQ: Can I ever plan further ahead than a week? By all means, yes! I have seen some Together Teammates, especially those who manage someone else's calendar, try to consistently look two to four weeks ahead. The benefit of doing this, even if you are not building your Weekly Worksheet that far out, is that it allows you to Forecast Forward and Be the Bird's-eye. Maybe there is a three-day week coming and it would be helpful to shorten meetings on your calendar or someone else's. Maybe you can look at the Comprehensive Calendar and see a huge team retreat deadline looming – and Rally the Team to get the prep done.

Now that you have created your own Meeting with Myself checklist, let's look at when to best conduct this meeting, and think about where and how you will want to accomplish it.

CREATE THE CONDITIONS TO SUCCESSFULLY MEET WITH YOURSELF

After training thousands of people in this weekly practice over the past two decades, we have seen a few possible barriers emerge to the Meeting with Myself practice. Time, motivation, interruption, guilt, the list keeps going. Basically, it is very, very easy to skip a Meeting with Yourself. This section will focus on creating the conditions to facilitate it happening consistently through picking the right location and time of day and then protecting your time accordingly.

Pick the Right Location

While this may feel like a picky technical item in relation to your Meeting with Yourself, we have seen it make all the difference in whether the practice sticks for people. Ideally, I want you to select a space where you can be uninterrupted, with all of your Together Tools (Goals, Year-at-a-Glance, Long-Term List, Weekly Worksheet, Project Plans, and more) all in one place so you can plan out your week in full.

Options for Where to Meet with Yourself

☐ **Onsite in your usual workspace.** This will work only if you are not regularly interrupted or if you have a visual cue to tell people you are focusing.

☐ **Onsite in a different location.** This is otherwise known as hiding – and sometimes that's what it takes. Maybe you have a colleague whose office you can use while your post is covered or a quiet conference room to plant yourself in. If this is your best option, you'll want to consider what materials you need to bring when you Meet with Yourself.

☐ **Offsite at a public location.** Some people prefer the friendly peer pressure of a buzzy coffee shop or co-working space. If this is the case, be sure you can bring your materials and spread out for an hour.

☐ **In a home work space.** The pandemic upgraded many of our work-from-home spaces, for sure. Some of you may remain in a hybrid work mode. If this is the case, you may find it more comfortable to Meet with Yourself from home. You may need to communicate electronically if you will not be available because you are focused on planning for the next week.

FAQ: How do I get "permission" from my manager or organization to take time to plan? I know, at first glance, Meeting with Yourself may not feel like (or look to others like) "actual work." And you're right: at first, pausing to plan could feel less valuable than immediately tackling everything in front of you. However, I think you can make a strong case to your manager regarding the value of planning ahead. In fact, let's even give you a bit of a script to help with this conversation.

■ *Manager doesn't understand Meeting with Myself.* "The Meeting with Myself will help ensure I close up loose ends from the week prior, and that I can look ahead for the coming week. This will help me prepare for upcoming meetings, prioritize my To-Do list, and make sure we have all the supplies we need for the coming week. Do you want to join me for a Meeting with Myself and we try it together?"

■ *Manager doesn't see value in planning time.* "Cleaning up the week behind me will ensure all meeting action items are logged and assigned, data is entered, and materials in the conference rooms are restocked. When I take the time to look ahead for the next few weeks, I can identify the preparation needed so we can use meeting time more wisely, I can solicit upcoming work from others, and we can give a longer lead time when we delegate work out. How about I try it for a few weeks and share my priorities and weekly plan with you after it's done?"

Reader Reflection: Where will you Meet with Yourself? Why is this your chosen location?

Pick the Right Time

Now that you have determined your where, let's focus on the when. In the early days of this work, we signaled Friday afternoon could be a helpful time, but over the years, we have seen that time is often when people are tired and feeling done for the week. Our current recommendation tends to be Thursday morning or afternoon. Your Meeting with Yourself will typically take an hour once per week.

Here are the reasons we recommend moving your Meeting with Yourself toward the end of the week (rather than Sunday night or Monday morning):

■ It leaves ample time to deal with schedule movement for the following week.

■ It allows time to follow up on meeting next steps and other quick hits.

■ It grants you time to ask other people about anticipated work they may be sending your way.

■ It lets you digest any organizational memos or communications that land at end-of-week that add to your workload.

■ It gives you a buffer so that if you miss Thursday, at least you can do it on Friday.

Of course, please take into account your overall context and role as you consider your When. A few examples that could drive your When might be:

■ A meeting with your manager or team on a particular day, and a Meeting with Yourself prior to that meeting could help you name your priorities, give status updates, and solicit incoming work.

■ You may receive a large memo on a regular basis from your organization or team that impacts your workload, and you may want to time your Meeting with Yourself after this memo lands to digest the To-Dos coming at you.

■ There may be an organizational weekly lull where perhaps you have access to a quieter time and space to process the week.

 FAQ: Can I also Meet with Myself each day? Yes! I have definitely seen Together Teammates do a mini-meeting with themselves to close out each day, wrap up meeting notes, and do a quick preparation for the next day. Sometimes people will even block it off in their Weekly Worksheets as 10–15 minutes before they leave for the day.

I encourage you to place your Meeting with Yourself for when it works best for you and the rhythms of your role and your life. What I do want to make sure is that you try not to wait to do it Monday mornings, because Mondays are often hectic, and can often entail last-minute requests or urgent needs from others. Most of us are in execution mode, not planning mode, on Mondays, and the week can then feel like it is happening to us rather than vice-versa.

Reader Reflection: When will you Meet with Yourself? Why are you making this decision?

Now that we have hit the Where and When, let's keep going with this invitation and figure out what materials you need to make your self-meetings most productive.

Bring the Right Materials

A common misconception for the Meeting with Yourself is that it is just a Zen, go-to-the-mountaintops exercise in reflection. While that could play a small part of centering yourself, really this is a clean-up-the-week-behind-you and prepare-for-the-week-ahead exercise, which means you need a particular set of materials. Let's build a list together:

- Whatever you need to center yourself (In my case, this is noise-canceling headphones and a five-minute meditation.)

- All of your Together Tools, as well as digital calendars, To-Do lists, planners, and the like

- Any Project Plans you lead or play a role in

- Any data that impacts how you may spend your week

- Checklists for recurring events or activities in your organizations, such as board meeting prep

- All of your inboxes (email, Slack, paper) that could influence your To-Dos

- Newsletters or memos you may receive from the organization that impact your To-Dos or priorities

- Any meeting notes or next steps that influence the week ahead

- Any ways you choose to show gratitude, such as thank you cards or messages

- Anyone else's calendars, if you manage those too

The idea of having everything at your fingertips is so that once you begin the Meeting with Yourself, you can honor the time without getting interrupted while you go digging for something. Dare I say it, some people even turn off their email and phone inboxes during this time to truly plan without interruption, like Brett did in the example shared above.

Reader Reflection: What materials do you need for your Meeting with Yourself?

 FAQ: How do I communicate to others that my Meeting with Myself is truly part of my actual work?

We have got to normalize the idea that people clearing the decks and planning ahead is actually one of the most valuable ways they can contribute to their organization's mission. This one-hour process each week will actually make you more useful to your organization because you are carefully figuring out how you can most strategically contribute your time to the organization. There are a few ways you can approach it with your manager or colleagues:

■ In looser organizations, just take the time and don't say anything. Plan ahead and that is that!

■ In tighter organizations or time-sheeted situations, share why you would like to take the time and what outcome it will have.

■ Create a deliverable to share with your manager that has actual data or results. For example, after your Meeting with Yourself, you may be able to say, "Next week I plan to spend X amount of time on the organization's website making those updates we've been talking about."

COMMUNICATING AFTER YOUR MEETING WITH YOURSELF

After you Meet with Yourself, you will feel like a million bucks. Completely prepared for the week ahead and on top of the world and ready for the weekend, I guarantee it. But there may be a case where during your meeting, you realize you will need to communicate with other people about your priorities and capacity overall. Let's look at a few examples, starting with Heidi, a member of the Together Team, and my book-writing collaborator.

Heidi's Post-Meeting with Herself Email

Heidi completed her Meeting with Herself and emerged with a few questions for me, as her manager. Let's peek into her thinking and see what we can learn.

Heidi exhibited several Together Try-Its in one sweep:

- **Forecast Forward.** Heidi saw a collision between a medical appointment and a one-on-one meeting, and proactively asked for an adjustment. This is much more Together than waiting and noticing at the last minute. As her manager, I certainly appreciated getting this heads-up several days before, rather than several hours before, our one-on-one was scheduled to happen.

- **Recommendation Ready.** She noted the website continues to be a priority and suggested what she could delay (spring classes and client tracker). This is much more helpful than just noting a delay and asking what could go on hold.

- **Pause to Plan.** Not to state the obvious, but Heidi paused to plan ahead to gain a sense of her week and then shared it with me to Show the Work for the week ahead. This allows me, as her manager, to know and trust she is deeply on top of her priorities and tasks.

 Reader Reflection: Do you need to communicate with anyone after your Meeting with Yourself? If so, what is the information you need to share and communicate? For what purpose?

✉ **Can we move our 1:1? -- and please check my priorities for next week!**

⊙ Heidi Gross   Today at 8:36 AM
To:

Hi Maia,

I just finished Meeting with Myself and need to check with you about a couple things for next week:

- Can we bump our 1:1 check-in to 3:00 PM EST on Wednesday rather than 2:30? I just realized my medical appointment prior is at a different clinic than I usually go to, so it'll take me longer to get home than I had initially blocked time for.
- The new website launch Project Plan calls for me to give final feedback and edits to Alter on the Courses, Resources, and Books pages. But it's been taking me longer to get through each page than I had realized it would, so I may only get to Courses and Resources. FYI that this may result in delaying the stakeholder round of feedback, but not sure yet. I'll keep you posted.
- Given that the website needs to continue to be a priority (and it's taking longer than anticipated), I need to bump a couple other items to the week after next: I was thinking I'd delay: 1) getting spring classes listed in Arlo, and 2) updating the client tracker. **Do you agree?**

Thanks for any and all feedback as I build my Weekly Worksheet for next week!

-Heidi

Figure 7.6 Heidi's Post-Meeting with Herself Communication.

While this is an example of a regular Meeting with Myself communication, sometimes you may be able to forecast ahead even further.

FAQ: What if I'm about to go on vacation or have a break? How do I stay Together then?

Inevitably, you will have a vacation or some organization-wide time off, and this can often feel like a sprint to the end. While it can be easy to finish on a Friday before a week off, gasp for air, claw for your bag, and leave, it may help to set yourself up for success when you return – perhaps through a Mega-Meeting with Yourself. If you find yourself in a very busy pre-vacation week, it can help to start jotting down priorities for when you return. If you really want to go for the Togetherness gold star, get that Weekly Worksheet done before you leave for vacation. Trust me, it will feel amazing to have this ready to go upon your return – and sets you up to really let the relaxing and rejuvenation begin.

Let's meet another member of my own team and see how she had a Mega-Meeting with Herself when preparing to be out of office for a vacation.

Kendra's Pre-Vacation Meeting with Herself Email

Kendra, a member of our Together Team, excels at communicating after she pauses to plan each week. Kendra often looks ahead multiple weeks to Forecast Forward for herself *and* the entire team (more on that in an upcoming chapter). Here is an example of her final countdown before a vacation.

This email was written as Kendra was Meeting with Herself and preparing to be out of office for vacation. The purpose of her sending this email was to align on prioritization with me (as her manager) on a final set of tasks before she headed out the door. Yes, this took Kendra more time, but it also prevented me from wondering what was still on her plate and also helped her prioritize that final set of tasks.

Hi Maia,

Below is my final list of to-dos for tomorrow. I've prepped emails for Heidi to send out, calender notes for you, behind-the-scenes steps for all the classes while I'm out, etc., but please flag if there's anything you're not sure about!

I have a hard stop at 3:30 PM my time (preferably sooner), and will officially be offline at that point. You'll notice my OOO popping on in the morning to buy me time with client emails.

Thanks!,
Kendra

- Assemble CCS
- Assemble Einstein
- Ship CCS & Einstein + send tracking #s to Catie and Danielle
- Work on CCS deck edits
- TA CFA + YMCA C1

- Call with Heidi to review what she's covering
- Schedule Logistics call with Legacy
- Send Coney Island SoW

Figure 7.7   Kendra's Pre-Vacation Meeting with Herself Communication.

FAQ: What if plans change after you Meet with Yourself?

Oh, they definitely will. The whole point of planning this extensively is so that you can effectively and quickly pivot as needed. Your calendars and To-Do lists are not meant to be static. In fact, part of planning so much for the next week is to allow you to see where flexibility and trade-offs can happen when things inevitably shift. Here is how this could play out:

■ "Thank you for sharing this request with me. . . . I had planned to do X, Y, and Z at this time, but if you are okay with a delay on that, I'll pivot quickly."

■ "Ahh, yes, this is an emergency and I will dive right in. Can I possibly have an extension on X deadline given this new priority?"

■ "This sounds super important. Is it okay if I bump this to end of day so I can finish A, B, and C first?"

The Meeting with Yourself is not designed to turn you into someone who has a rigid plan that you won't deviate from; that would be the wrong takeaway. My goal for you is that you will be someone who has a plan that empowers you to be flexible. The more planned you are, the more flexible you can be; along with that flexibility you can be keenly aware of the trade-offs required when things change.

TURBO TOGETHERNESS

We don't like to play favorites out here in the Together-verse, but after almost two decades of Togetherness, we believe the routines of pausing to process and plan (through your Meeting with Yourself to build your Weekly Worksheet) will help you reap the benefits of *all* of your Together Tools. It will feel tempting and easy to skip it, but I assure you that you will absolutely feel the difference between weeks you plan for and weeks you don't. Time and time again, class participants have told us how self-reinforcing this is. One of these participants recently said, "It made all the difference in my week and now I am hooked on doing it moving forward." Once they built time for this type of self-check-in and saw the difference it made in their week, they were committed to finding time on a regular basis. Here are your steps to get started:

- Create a checklist of steps that will help you process and plan that is specific to your role.

- Select a day, time, and location for your meeting.

- Determine what materials you need to effectively meet with yourself.

- Communicate the purpose of this meeting to people around you.

MANAGER MOMENT

The number one thing we can do as leaders (in my opinion, and as it relates to my area of expertise) is to create a culture of planning on our teams and in our organizations – especially for the folks whose roles are to make things happen, ensure the trains run on time, and keep the supply closets stocked. So, how exactly can we ensure that we and our teams Pause to Plan on a regular basis?

- **Model it.** The first step is simply Meeting with Yourself, sharing that practice with others, and then naming the outcomes – a well-built week designed to align your time with what matters. Please do not declare a mandatory Meeting with Myself until you try it yourself, get hooked, and really feel the benefits deep in your bones. Peek at *The Together Leader* if you want more models of leaders Meeting with Themselves.

- **Co-work it.** Have an assistant? A team? Consider creating a virtual or physical space to plan together. This could be as simple as looking ahead on a team-based calendar, or working with your assistant to get support in planning your week while supporting them to plan theirs.

- **Create it.** I have seen organizations have luck creating – from the team leader level – a specific time and place for the entire staff to Meet with Themselves. The benefits of this are numerous. Perhaps most importantly, it specifically names a cultural value – planning – by giving it time. It also adds accountability and permission for everyone to take time to clean up the week behind them and thoughtfully prepare for the coming week.

Together Tour

Brett
Regional Director Of School Operations
Kipp Socal Public Schools
Los Angeles, California

WHAT IS YOUR MOST USED TOGETHER TOOL TO KEEP *YOURSELF* TOGETHER?

Hard to choose, but I really rely on my Flexy Friend (a soft covered binder), where I keep a paper copy of my Daily and Weekly Worksheet and Thought Catchers. Overall, I use a mix of digital and analog. But I really like using an analog daily and weekly worksheet to capture and organize To-Dos.

HOW DO YOU RE-TOGETHER YOURSELF WHEN UNEXPECTED THINGS POP UP?

Pause to Plan, Pivot Powerfully. Because I have built the habit of Daily Roundups and Weekly Meetings with Myself, and I'm planned ahead, I feel confident that I can jump into something unexpected/urgent. I know that either in my next Daily Roundup or at the latest in my Friday self-meeting, I will be able to reorganize and reprioritize.

WHEN IS A TIME YOU HAD TO ADJUST YOUR TOGETHERNESS PRACTICES AND WHY?

When the pandemic hit, with all the personal and professional uncertainty, I found it very hard to plan ahead for a month, let alone a week. (I also didn't have access to a printer at home and I usually print out my Weekly Worksheet and monthly Priority Plan.) I took the advice in one of Maia's blogs and really shifted to a very simple daily worksheet – handwritten. I would review and refresh it every day. This really helped.

HOW HAS TOGETHERNESS HELPED YOU COMMUNICATE AND WORK WITH OTHERS?

I think it's fundamental to my work with others. When I was a first-year director of school operations in Brooklyn, I quickly realized I was not Together. While the main impact was on my own feeling of drowning, it also impacted many others, including my direct reports. It's hard to provide coaching to others when you don't feel Together. Also, as a member of the school leadership team, staff members could sense when I was frazzled and that really did not inspire confidence in the entire institution and team.

Stand in the Shoes of Others. While certainly not perfect, my Togetherness today allows me to plan effectively for projects, check-ins, meetings, etc. Also, I consider a major part of my job to be setting direction for my team and this requires being able to look ahead to the next few months (still working on getting ahead a few years).

HOW DO YOU HANDLE WORKING WITH COLLEAGUES WHO ARE SLIGHTLY LESS THAN TOGETHER?

Close the Loops. In these occasions, I adjust my approach by proactively setting ticklers or follow-ups. For example, if I send a request to a less-than-Together teammate, I might add an all-day event a few days later as a reminder to myself to follow up with them because I can't yet rely on them to respond. If it's a team member who may come to meetings unprepared or even forget about them entirely, I might message them the day before or a few hours before to share the agenda. And instead of relying on their ability to capture next steps, I may send them an email recap myself of the next steps.

WHY DOES TOGETHERNESS MATTER TO YOU AT WORK AND AT HOME?

Togetherness allows me to enjoy work and life more. I'm more likely to feel confident in my decisions about how I spend my time. I can be more present in any given situation, with a coworker or with my kids and wife, because I'm confident that I am clear on what needs to be done and know that I have a system to do my best to get the most important things done, as best I can.

Put It All Together: Build Your Together System

Well, that was a fun whirlwind through your Together Tools in Section 2. Before we move on, let's pause in this section and do a check on your Total Togetherness System.

CUSTOMIZE YOUR OWN TOGETHER SYSTEM

All of this talk of build-your-own aside, we have found some people just crave being handed something that works! As you build your Together System, you may get really excited about a bespoke system that you design to be perfectly tailored to you, or you may just want to use a fairly standard set of tools many of you may already be using. Here are a few questions – choose-your-own-adventure style – that will help you select the right Together System for you. And yes, of course, you can start with an idea and then shift it later. In fact, Together Tools are meant to be updated frequently, anytime you realize there is a way that your system could serve you even better. Let's have you answer a few questions to get a sense of your own preferences.

The following questions may help you consider your best Together fit.

Reader Reflection: Your Togetherness Preferences

■ Do you prefer writing on paper, or inputting items into a phone or computer?

■ When you get to work, do you prefer to look at a list first or at your calendar first?

■ Are you in one place most of the day, or are you moving around a building or a city?

■ How fluent is your technology ability? Do you delight in learning new products or systems?

■ How much of your day includes interruptions versus being protected for focused work?

■ Does your brain like to organize information in lists, tables, or charts?

■ How are tasks or projects handed to you? On the fly or in meetings? Or other methods?

■ Do you like to color-code items or keep them in gray scale?

■ Do you like to see things beautified or prefer them simple?

■ When referencing or reading papers or documents, do you prefer hard copy or on a computer?

I use the word "system" deliberately to name the fact that one singular tool usually cannot stand up to the complexity of your jobs. Using the analogy of the Trapper Keeper (any other '80s kids out there?!), I encourage you to create a one-stop shop that allows you to segment your work into calendars and lists, short-term and long-term. Frankly, a Together System is anything that works to help you plan, prioritize, forecast, respond, and be flexible in the moment. This can look different depending on your environment, your particular role, and your own personal preferences. In our experience, standard off-the-shelf tools for "productivity" (I abhor this word because it assumes that productivity is the end goal, as opposed to results, fulfillment, balance, outcomes, etc.) don't really work for people in roles like yours. My charge to you is to create your own Together System that works for you, for now, in this role, and at this point in your life. It may change over time, it may look very different than a colleague's, but what I care about the most is what works for *you*.

Quick Tool Confirmation

You have likely been reflecting in each chapter, but let's lock it in and make sure you have something that works for you.

My Together Tool	Sample Answer	Your Tool Selection
Goals	In a Google Doc shared with my manager	
Comprehensive Calendar	Google Calendar	
Long-Term List	Google Sheet	
Weekly Worksheet	Printed out version of my Google Calendar for the week	
Project Plans	Google Sheets	
Meeting with Myself	Google Keep Checklist	

We can recommend a few baseline models or "starter kits." Here are a few ideas for you to ponder:

■ *Outlook Calendar + OneNote.* This obviously works well if you are living in an Outlook environment. I recommend OneNote over the Outlook Task feature because we find the notebooks and tabs easier to work with.

■ *Google Calendar + Google Keep + Google Tasks.* This is another common Together system we see in Google environments. It is easy to also layer in multiple calendars to have personal and professional all in one spot. This is the example shown in the table.

■ *Digital Calendar + some kind of task software such as Asana,* monday.com, *Smartsheet, Trello,* or *Workflowy.* We see this often for people who identify more as "What-ers" (from the Weekly Worksheet chapter) or are in roles with more tasks and fewer meetings where their list-making situations need to be robust.

■ *Physical or digital notebook with multiple dividers.* Notebooks come in all forms these days, so whether you have a beloved Moleskine notebook with colorful tabs or a digital Rocketbook or Remarkable notebook, you can usually arrange sections within your notebook for each Together Tool.

■ *Clipboard with printouts of digital tools.* If you prefer to use partial paper and partial electronic systems, printing can be a way to put it all together.

■ *Tiny pocket notebook and then larger digital system.* This is actually my husband's preferred method. He is all digital with Outlook + Workflowy, but he also likes a tiny notebook that fits in his back pocket to "catch" items that come up all day and then he calendars them later.

There are many options out there – almost too many – and my hope is that, by viewing multiple examples and deeply examining your own habits, you can select or invent what works best for you right now.

FAQ: What if my organization mandates that I use certain tools or systems or software? I get it, and in many cases – such as shared digital calendars or certain project management software – this makes sense. Often this means that you will want to take the required tool, system, or software and use that as your starting point as you are building your Together System while working through this book. If you find that you are mandated to use a certain system, and then you end up having to create *another* system to actually manage your work, you may want to (nicely) ask:

■ What are you trying to achieve by having the team complete ABC each week?

■ Could we achieve it instead by this system XYZ I already use?

■ Could I walk you through how I keep myself Together?

CHAPTER 8

Get Those Inboxes in Check – Set up Your Digital Life

Picture a world where anytime you need to find a file, email, or piece of information, you know exactly where to go to find it. No scrambling through your sent messages or taking wild guesses while inserting various search terms in Google Drive. As a Together Teammate, others will count on you to locate, organize, and distribute information quickly. As you consider which Together Tools you will put in place to manage your workload, I don't want to shortchange getting your digital universe set up for success. While I would never mandate Inbox Zero or a computer desktop empty of files, I do care that you have a plan to have your materials at the ready, you have filed your documents moderately in order (at least enough so you can locate things easily), and you can access them handily.

In this chapter, you will learn how to:

- Set up your inbox(es) for effective and efficient storage and recall

- Create a plan to ensure your digital life is organized intuitively and clearly

- Deal with additional digital clutter that comes your way

As you read this chapter, consider the state of your computer desktop and your email inbox. Are they serving you, or is the chaos slowing you down every time you need to find a file or email? I know personally my Dropbox is very carefully ordered (thanks to the Together Team for ensuring this), but Google Drive – which is a blend of both professional and personal documents – could use a little . . . love. Take a few immediate notes about what you notice. As always, you can also note comments in your Reader Reflection guide.

SET UP YOUR INBOXES FOR SUCCESS

To folder or not to folder? To label or not to label? I see many different strategies here, but generally it makes sense to have strategic folders (Outlook) or labels (Gmail) for items you need to recall easily for reference or compliance reasons.

What about basic inbox setup overall? Let's just hit the basics here. This section focuses on Outlook and Gmail options to proactively organize, sort, and possibly file the incoming messages.

Reader Reflection: Questions to Consider

- How many emails do you send in a day?

- How many emails do you receive in a day?

- How often do you need to reference past emails?

- How far back do you need to reference past communications?

- Are you on lots of listservs or group message threads?

- Are you in charge of finance, grants, or other areas that need clear documentation?

- Do you often receive communications that need to be frequently referenced or returned to?

- How much of your work is generated from your inbox? Do you like to answer it directly from there or do you prefer to sort it somewhere first?

Your answers to these questions may help you decide:

- If you find you receive many communications that need to be handily referenced, you may benefit from a more extensive folder or labeling system.

■ If you receive a lot of quick questions via email that can be answered in one fell swoop, you may benefit from creating an email folder called "Answer at End-of-Day."

■ If people are always reaching out to you with, "Do you have that email that . . ." you may find you want to set up particular Categories or Labels.

Now that you have reflected on your own email needs, let's take a peek at a few specific systems in which individuals carefully considered their needs and organized themselves accordingly. My hope is you can look at their samples, and not mimic or copy them, but operate with the same level of intentionality.

Brett's Gmail Inbox Designed for Action and Reference

Brett, an operations leader in Los Angeles, sets up a simple set of labels in his Gmail inbox to keep himself organized. Let's peek into this inbox and see what we can learn. Keep in mind, all Togetherness Tips are simply offerings – it is up to you to customize to your own needs and liking. I asked Brett his overall inbox goals (yes, these are the kinds of questions I ask people), and he referenced one of my favorite strategies, Yesterbox (made popular by the late founder of Zappos, Tony Hseih), which is to get through *yesterday's* inbox today. Meaning don't try to keep up with all the items incoming today, but rather make it your goal to be reliably responsive in a 24-hour period. This is also my goal! I love this strategy because, well, you know that horrible feeling of your inbox filling up as fast as you clear it [insert deep groan]. Instead this gives you a finite goal of clearing yesterday's mail – which you can make progress on and *actually complete*. Let's see what else Brett does to set up his inbox for success.

Figure 8.1   Brett's Gmail Inbox Labels.

Brett set up a few systems to keep his email messages organized, searchable, and sortable:

■ **Set up clear and simple labels.** Brett has categories such as Action (more on that in a minute), Receipts, and Waiting For. The Waiting For category is a callout to David Allen's method in *Getting Things Done*, a popular productivity book. What Brett is doing is using his Gmail inbox for both In-Progress Folders and Reference Folders. What I mean by this is kind of a flashback to old-fashioned manila folders on a desk. You likely had a set of folders for "action," such as "pay" or "distribute" for actions. And then perhaps you had a filing cabinet (or still do) with items you might want to reference. These are your less active files. Brett knows that anything tagged Action still needs his attention.

■ **Create appropriate sublabels.** Brett then has a nested set of labels underneath Action. For example, as he receives email messages with items for the Ops/SL (School Leader) bulletin, he receives them, labels them, and then can reference when he writes his bulletin.

FAQ: How can I use my inbox to Close the Loops? Ahh, great use of a Together Try-It! As Brett did with his Waiting For label, your inbox can be a super place to keep track of Loops that Need Closing – especially if you are assigning tasks to others via email. You have a few options:

■ Similar to Brett, each time you assign a task, you can either drag it to a label or folder that has a title like "Waiting For," or "Pending." Then assign yourself a time once per week to review the folder/label and bring the task back to the world if it still hasn't been addressed.

■ Some platforms allow you to turn an email into a Task or To-Do, which often live beside your inbox.

■ If you are a super calendar person, you can also move your emails into specific days on your calendar when you want to remind people.

Reader Reflection: Whether you exist in Google or Outlook (or like me, both!), do you need any Action folders? How about Reference? What subfolders do you need underneath each? Can you jot a quick list of what labels or folders you may need?

Let's move into a slightly more complex labeling system within Outlook this time.

Katie's Outlook Inbox Ready for Action

Katie has similar folders for reference, but what about setting up your folders or labels for action? You know, for those emails you can't get to in the moment.

Katie has set up her folder system such that she can move messages into the following locations:

■ **Today.** These are for emails that must be answered today, most likely at the end of Katie's day or during an email block on her Weekly Worksheet.

■ **This Week.** This folder is for items that need a response at some point this week. Hey, not every email needs to be answered immediately!

■ **This Weekend.** Whether or not you work on weekends is a personal choice, of course. Katie has a folder for weekend correspondence, likely less time-sensitive items. Maybe for emails that are a bit more . . . fun?! There, I said it.

■ **Next Week.** She can pop over truly not time sensitive stuff, such as ideas people send her and so on.

■ **Later Follow-up.** The true later emails!

Of course, a folder set up like this is dangerous if you don't actually return to it. Out of sight, out of mind and all that. But if you diligently set time in your Weekly Worksheet and systematically return to your folders at the appointed times, this will set up your active inbox for success!

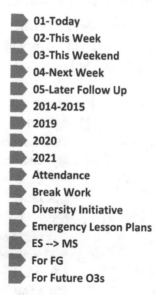

Figure 8.2   Katie's Outlook Inbox Folders.

FAQ: What if I want my folders or labels in a specific order? Oh, we hear that, and the alphabetical order can be an annoying default. It's no fun to scroll to the bottom of a huge folder list for your most frequently referenced topics. I've shared a model in the image here. Easy-peasy, and now your folders are in the order *you* want them!

Figure 8.3   Ana's Outlook Inbox Numbered Folders.

Now that you have seen two inboxes set up for Action, let's also take a look at how people use their inboxes for Reference.

Clara's Gmail Inbox Designed for Easy Reference

Clara, a director of operations in Boston, manages teacher cohorts that cycle through on an annual basis. She carefully organizes her Gmail inbox with the communications she sends to and receives from each group. Let's peek at her approach and see what we can learn.

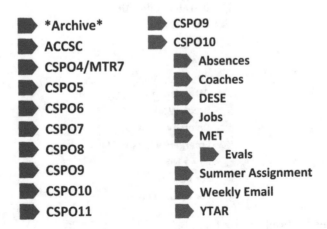

Figure 8.4A & 8.4B   Clara's Gmail Inbox Labels.

Clara organizes her inbox in a few ways:

- **Chronologically.** Clara has each year of her training cohorts laid out with clear nested sublabels. She says, "In my role as director of operations, I organize many of the emails in my inbox by year, or trainee cohort. For example, CSPO11 is this year's cohort. In each CSPO folder, there are pretty much the same sublabels, so that I can keep things organized by year, and also color-coded the same. This is especially helpful for things like the Weekly Email that I send to the cohort every week – I can very easily find the same Weekly Email that I sent to last year's cohort exactly a year ago, to see what reminders I need to give the cohort for that time of the year." Hello Systems Spotting!

- **By Topic.** Clara has a clear sense of the groupings of labels she needs for her teacher cohorts. For example, she has "Absences," "Coaches," "School Visits," and more. As her messages stack up each day, she can quickly give them the correct label and have them at her fingertips for the future. This way, when a coach or her manager says, "Who will be absent at tonight's class?" Clara can quickly pull up emails with this label and list the folks who will be absent.

In order for Clara to do this, she needed to have:

- A clear sense of items she may want to recall, such as the Weekly Email

- An understanding of the overall topics, which allows her to create the sublabels

- A little bit of time to file everything by either attaching the label in her inbox or simply dragging the email over

 Reader Reflection: What can you learn from Clara's approach? Do you have any repeated communications that would be helpful to organize for annual recall?

Let's take a look into someone else's inbox, one in Outlook, to see a different approach.

Erin's Outlook Inbox and Folders for Easy Recall

Erin, a senior operations leader for a network of schools in the Northeast, operates in an Outlook environment. She clears out her inbox throughout the day, but she also adds a set of Reference Folders for each school she works with. Let's check it out!

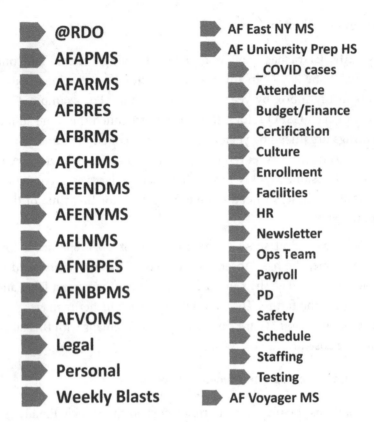

Figure 8.5A & 8.5B   Erin's Outlook Inbox Folders.

As you can see, Erin has a few things to keep her inbox manageable and searchable:

- **Limited number of folders organized by groups.** In Erin's case, this is all of the schools she works with, since she oversees the operations at each of these sites.

- **Subfolders.** Underneath each school, she has a set of folders of items she needs for compliance reasons, such as legal documents.

- **Weekly blasts.** Erin receives a number of weekly memos from her schools, and this enables her to sort them directly there.

Erin says, "The folders in my inbox match the folders in my documents folder on my hard drive and generally the top priority focus areas that I talk about with my team on a regular basis. I'm copied on a lot of emails, so it's efficient for me to file them away by subject area within the school's folder so I know exactly where to look when I need them as a reference. I know some people prefer to set their inboxes up by sender, but for me when I'm thinking about a message, I always think about the subject first, so that's how I've defaulted to organizing my messages."

Most frequently, I see Reference inboxes organized in one of the following ways in terms of emails that have been completed and no longer need action taken:

- **If your email bias is toward simplicity,** you may choose to have *one* massive Archived (Gmail) or Processed (Outlook folder) folder for anything that is dealt with but you may want to recall.

- **If you prefer to know generally where you store your items,** you may want a few key folders or labels for items that you most frequently reference, like key legal documents or pricing sheets.

- **If you want a precise location for each document**, you may wish to organize by topic or category. This works well if you work with a number of like things (field offices, schools, cohorts, trainings) and you want everything related to specific categories.

FAQ: Can I set up filters or rules to direct incoming messages directly to folders or labels? You can definitely do this, and you may want to, especially if you are part of many listservs. This is a great way to slow down the deluge of messages and get the Reference ones right where you want them to begin with. The one challenge of this – especially if you have Actions within any of them – is that you have to remind yourself to review these actual folders at some point (hint, hint: your Weekly Worksheet can help you there!).

Reader Reflection: Do you fall on the simple or complex side of email setup? Why? Either way is okay as long as you are intentional about your plan and it fits with your role and work.

GET YOUR DIGITAL DOCUMENTS IN ORDER

Gulp. There are entire books written about this exact topic, and we are only going to scratch the surface on this one. Whether you are thinking about your hard drive, your digital desktop (anyone else have a lot of PDFs hanging out there?), your Google Drive, your phone albums, or your Dropbox or shared drive, there is a plethora of digital documents. You need good ways to organize them so you can find what you need when you need it, avoid version control issues, and share documents easily with others. In this section, get ready for some document naming conventions, folder structures, and more. While this may not be the sexiest part of Togetherness, it sure saves hassle later.

 Reader Reflection: List all the digital documents you keep track of in your role. Where do they all live?

Clara's Google Drive

Before you dive into organizing your files into a million folders or giving documents super-specific names, I would start by asking yourself what is your goal with document organization? Is it to train others? To collaborate on documents? To pull items up and use them in the future? Like with email, you want to match your solution to your actual needs.

Clara, the same operations director featured in a previous sample, notes that she organizes her Google Drive by cohort year and shares with various folks who also collaborate on documents.

My Drive ▾

Name ↑	Owner
📁 2012-2013 (Training MTR5 & Coaching MTR4)	
📁 2013-2014 (Training MTR 6 & Coaching MTR 5)	
📁 2014-2015 (Training MTR7 & Coaching MTR6)	
📁 2015-2016 (Training CSPO5 & Coaching MTR7)	
📁 2016-2017 (Training CSPO6 & Coaching CSPO...	me
📁 2017-2018 (Training CSPO7 & Coaching CSPO...	me
📁 2018-2019 (Training CSPO8 & Coaching CSPO...	me
📁 2019-2020 (Training CSPO9 & Coaching CSPO...	me
📁 2020-2021 (Training CSPO10 & Coaching CSP...	me
📁 2021-2022 (Training CSPO11 & Coaching CSP...	me

Figure 8.6 Clara's Google Drive Folders.

Similar to her Gmail inbox featured previously in the chapter, Clara names (and color codes, which you can see in the full version found on this book's website: www.wiley.com/go/togetherteammate) her Google Drive folders by the cohort year. This allows Clara – and her colleagues – to quickly find everything they need related to the cohort by year. Very practically, when recruitment begins, they can go into last year's folder and then pull out relevant documents, revise or change, and off they go.

Sara-Kate's Microsoft Folders

Perhaps your organization doesn't use Google Drive, but rather a Microsoft shared drive. How on earth do you organize this to best meet your needs? Sara-Kate, a virtual chief of staff, shares her folder hierarchy in this image.

Sara-Kate numbers her folders in a similar way to Katie with her Outlook inbox. This allows her to have say over the order of the folders, thus making it easier to grab more frequently used items.

Sara-Kate reminds us, "Always have an Archive folder where you can save past versions. You never know when someone might say, 'I liked the past version of this sentence.' But also

Figure 8.7   Sara-Kate's Folder Structure.

0. Meeting Materials
1. Client Artifacts
2. Shared Resources
3. New Structure Development
4. Surveys and Findings
5. Miscellaneous
Z. Archive

Figure 8.8   Sara-Kate's Archive Folder.

keeping old things in this folder ensures you don't have to spend time locating the current version you are working on [amidst many versions]. I also number folders in addition to naming them so the most important/relevant items can be accessed most easily." Good old-fashioned version control!

Reader Reflection: Based on your observations of Clara's and Sara-Kate's digital document storage systems, sketch out how you want to structure your folders to best meet your needs.

Now that your folders are set up, let's go big and see how an entire team set up their digital documents.

Adelante's Digital Storage System

No doubt your organization is not limited to one single place where all digital documents live. Imagine my delight when Jordan, a founding director of operations in Indianapolis, shared his shared drive structure with me. If only I had this guidance 25 years ago when starting my career! Let's see what we can learn together from walking through this example.

I'm enamored with the Be the Bird's-eye and Forecast Forward Together Try-Its exhibited in this one-pager. Jordan and his team at Adelante were thinking about how to ensure learnings are captured, receipts are reconciled, and audits are properly prepared for. To do all these things, they need to have files exactly where they know they can find them.

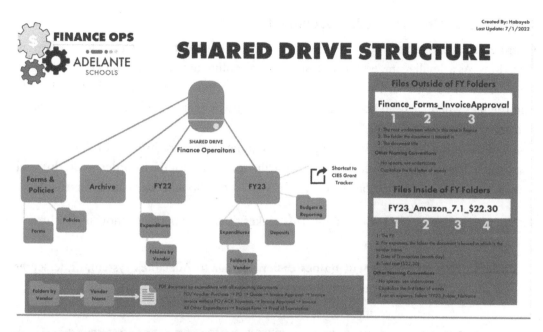

Figure 8.9   Adelante's Shared Drive Structure.

There are a few things I love about this:

■ **Clear lead folders.** The fiscal year folders, often used for audits, are separate from the forms and policies – which people may need to dip into more often.

■ **Strong vendor organization.** This becomes useful if you have multiple people reaching out to various vendors or need to pull invoices or purchase orders quickly.

■ **Crystal-clear naming conventions.** Right down to no spaces, use underscores. Imagine if you were new entering this organization, how quickly and easily you could find everything you need, not to mention know exactly where to put files you know need to be saved.

Of course, this is easier to do when you are building an organization from scratch, but I'm struck by the intentionality, planning, and Togetherness of considering how the digital documents should look across an entire finance and operations team. No more do you have to worry about important documents stuck on an individual's hard drive, receipts missing, or scattered financial reports. Let's get it right the first time.

Now let's peek inside the folders and figure how to best name your documents.

The Together Group's Digital Documents

Over here in the Together-verse, we have quite a lot of documents moving in a lot of different directions. As a small team, we are all responsible for filing our own documents. This means we all need to be on board with some naming conventions, so that we all know where to find the files when we need them! As an example, I invite you to peek at our receipts folder and see what we have learned.

We deal with a lot of receipts, people, and supplies over here in my world, and we are responsible for sending our receipts for reconciliation each month. In order to do this, our team set up naming conventions to make it easier on our bookkeeper – and ourselves!

■ **Document names start with a date.** This makes them automatically show up in chronological order for us.

■ **Underscores make document names easier.** Similar to Adelante's system, underscores help make document names easier to read and file.

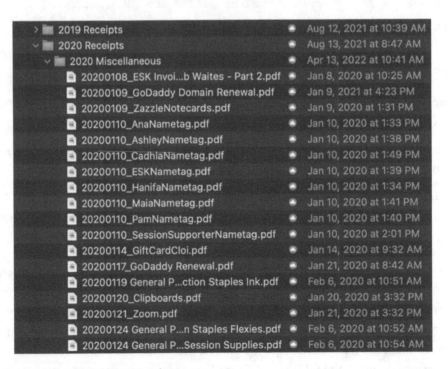

Figure 8.10   The Together Group's Naming Norms.

FAQ: What is my role in helping my organization do a better job with shared files? Ooh, I love the Deep Ownership and Systems Spotting behind this question! If you are motivated to do this, you may be a good person to research the best system to use and propose options to others. After everyone is on board with using the same methods, you could also go a step further and consider how the overall organization names and organizes documents for use.

 Reader Reflection: What are your next steps for naming conventions – either for yourself, your team, or your organization?

DEALING WITH ALL THAT OTHER DIGITAL CLUTTER

I get it. Nowadays clutter goes beyond just the inboxes and the digital documents – there are certainly more items to keep track of, and digital tools can help you with the following areas:

- **Password managers** help ensure your passwords are secure but accessible.

- **Tab managers** keep all of those digital tabs at your fingertips (and mean you don't have to be scared to close your computer).

- **Apps that turn paper or photos into PDFs or other documents** are a lifesaver when dealing with receipts, artifacts, or meeting notes on whiteboards.

- **Photo folders on your smartphones** enable you to have an album specifically created for pictures of how the conference room should be set up.

The technology for all of the above changes frequently so I am deliberately not writing out an exhaustive list of tools (hello Google, and check out some of our favorite options on this book's website and my blog). But I am asking you to keep track of what causes you to lose minutes digging around, and see what small time-savers you can put into place.

TURBO TOGETHERNESS

This chapter took you on a journey through how to set up your digital spaces to act responsively, reference thoughtfully, and sift through some of the deluge. Of course, setting up these systems may take a bit of trial and error, and no job is alike in terms of what systems are needed. If you are sitting on a digital desktop full of random PDFs, an inbox that feels like it is never-ending, and a stack of papers that needs to be scanned, start small and make a few small moves each day. Or consider finding a few hours of what my team calls Together Tidy Time, where you block time to sort through the piles and create structures for the future. The time investment for some tidying will pay off, I promise!

CHAPTER 9

Plan for the Pivot –
Deal with the Daily Deluge

So, you made your Weekly Worksheet – pulling from your Comprehensive Calendar and your Long-Term List, perhaps peeking at your Year-at-a-Glance and Project Plans – and you're feeling on top of the world! You've even put all your inboxes and files in order! You've got this; nothing's going to stop you from the perfect Together Week. But here in Together-Land we live in the real world, and we know Together Teammates are often on the front lines, dealing with the crisis of the day, and problem-solving for people right and left. Let's go ahead and call this the Daily Deluge. This is something teammates may uniquely experience given our customer-service focus and operations/assistance roles. My hope is that this chapter helps you find the right balance between systems and spontaneity, and the ability to pivot gracefully when called for, *or* stay the course when required.

What do I mean by Daily Deluge? I bet you know (and can probably feel it in your bones), but in case you don't: I'm talking about the incoming urgent email, the person who needs your help immediately, the meeting location change at the last minute, the agenda with the misprint that requires reprinting. Do you see where I'm going with this?

In this chapter, you will learn to:

- Plan your week such that it has room for preplanned work *and* time for the unexpected
- Design structures that allow you to do your work with focus and efficiency
- Anticipate and predict last-minute work that comes your way
- Triage last-minute requests and communicate the pivot accordingly

If you're savvy, you actually do not expect days to go exactly according to plan. In fact, you plan *so that* you can pivot thoughtfully, propose trade-offs, and be nimble – without tossing your plans completely out the window – even though it may feel like you want to. In this chapter, we will explore several examples of how you can both plan (like in the chapter you read previously) and also pivot when the Deluge comes. I assume you may get "interrupted" in many different ways, such as the hallway or cubicle friendly ambush, incoming phone calls or text messages, and frantic emails.

This chapter will help you figure out how to deal with the inevitable Deluge while not completely abandoning your Weekly Worksheet and other Together Tools. Toward the latter part of the chapter, I will focus on how you handle true emergencies and share some strategies to reset yourself when they inevitably occur. Let's start with what often crashes the best-laid-plans: the innocent interruption.

THE INNOCENT INTERRUPTION

Many of you have desks or workstations in relatively open spaces, or if you're lucky enough to have an office, the door may always be literally and figuratively open. The challenge with this is that it can prevent you from focusing on that deeper work. I'm certainly not suggesting that you try to eliminate all drop-bys because that is not realistic. What I do want to encourage is that you try to protect some snippets of time for focused work, and this will not happen magically. You may have to take it upon yourself or rally some colleagues or a manager to help you protect a bit of time.

Create (Subtle) Visual Signals

I'm a longtime fan of a visual cue to help people know when I'm in a focused work time. (Just ask my kids what they're supposed to do if they see Mom wearing noise-canceling headphones!) Amanda, an operations teammate based in Brooklyn, New York, who is often in the front office of her school, described how she and her team use purple feather boas to signal when they are focused on something that is a high priority, while still ensuring a member of the team is available to help.

Amanda says, "I want to help my team create a safe space to hold sacred time for their work – as well as jump in and help each other." Of course, you don't have to go all feather-boa-all-the-way. But the idea here is that a visual cue can nicely redirect people. Of course, you don't want to go tossing on the proverbial boa when people are streaming through your front office or rapidly submitting urgent tech tickets. (Side note: feel free to peek at the boa photograph on our book's website.) The key here is to be strategic and consider your Weekly Worksheet, what you know about the rhythms of your role, and your particular physical space. You may want to have a conversation with your manager and colleagues (more on this coming up) about the one hour a day where you can most likely have a bit of protected time with as little impact on the team and mission of your organization.

 Reader Reflection: Look at your Weekly Worksheet. Do you see any natural lulls in the Deluge that could be a home for focused work time? Would any visual cues support your ability to protect your work time?

Maybe visual cues are too subtle for you, and you need specific tools that you use with your team to help the entire team protect their time – enter some signage across your organization!

Create Shared Signage

If feather boas are not your style (and I understand, though I can't say I relate), perhaps you could benefit from designing signs to post on your office door or workspace that signal when you are available and not available. I have seen many teams work together to create agreements that help others protect their time, while also still providing top-notch customer service. Let's look at an example of a front office in the next image. (As a reminder, if you ever want to view our images and photos in color, pop on over to this book's website at www.wiley.com/go/togetherteammate).

Amanda – from the prior example – worked with the entire front office team to develop a red, yellow, green symbol at their cubicles. This showed who was in a Do Not Disturb situation (busy doing focused work), who was out on vacation or in a meeting, who was on a break but would be back soon, and who was open and ready to assist.

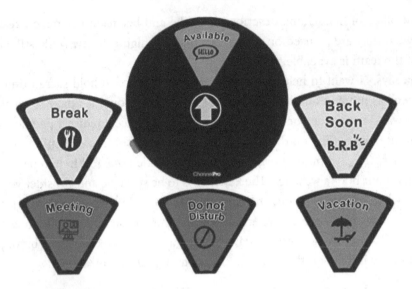

Figure 9.1 Coney Island Prep's front office staff availability.

This visual signaling helps let folks who signal "red" get the focused work done, while letting others who enter the office approach the team members on "green." The key here is to make sure someone is always on green and approachable for people who have questions.

 Reader Reflection: How could a team-level visual signal help you and your team members?

Some of you may crave something even more formal and structured. Well, I bumped into a team using an on-call schedule. Let's look at that next.

Design an On-Call Schedule

I was once in a team meeting with a nonprofit executive team when there was an emergency from one of the regions, and every single executive team member jumped up and worked on solving it. Well, guess what happens when all of those folks are dealing with an emergency? The mechanics and mission of the organization get put on the back burner and crisis mode becomes the normal way of operating. I am a strong advocate of not having every member of a team called or paged when there is an emergency or crisis. So how does this work? Erin, an operations leader in a charter network, created a front office on-call schedule in order to assist others – and protect their time.

	HL	CR	NM	RM	SM
	DIR	**OA**	**SSM-C**	**PEA**	**SSM-A**
7:00 – 8:00	MO		W: LS Atten	7th Crnr	Busses
8:00 – 9:00	MO			MO Crnr	
9:00 – 10:00	MO		MO		MO
10:00 – 11:00			Attend	LIB	Attend
11:00 – 12:00			MO	SUB	MO
12:00 – 1:00			Attend		Attend
1:00 – 2:00	Coach		MO		MO
2:00 – 3:00			MO Attend		MO Attend
3:00 – 3:45	ES Crnr	MO Crnr	5/8 GBR	6/7 GBR	MO

Figure 9.2 Erin's On-Call Schedule.

Erin said her team was constantly all jumping up to assist when someone entered the main office (MO). So they created a staffing schedule, as shown in this image, so you can see the "Main Office on time." The five operations team members had times of day where they were the lead main office greeter, and the other team members alternated with attendance. By laying it all out, each team member could see who was responsible for what and pitch in. If you peek at a few pictures of the main office setup (available on this book's website), you'll see how the office remained a welcoming environment. This ensured that the front office remained customer-service friendly, but that other team members could continue working on regular responsibilities.

 Reader Reflection: Would an on-call schedule help you? What would it take to create one with your team?

Now that we did some preventative work on incoming interruptions, let's dip into the actual day and what happens as things start flyin'. Pause your inbox for a minute and let's consider how to handle that Deluge.

It's a Bird, It's a Plane, It's . . . More Messages

In support roles, you should expect that last-minute requests will pop up, and you can't let that throw you. It is your job to be nimble. Assuming you have a clear sense of your role and goals from earlier in the book and a strong Weekly Worksheet, you can absorb the request, but also look at the rest of the day or week and see what can be shifted to accommodate.

One of the biggest parts of the Daily Deluge is all the incoming communications landing on you at every moment of the day, via your inbox(es), your phone(s), and the like. While likely a significant aspect of your role is being responsive, there is a difference between being immediately available at every single moment and being reliably responsive. My hope for you is that you can find the difference and then the middle ground between the two, figure out who does require immediate responses, how to batch process your communications, and what can wait for a little bit. This may mean not immediately dropping everything the minute a new message comes through, and that takes discipline, communication, and patience. Intrigued? Skeptical? Let's give it a try.

I mean, this is a harder topic than it used to be. Just 30 minutes of trying to write this chapter found me checking my email at least 10 times, WhatsApp 5 times, and so on (kidding – maybe). The point here is that all of the various methods of communications at our disposal these days can cause us to feel constantly on, being expected to check on our phones, tablets, and computers, which leaves us unable to make any progress on our bigger projects.

To get beyond this default of constantly checking and responding, let's figure out what you actually need in the context of your role. Here are some questions to help you determine what your communication routines should be. Keep in mind that these are not your routines forever, just for right now, in this job, in this particular place. I cannot and will not try to tell you how many times per day to check your communication options; I only ask that you think deeply about your habits and be intentional with your approach.

Reader Reflection: Communication Routines Reflection

- What are the actual expectations in your workplace? Are they spelled out anywhere?

- If not, and you find yourself checking all the time, what are the expectations you place on yourself? Where do these come from?

- Do you have specific time blocked in your Weekly Worksheet for checking email or other communications tools?

- When do you find yourself drawn toward your communications? Is it because of need, or something else?

- Do you keep notifications on? Are they necessary?

- How effective are you at the Get In/Get Out method (this means going directly in to your online tools with a very specific purpose, doing that thing, and then closing down) with your communications? In other words, if you *have* to check something in Slack or any instant messaging while working on a different project, do you dip in and out quickly to just grab what you need?

- How often do time-sensitive items come in to you in each of your methods of communication? For example, do you have to check trouble tickets each morning, or can you anticipate a last-minute scheduling request via email from your manager?

Based on your answers to the previous questions, you can start to think about developing your communications habits in accordance with your actual job needs. Let's start with how often to check.

Determine Which Device to Check on and Why

Given the proliferation of personal mobile devices of all sorts (watches, tablets, phones, laptops, and more) – only some of which are actually helpful for communications – it makes sense to be intentional about which device you are using to check in any given circumstance.

Why? Well, without intentionality around which devices you are using when, it can be tempting and inevitable to check on *all* devices *all* the time – which flies in the face of all we know about attention and focus for project work. Additionally, not all devices are necessarily useful or relevant for the incoming communication. For example, maybe I check a message on my iPhone, and it requires a very complex answer directing the recipient to Google Drive, some attachments, and so on. Perhaps I should have just checked that from my laptop, which is where I'll actually want to respond from.

 Reader Reflection: How do you prefer to check messages? For instance, I like to do a quick pass-through, but often flag or star items to return to later.

■ Which devices do you like to use to check messages? (For example, I prefer to scan on my phone, but answer everything from my computer.)

■ How often do you prefer to check? Be honest here, people! (For example, I wish I could say three times a day, but I always flip to email or Slack when I'm focusing on a harder project. #guilty).

Once you have established which device and how often to check, it still will not be easy. You will likely have to do a few Jedi mind tricks on yourself and also utilize good old-fashioned communication with your colleagues to ensure that you can live within the boundaries you set. If possible, you may want to experiment with turning off your Wi-Fi or pausing your inbox. And don't be afraid to communicate to your team that you are going into some focused work, but they can call you if there is an emergency.

 Reader Reflection: What are your communication boundaries? How will you gently share them with others?

I'm going to warn you, this one will feel *very* challenging because we are now conditioned to jump when we hear a ding, to respond immediately, to rapid-fire run to the request. It *is* possible to be reliably responsive without being immediately responsive. And sometimes the issue when reviewing your communications is getting clear on what you are actually doing with them. Are you trying to process toward the famous Inbox Zero? Are you trying to clear yesterday's messages (Yesterbox, mentioned in the previous chapter)? Are you intending to respond only to volunteers from an event? Or are you just in a triage mode? Know your intent first and *then* dive in.

AVOID DISTRACTIONS

There are many resources out there about avoiding distractions, often written by psychologists or neurobiologists. Some of my favorites include *Deep Work* by Cal Newport, *How to Break up with Your Phone* by Catherine Price, and *Stolen Focus* by Johann Hari. The synthesis of suggestions includes:

- Turn off your notifications on all devices. Gulp.

- Use technology solutions such as Inbox Pause, Freedom, Do Not Disturb, Boomerang, or Delayed Delivery to pause incoming mail while responding to messages.

- Be selective with which methods you are checking and when. Get in and get out.

- Communicate your boundaries with colleagues and ensure these boundaries work in your organization.

Okay, that was a quick tour through your inner psychology, your actual team or organization, and your own preferences. But hopefully you have a handle on your habits now, so let's focus on exactly how you will tackle that incoming Deluge from others.

Brett's Inbox Pause

Remember back in the day when Wi-Fi on airplanes wasn't a thing? And therefore flights gave you precious disconnected time to read, watch movies, or perhaps unbury that inbox knowing that you'd only be getting ahead, with nothing new coming in until you were back on the ground? Those days are behind us, so now it's up to you to take matters into your own hands and create your own intentional disconnected time.

In some cases, you may find it helpful to quite literally pause your inbox and other communication channels. That could look like turning off your Wi-Fi (gasp), putting your phone on Do Not Disturb, or using technology such as Inbox Pause, various apps that limit your internet wanders, and other ways to slow the Deluge. Brett, an operations leader in southern California you met previously, uses Inbox Pause to slow communications. Inbox Pause is a tool that "gives you control over when emails appear in your inbox" and can be used with both Outlook and Gmail. I've shared a quick image so you can see it in practice.

Inbox Pause by Boomerang ⊘

⊘ Turn on Auto-Responder   ⬤ Hide label ⊘

⬤ Delivery exceptions   ⬤ Bring messages into Inbox on a schedule

While paused, continue delivering messages   ☐ Weekdays only

from addresses: 7:00   AM

                                  8:00   AM   ×

or addressed to: 8:45   AM   ×

                                  12:00   PM   ×

or from domains: example.com   1:00   PM   ×

                                  3:30   PM   ×

or with words: urgent   6:00   PM   ×
                   emergency
                                  Add Time

⊘ Unpause automatically   After 2 hours   **Pause**   Cancel

Figure 9.3   Brett's Inbox Pause.

Worried that this is not realistic or possible? Start very small. Maybe you pause for just 15 minutes, and see what happens. Use what you learned earlier in the chapter around asking for some focused work time, and also alert others that during this time, your communication channels (with maybe the exception of your actual *phone*) will be shut down so you can focus on . . . the data report? The Project Plan for the end-of-year-potluck? The preparation for the audit? You get the idea! And if you are worried about a few VIPs not being able to reach you, you can set exceptions for who can "break through," as Brett did.

 Reader Reflection: How and when will you pause your inbox so you can gain some Focus Time? What will it take for you to practice this and communicate about it with others?

Can't Pause? Well, Determine Your VIPs

Typically, in jobs like yours, you are not able to disconnect for hours at a time. Most of you likely need to do frequent scans of inboxes or channels, but the trick here is that not everyone requires an immediate response. Perhaps you have some VIPs in your environment, like a manager or donors or tutors. Or maybe there is a group of people who always receive priority because they are in the field and may be contacting you with time-sensitive requests. Or maybe you work on the fundraising side, and donors get an ASAP response. In my past life supporting schools, our school leaders were VIPs, and the superintendent made it clear that a phone call or email from a principal required a near-immediate reply – as it should.

There also may be certain times of day or year when you need to have your VIP access channel wide open. For example, on my team, in the 48 hours before we roll new courses, there are a barrage of last-minute questions from our class participants. For this period of time, our students are our VIPs and my team needs to be very available for last-minute questions, registration shifts, or substitutions. This means our team needs to block time on our Weekly Worksheets the day before, during, and right after our first class of a course; know the Deluge is coming; and be ready to respond immediately to every email from a course participant in that period of time. Consider your VIPs as seasonal and shifting, and try to be aware of known Deluge time.

 Reader Reflection: Who are your VIPs? Have you communicated with them which methods are best to reach you for an immediate response? Are there certain times of day, or seasonal VIPs?

As you get ready to handle multitudes of incoming communications, I want to offer an additional strategy knowing as "batching," or completing similar items at the same time. You know, like when you meal prep an entire week's worth of lunches on a Sunday afternoon.

MOVE SWIFTLY THROUGH YOUR INBOX(ES)

No doubt throughout your day, you will want to move swiftly and efficiently through your inboxes. Why does this matter? Because the amount of information, messages, and requests coming at you in different directions all day long means you have to be able to scan, sort, and act quickly throughout the day. My hope is this section helps give you strategies to set up your inbox to fly through it with ease.

Create Specific Templates

Ever found yourself writing the same email over and over again [guiltily raises hand]? You may be able to save yourself a bit of time if you can create some templates to reuse. For example, over here at the Together Group, we keep templates of all pre- and post-class emails in a Drafts folder. Then when we are preparing for a specific class series, we can simply copy the entire folder of templates into the main Drafts folder and have the emails ready to customize. Efficiency at its finest.

Flag, Star, or Designate Emails as Important

Ever scanned through your inbox from your smartphone or quickly during a meeting, and been like, "Dang, I need to return to *that* one ASAP." Well, enter your Flags (Outlook) or Stars (Gmail). Each of those features enables you to quickly click on that email and have it ready for later. The challenge with this, of course, is that if you overflag or star your inbox, you will become immune to the stars, rendering the system ineffective. If you do choose to flag or star as a means of noting emails to be answered later, do yourself a favor and add it to your Weekly Worksheet to return to them at the end of each day. Sort your inbox by flags or stars, and voilà – your priority messages are right there waiting for you!

FAQ: What if I simply don't know how much time some of this routine Deluge work will take? In some of your roles, especially those of you with a heavy customer-service component to your work, many of you will spend a lot of time answering standard questions, processing invoices, registering participants, responding to scheduling requests, attending to trouble tickets – insert your particular job tasks here. If you are not sure how much time you need, it may be helpful to time yourself clearing the inbox every day for a week to check yourself. After averaging for a week, you will have a sense of how much time to budget on your Weekly Worksheet. After this, you can think through how often it makes sense to check. For example, a member of the Together Team, Lauren, who is responsible for our general workshops inbox, has learned that when we are in regular class sessions, she can respond to everything in this inbox with two 30-minute blocks per day. The first week of classes is heavier, so on those weeks she schedules two 45-minute blocks per day.

Batch Similar Messages or Tasks

Ping-ping-ping, notifications are designed to make you notice them and it can be very tempting to go ahead and deal with each thing as it comes in.

Sure, you see the barrage of emails or tasks coming in and you know how to answer them. You might even think to yourself, "This will only take thirty seconds to answer!" but not all replies can be (or need to be) answered in the moment. Some require time, some require getting information from other people, and some require some longer-term work. And sometimes responses can be strategically delayed to allow you to manage your work more efficiently.

Let's play out a case study from our own team. (The Together Group loves getting meta about our own practices!) Ana, a member of the Together Team who focuses on our class design and instruction, could easily spend her day pinging between messages and tasks related to homework assignments, checking the class discussion boards for feedback, scheduling interviews for our blog content, or reviewing training decks for me. Taking five minutes here and there sounds good in theory, until you find your brain completely fried and unable to focus on anything, and you realize you've been pinging around so much that you've lost any ability to focus on a sustained project. Given that your roles often require both proactive work and reactive responses, I want you to find a middle ground to help you handle the Deluge. In Ana's world, you can easily imagine how immediately responding to each thing could make for a choppy day with very little focus time. At the same time, some of this stuff is time sensitive.

Let's look at an expanded version of Ana's inbox from the FAQ about numbered folders/labels previously. Sometimes it can be helpful to categorize emails as they come in. For the

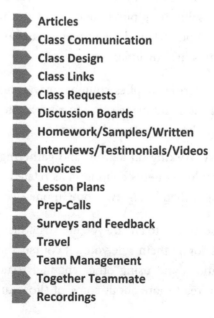

Articles
Class Communication
Class Design
Class Links
Class Requests
Discussion Boards
Homework/Samples/Written
Interviews/Testimonials/Videos
Invoices
Lesson Plans
Prep-Calls
Surveys and Feedback
Travel
Team Management
Together Teammate
Recordings

Figure 9.4   Ana's Categorized Inbox.

sake of efficiency, I'll use the word "tag," though Outlook calls these Categories and Gmail calls them Labels. Let's see how Ana does this in the example here.

When Ana wants to answer her email (perhaps she even has time blocked on her Weekly Worksheet, so that she can quickly see, "Oh, it's time for me to answer all homework submissions"), she can pivot there and wipe them out in one sitting.

In other words, Ana can "batch" her work into categories for the day or week. Bonus points for Ana for considering her physical location and mental load. Ana could consider:

- Earlier in the day, a 30-minute block of time for **Lesson Plans.** This takes Ana a deep amount of focus and concentration.

- Once a week, a 30-minute block of time to process **Class Feedback** for the next week. This is more efficient than doing it in bits and pieces.

- An hour to review incoming class homework and offer feedback. Ana needs to have two screens in front of her to review the homework on one screen and write feedback on another, so she needs to make sure she is in front of her home workstation at this time. Because Ana has labeled each of these emails over the course of the past few days, she can quickly sort for **Homework** and batch those replies.

Your day is obviously different from Ana's, but you can learn from how she tries to structure her day to batch process. Consider different categories of your work and think about what or when you can batch process. Maybe it's paying invoices weekly, or responding to scheduling requests daily, or submitting purchase orders two times a week. You see where I'm going with this. Consider your categories and plan accordingly.

Some other examples of this may include:

- Perhaps all requests for ordering supplies come your way, and you place supply orders twice per week? Well, then it could make sense to have a category or label called Supply Orders, and then swing to those emails at that time.

- Or let's say you were busy working on a grant and gathering pieces of information via email. In this case, you could tag items coming in as related to a specific grant, let them hang out in your inbox, and then thank everyone in one swoop.

The overall point of this section is to ensure you are structuring your digital communications so you rule them, and not let them rule you. Of course, there are many best practices around turning off notifications and using other channels (such as Slack, Teams, Zoom messages, etc.), and you can read more about some of those in the upcoming chapter on communications.

Of course, you will continuously receive emails and other communications that generate new work. In this case, you want to reply, and then add work time to your Weekly Worksheet between the date and deadline.

SYSTEMATICALLY CAPTURE INCOMING NEW REQUESTS

Inevitably, it will happen. You plan your week or day, you know your routines for incoming work, and then take an innocent trip to the restroom and boom! Someone will have a quick request, a great idea, or a random thought to share with you. To be a true Together Teammate (which is your goal, right?), I want you to have a way to capture these items in the moment – even if you cannot act on them immediately. So how can we deal with the mobile inbox, so to speak? Likely you need a way that your Together System is always with you.

DETERMINE THE SOURCES OF YOUR REQUESTS

Your first step is to identify the sources of your incoming requests. Usually, they can come:

- Via email, text, or messaging app
- During formal meetings, such as a one-on-one with your manager
- During larger meetings, such as a board meeting or a regional team
- During informal meetings or stop-bys
- From Project Plans created by yourself and others
- From various memos or publications that may have To-Dos for your role

No doubt, your role likely has its own sources of incoming requests. Pause and add anything else to this list.

Now that you know all the places your requests come from, you can figure out how to "catch them." The instinct can of course be to either try and remember them or jot them down on whatever is in front of you at the moment. In my experience, this *can* work – to a point – but in your roles, the requests can come fast and furious, at many times of day and in many formats. Don't waste your valuable mental energy on retaining them! For example, if you determined that many of your requests come through email when at your desk, you may be able to pop them into your digital Weekly Worksheet. Or maybe a bunch of action steps come out of meetings where you don't have your laptop, so you need to quickly catch items in a notebook to bring back to your digital Long-Term List.

Let's look into how various individuals have assessed their situations and determined what works for them. As always, these examples are not meant for you to emulate exactly, but for you to witness the thinking process and then extrapolate for yourself.

Caught on a Weekly Worksheet! Incoming Communications Requiring Additional Work Time

Lauren, a former executive assistant in Brooklyn, is used to responding to lots of incoming requests, and she prepares for them by blocking time for the priorities of her role. In the example below, she receives a request from her manager (Angela) for a table displaying data for an upcoming meeting. Luckily, she has already blocked time to help assist with preparation for this meeting.

Let's see how Lauren handled the incoming Deluge that was time-sensitive, from her manager (a VIP in her world), and a new request:

Acknowledged the request. Lauren replied and said she was on it. You could argue that perhaps this is not necessary, but when you have a fast-moving request from your manager, I think an acknowledgment is helpful. This is a prime example of Show Your Work, a key Together Try-It that builds trust with others.

From: Lauren
Sent: Thursday, December 07, 2017 11:04 AM
To: Angela
Subject: RE: FW: FYI: Sharing YOY Math Data Tomorrow

Thanks, Angela. I'll have this to you by EOD 12/12.

From: Angela
Sent: Thursday, December 07, 2017 8:42 AM
To: Lauren
Subject: FW: FYI: Sharing YOY Math Data Tomorrow

Hi Lauren,
When you get time, could you put together the same chart in the attachment, for ELA and math, for my schools?
Thank you 😊
Angela

From: Anna
Sent: Wednesday, December 06, 2017 10:20 PM
To: Jessica, Michael, Angela
Subject: FYI: Sharing YOY Math Data Tomorrow

Hi Jessica (Michael, Angela) –

Given we have hot off the presses math data, I wanted to be able to share YOY data with principals and deans tomorrow. Attached is what I'm planning on sharing. Please let me now if you have any questions or concerns about me sharing. I would LOVE to be able to get this data in front of principals tomorrow, but **if you feel strongly that we shouldn't, let me know and I won't.** Just text me in the morning. The true purpose of tomorrow is to put the data on stage publicly, name we've seen some movement and that now we need to build momentum towards more gains.

Thank you!
Anna

Figure 9.5   Lauren's Deluge Rapid Response.

Stated the next step and timeline. Lauren said she would have it by EOD (end-of-day) on 12/12. This lets Gina know when to expect the deliverable. Lauren is Closing the Loops.

Checked for time on your Weekly Worksheet. Lauren also named to herself that she could add the request to existing work time for a cohort already in place. If you are more of a What-er, you could make sure this goes on your list to complete by end of day.

Lauren is in front of her desk often, with her digital calendar (aka Weekly Worksheet) right in front of her, so she chooses to capture the incoming work right there in her Outlook calendar.

 Reader Reflection: What can you learn from Lauren's process?

Caught on a Tracker! Teresita's Categorized Request Tracker

What about if there is a pattern of one-off requests? One of the biggest challenges of your roles is tracking incoming requests, which often feel like they are flying at you – all day long and from many different directions. Successful Together Teammates are lockboxes with these requests: tracking them, communicating them, and acting on them.

Teresita, an executive secretary for a large school district in San Antonio, carefully tracks requests from her manager, Ms. Romero. Teresita knows there will always be different requests coming in all day, and she has identified the categories they will typically fall in, which correspond with open spaces on her Weekly Worksheet. Since Teresita is often at her desk and has her Weekly Worksheet up and open – and is more of a What-er – she can easily plop any new requests from Ms. Romero into these sections. She shared a snippet of the categories (and hyperlinks) she created to capture all the requests.

Teresita built these trackers right on top of her Weekly Worksheet, with hyperlinks to capture the tasks as they come flooding in. These hyperlinks lead her to categorized Google Docs so she can record them in one place. This means she can serve as a thought-partner to her manager, Ms. Romero, and track the Parent Concerns, the Calendar requests, and the emails to answer. Because Teresita is aware of the different types of requests, she is sorting

DAILY PRIORITIES/AM

MS. ROMERO'S REQUESTS					
PARENT CONCERNS					
LOG NEW ASSIGNMENTS					
CALENDARING					
EMAILS					
ZOOMS					

Figure 9.6 Teresita's Requests Tracker.

through the Deluge as it comes in. She is setting herself up to batch work very effectively. When it is Calendaring time, Teresita can fly through those requests with efficiency.

 Reader Reflection: What categories of requests do you get throughout the day? Can you capture your requests in an organized fashion so they are easier to batch later?

Let's have a look at another method for catching notes on the fly.

Caught on the iPad! Kevin's Requests Tracker

Kevin, an operations team member in Brooklyn who is often on the move down hallways, in supply closets, and around the front office, has gone all-digital to capture his incoming requests during the day. Using his trusted iPad, Kevin catches the incoming Deluge that comes at him all day long.

Kevin captures his requests as they come in chronologically and in separate digital notebooks. Kevin says, "I use an iPad very religiously in my work now in my day-to-day life as an associate director of operations. I utilize GoodNotes, where I have a planner and I utilize my different notebooks in my planner to allow me to capture my requests and chunk it that way." (You can read more about GoodNotes in Kevin's Together Tour.)

Once you capture the shifts and requests on the go, then you have to go back and process them. No matter how you have gathered them up, when you return to your desk or workstation, you will need to sift through each of them and distribute accordingly. A task that will take two hours? Add to your calendar. A quick email to send? Jot on your Weekly Worksheet. A long-term discussion topic with your boss? Pop into a Meeting Agenda.

 FAQ: Can't I just hold all of the information in my head? Likely no. Our brains can only accommodate so much, and with multiple things flying at you, inevitably something will get forgotten unintentionally and erode trust with colleagues, vendors, or managers.

NEED A THOUGHT CATCHER?

If you find yourself catching a lot of stuff throughout the day, you may find you need an even more systematic method that I call Thought Catchers.

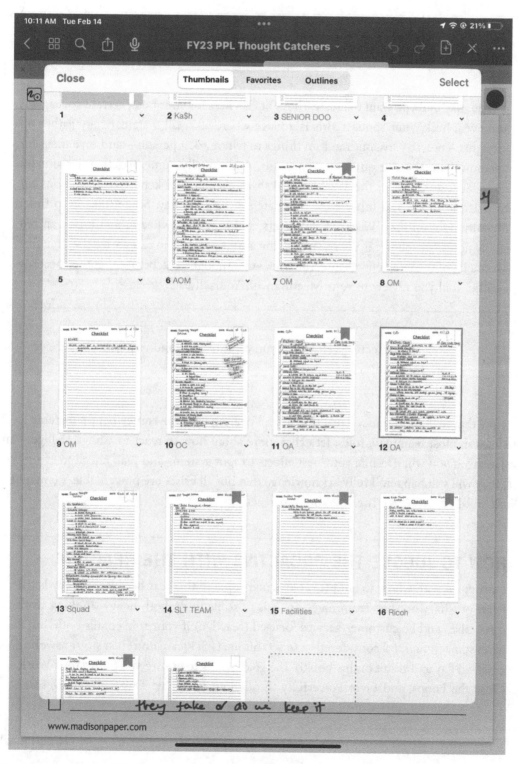

Figure 9.7   Kevin's Thought Catchers in GoodNotes.

Thought Catcher: A place to record and revisit your thoughts for people, teams, or topics for future reference.

You may find you want to create Thought Catchers for your boss, certain colleagues, and even, heck, your spouse! This is a place where you will systematically gather up thoughts – not To-Dos, but random things to tell or ask a person – and save them for upcoming meetings or quick conversations. Additionally, some Together Teammates do what Jazmin did in the Weekly Worksheet chapter and kept special sections for Newsletter Topics and other ideas you catch during the day. Some folks keep them digitally right on their Weekly Worksheets, and others may keep them on organized sticky notes. The choice is yours, but having a routine place to categorize the thoughts saves a lot of time and effort later. The trick with Thought Catchers is that they become another tool you review in your Meeting with Yourself each week.

Reader Reflection: How will you capture FYIs and requests you receive on the move?

Now that we have discussed reacting to and dealing with the somewhat predictable level of chaos in most teammate roles, let's chat more about how to react to a huge Deluge – an avalanche, if you will. Despite your best efforts to spot systems and plan ahead to avoid crises, they will still happen. I fully acknowledge that not all crises are preventable. Remember, Work and Life are Never Together, but our reactions can be.

HOW TO JUGGLE THE PROACTIVE WITH THE REACTIVE

I struggled with where to land this particular topic in this text because it really is the heart of what Together Teammates do. It is possible to do both heavy thinking work (proactive) and be customer-service focused (reactive) if your role entails both, but it takes some thoughtful consideration to set this up. (PS: Please don't just stop answering email all day as a result of this book!) The goal here is to ensure you Show Your Work, Close the Loops, and Pivot Powerfully throughout your day. This will require some

(Continued)

thoughtful evaluation of what you know to be predictable work, and what you can anticipate will be the reactive stuff. You may find that it will help to:

☐ Set up super-clear roles and responsibilities and find yourself coverage for a few times during the day, like Erin and her team.

☐ Tell your colleagues and manager your intentions or goals for the following day at the end of each day. That can be a great way to wrap up your daily or weekly Meeting with Yourself. For templates, you can look here: www.wiley.com/go/together teammate. This helps others know what to expect in terms of your communication availability, and also serves as an accountability tool for you.

☐ Turn off notifications and other items that beep, bloop, or buzz. You may want to set filters so that some very important people can get through, but not everyone needs an immediate solution.

☐ Set up some templates or self-service options if you find you are writing the same messages over and over again.

☐ Remind your manager and colleagues (kindly) of different ways of reaching you. For example, you may say, "I am not checking emails in the evening, but please call me until 10 p.m. in case of an emergency."

PAUSE TO PLAN YOUR PIVOT – AND THEN COMMUNICATE

Inevitably, the work will shift over the course of the day and week. The point of this book is not to set you up to create a Weekly Worksheet and then send you into robot-execution mode minute-by-minute. The point is that you plan in order to be flexible.

What to do when you have too much to do? You know the drill; it may happen every day. We have a plan for the day, room for emergencies, and then *boom,* something comes up that forces us to pivot. While our instinct can be to groan, work later, or build silent resentment, we have to have a plan in place for these situations:

■ *Evaluate the level of the emergency.* To do this, you have to have a clear sense of your own priorities, your manager's priorities, and the organization's priorities. If you are not sure, you can ask questions like, "Is this a right now, later today, or tomorrow situation?" to get a handle on the time sensitivity. You can also ask, "Is there a particular method you prefer to have this solved?" (e.g. "I can pull a polished version of the data, but it will take me X amount of time.")

- ■ *If it is a true priority, then communicate the change of plans.* Once you have established that a shift in priorities is required, then it falls on you to communicate the change of plans, including asking for help and establishing clarity around deadlines.

- ■ *Communicate your needs to make the priority happen.* This might mean a quiet workspace, additional supports, or a little grace with your colleagues. Let people know via land, sea, and air what you will need to finish the board report, knock out that grant, create a hot cocoa bar, or [fill in your priority here].

Let's look at two examples from my own small team when someone pivoted from the original plan and reprioritized, whether because of a change in circumstances or because of an overflow of priorities.

Kendra's Midweek Pivot

To see this in action, let's peek behind-the-scenes at the Together Group when our beloved senior director of operations shifted priorities to onboard a new team member who would staff some of our additional classes.

This request came from me and was of highest priority because it connected to our main organizational goal: to deliver excellent instruction in the area of Togetherness. Kendra sent the email you see in this image to me directly after I dropped a glib, "We have hired a new person!" on her in, I'm slightly ashamed to say, a text!

Let's break apart the anatomy of what makes this a Powerful Pivot:

- ■ **Names priorities clearly.** Kendra names the immediate priorities for the day, which in this case are onboarding steps for Erica (my request) and deck work for next week's classes. Kendra is clear that both are priorities because she aligned in her Weekly Worksheet when she Met with Herself.

- ■ **Gets recommendation ready.** Kendra proposes what will be delayed and her rationale for this decision-making. This was much more helpful than just asking me what she should delay.

- ■ **Asks for input on the adjustments.** Kendra gives me (her manager) a chance to weigh in on any adjustments I would like to make.

 Reader Reflection: What will you do the next time you have a legitimate change in priorities?

From:
Sent: Thursday, September 9, 2021 8:10 AM
To:
Subject: FYIs for today / let me know of any changes

Hi Maia,

Quick heads up that today I'll be working on:

- Onboarding steps for Erica
- Deck work for next week's classes
- TPM samples / templates branding steps *(I will double check with Maggie on when this is due!)*

To fit in Erica steps, unless I have time leftover, I'm delaying:

- Emails that have come through since last night, unless directly related to the tasks listed above
- Contracts (except for Erica's)
- Class website steps for next week's classes (will create a weekend work block for these)
- Host site feedback summary emails
- Updating the Online Class Supporter manual with new breakout room info and screenshots

Let me know if any of that looks off or needs to be adjusted.

Thanks!,

Kendra

Figure 9.8 Kendra's Midweek Pivot.

Granted, it took a certain amount of courage and trust for Kendra to send such an email to her manager (me!). If you read this thinking, there is no way I could ever send this to my own manager, I encourage you to start small and think about how you might simply articulate trade-offs when new work comes your way.

Let's look at a larger-scale example of another member of our team who was swirling in priorities and took a moment to Pause to Plan – a key Together Try-It.

Heidi's Reprioritization Email

Sometimes you may feel like you are drowning in tasks and need to align with others around you on priorities. Heidi, a member of the Together Team, had this happen to her recently, and she took some time to rise up from the day-to-day turbulence. I received the email seen here.

Hi Maia,

Feeling newly resolved after out team meeting today, can I ask you to help check my prioritization below?

I have them listed in what I consider to be priority order, top to bottom.

Please let me know of any feedback!

Thanks so much,

- Heidi

Task / Project	Heidi notes	MHM
Public Sessions – TL & Teams • Support new registrations • Book order • Invoice reminders	Essential	
Wellness blast	Essential by Saturday night!	
Together Teacher promotion	HIGH HIGH HIGH	
Create first draft of job description	Won't take long, will just get it on its way around our team	
FAQs, Bios, Testimonials to Jade / Sean	Needs to happen but may need to wait a few days while I promote Together Teacher!	
March newsletter	Essential but may need to be last-minute (working around your OOO)	
Add media release to Arlo registration form	Not sure how long this will take but can maybe wait a week or two? (Reality is we've already recorded the classes we're using with Jeff!)	
End-of-month Course Profit Dashboard		
Next steps with CMS • Email for Maia to respond about tags • Timeline for Heidi	This can be delayed	

Figure 9.9   Heidi's Reprioritization Email.

This is honestly one of my favorite samples in the entire book because it exemplifies every Together Try-It we hope a Together Teammate does all at once. Heidi's head was aswirl with many priorities and tasks, and whose isn't on certain days?! Let's see what Heidi did here after a team meeting when we looked at overall team priorities:

■ **List out everything that is causing your brain to swirl.** I call this a good old-fashioned brain dump. You may be able to get it from your Weekly Worksheet, or new items may have popped up. Regardless of *where* you write or view all of the To-Dos, fully empty your brain so you can thoughtfully look at the list in totality.

■ **Pause to plan and reassess.** I want to underscore this Together Teammate move. It is so tempting, and often easier, to go through and just keep trying to cross things off the list. When you realize, "I have no idea what goes first, second, third" – or you *think* you know, but want assistance to align with others, it makes sense to pause, write it all in one place, and seek alignment with a manager, your peers, or colleagues.

■ **Propose priority level.** Heidi went through and proposed priority level, using her own language like "Essential," and "High, High, High." By even pausing to do this, she was able to enter a thought process in her brain to slow things down and assess not only the priority, but to recalibrate what the workload actually was. She used this to align with me, and flag things as essential, but that maybe can be done at the last minute.

 Reader Reflection: When you feel the work whirlwind blow over, what is your plan to Process, Pause, and Propose? Do you need a sign above your computer that reminds you what to do in these situations? This is a friendly reminder that sometimes stopping the work for a minute will actually help advance the work.

Is the Daily Deluge still blowing around you? I know, I know. You cannot always control it, but you can try to Forecast Forward based on your past knowledge, you can Pause to Plan and reassess, and you can build trust with your colleagues by Showing the Work and Pivoting Powerfully. Remember, the more planned you are, the more flexible you can be.

TURBO TOGETHERNESS

Well, that was a whirlwind (just kidding – Togetherness Jokes). But I hope this chapter helped you to get clear that interruptions are routine, and while some of them are avoidable, some of them are definitely not. It may take an honest conversation with yourself and others to slow down the Deluge, handle the requests with grace and authority, and ultimately deliver on behalf of those you serve. To get a quick handle on the Deluge, here are your action steps:

Use your Weekly Worksheet to plan to protect your focused Task Time. Consider explaining this to your manager, saying something like, "In order to process all the receipts for four different colleagues – and to keep this error-free and on time – I will be pausing my inbox and closing my door for an hour once per week on Thursdays. If you need to break through, please call me directly and I can answer. If I don't take this time, we can risk me submitting reports to the finance team late or making errors. If this doesn't work for you, can you propose a different plan so I can accomplish what I need to do?" I know it may feel scary or not possible, but I would encourage you to try. If my script doesn't work for you, give your own a try.

Ensure your Together Tools can hold up to your particular version of the Deluge. Only you know the ins/outs of your role. Perhaps people stack up at your workspace at the beginning of the day for questions. Or maybe the two days before an event, you know you get a ton of last-minute requests via text. Or maybe your inbox fills to the brim when a board meeting is a week away. No matter what your role, your Together Tools need to withstand the strain now and again. This may look like a notebook you always take with you to a particular event when you will inevitably gather questions for immediate answers. Or it may look like opening up your calendar at certain times to invite the interruptions (more on this in the Systems Spotting chapter coming up).

Practice figuring out and communicating the priorities of your role on a consistent basis. Show Your Work! Maybe each week after you Meet with Yourself, a particular communication goes to your managers that includes your priorities. Perhaps your Weekly Worksheet has a big sticky note on it that says, "This week the following three things matter THE MOST: _____." Or maybe you simply verbally share in a meeting with your manager your top areas of focus and seek alignment. The larger point here is that only you know what matters most in your role – and only you can make time to make it happen. Yes, you will need help and support, but that starts with naming what you see as most important. And if you want support in meeting your priorities, you will need to communicate that to those around you as well.

Track the patterns. You plan your week, you respond flexibly, you leave empty space for last-minute crises, and yet they still seem to interrupt you *all day long*. It's time to track the Deluge and look for patterns. Maybe it is a certain time of day that is prone to interruptions and your focused time is scheduled wrong. Maybe a certain human or two are behind 80% of the Desk Drop-bys or Electronic Pings, so perhaps a regularly scheduled meeting with them would help.

Each of the ideas in this chapter can take a little bit of time and often a lot of courage. That said, over 20 years into this work – and with hundreds of organizations, companies, and teams served – I remain wholeheartedly convinced that we can both have systems *and* handle the Daily Deluge that comes in.

MANAGER MOMENT

Perhaps you read this entire chapter and gently ducked your head in embarrassment, realizing you could possibly be the source of the Daily Deluge for your Together Teammate. Or maybe you realized that you didn't have information or data about whether your teammate was interrupted or not all day long. Or maybe you realized that this is a culture that exists on your team or in your organization and you need some structural or culture shifts to improve this for everyone.

Starting small, let's consider some team culture assessments you could make to look for opportunities to calm the Daily Deluge – for your teammate and others.

Are YOU personally bursting into someone's office or casually doing Desk Drop-bys all day? While I love the relationship-building aspect of this for you, I wonder if you could use Thought Catchers or an ongoing shared agenda (fast forward to the chapter on Meetings if you want to see what I mean) to capture the thought for later. (Fun fact: my husband, Keith, and I both work from home, and I used to interrupt him quite often with random work and life thoughts. I now keep a Keith section on my Weekly Worksheet to store up the thoughts and share them at an appropriate time.) Yes, this takes discipline and perhaps an extra minute of your time, but it also means you may get more effective answers or results.

Does your entire team/division/office interrupt each other all day long? The good news is they like interacting; the bad news is research shows it takes our brains a long time to recover from distractions – and your entire team likely has focused work of some nature that they need to do. Consider a visual cue people can wear or another way to signal when they are focusing. Or you may want to institute team-wide Quiet Hours for an hour a day or at a certain time a week. I learned a lot from a team in Texas that created Dark Days once per quarter for their team to do strategic and focused work. This meant no internal communications because the assumption was that everyone was working on a more focused task or project. You could also consider some Communication Agreements so the expectation of how quickly a response is expected and via which medium is clear and transparent for all team members.

Do YOU interrupt yourself all day long? While this may sound like a silly question, I know I can be super prone to creating my *very own* Daily Deluge when I interrupt myself by checking email often, peeking at my WhatsApp threads from my girlfriends, or checking the news cycle too much. You may want to consider where you physically set up for which kinds of work, using the Pomodoro method (google it or take a peek at our blog), using various apps that block the internet, and maybe setting some predictable office hours so you know you can still be available to others. You play an important role in modeling for the rest of your team.

The larger point is that the Daily Deluge can usually be reduced for yourself, your team, and in particular – those I'm calling your Together Teammates. It may take some additional work or structures, but it will help some of the most put-upon people in your organization feel as if their time matters too. (PS: For more tips on this, I definitely recommend you grab a copy of *The Together Leader*.)

Together Tour

Fiama
Program Management Specialist
University of Maryland
Baltimore, Maryland

Fiama Romero

WHAT IS YOUR MOST USED TOGETHER TOOL TO KEEP *YOURSELF* TOGETHER?

My top tool is paper – my small spiralbound notebook. When a thought pops into my mind, when someone makes a request, whatever the case might be, it takes too much time and mental effort in the moment to figure out the perfect online place for those items to live. Paper (my notebook) gives me the freedom and flexibility to place those thoughts anywhere I want!

Depending on what I'm jotting down, I might add it to the list of things I'd like to knock out today. If the thought is completely random and unrelated to what I'm working on, I can place it in one of the margins.

Close the Loops. I know that as long as it makes it into the notebook, I will have time to get back to it and either execute or move it to another planning list or project system I might use. The most important thing is to make sure it's captured, and my notebook allows me the ability to capture it as quickly, freely, and unedited as it comes to my mind. (FYI, everything in my notebook gets crossed out once it either gets completed or gets moved to a new list, so anything that is not crossed out is begging for attention.)

Some added bonuses to using pen and paper: While I have an online tracker for my project To-Dos, I like to write the things I'm working on the day/week in my notebook. If something doesn't get completed one day, it gets rewritten onto tomorrow's list. If I am rewriting something too many times, I need to evaluate why I haven't gotten it done and consider: do I need to prioritize it, delegate it, or add it to a later list and forget it for now?

Spot the Need for Systems. This is also really helpful, by the way, when it's time to create process plans after the fact. I've realized the initial plan I created in my online system often misses all the tiny details. But by keeping all my "random" notes/thoughts/to-dos in the notebook, when it's time to finalize the process plan for next year, I can skim through my old pages and look for items that were so small they never made it onto the formal process plan.

HOW DO YOU RE-TOGETHER YOURSELF WHEN UNEXPECTED THINGS POP UP?

Just recently, I had my Wednesday perfectly planned, and it was important for me to stick to that schedule because Thursday was a work holiday celebration and Friday I was leading a virtual work event, which meant I would have limited focus time to work on Thursday and Friday. Towards the end of the day, I received an email from my boss – we had forgotten that Thursday's celebration, which would start as a team meeting, would require each department (including ours) to present updates on their progress YTD. Could I put together some slides for that presentation? (And of course, she needed those ASAP so that she would have time to review/edit/etc.)

At that point, everything else that had to be done did not take precedent.

Pivot Powerfully. To minimize the time I spent frazzled and bemoaning the unexpected-but-very-important task, I grabbed my notebook, and quickly reworked my list of "to dos" for the day. I made a line across the page to indicate a new section with new lists. "Slides" was the only thing on the new Wednesday "to-do" list. Everything else that was on the list was rewritten into either a "Thursday," "Friday," or "Next Week" list. (I knew I would only have a couple of hours to work on Thursday and Friday, so it was important to be explicit about what my "bare minimum" for each day would be.)

This allowed me to jump right into the Most Important Task, knowing that I had made a plan for all the other items I had hoped to get done that day.

WHEN IS A TIME YOU HAD TO ADJUST YOUR TOGETHERNESS PRACTICES AND WHY?

This year, I have had to adjust my time to support another department that was (expectedly but still unfortunately) understaffed. This meant that in addition to doing the routine and unexpected tasks needed for my own department, I was also supporting with grant submissions for another department. (I am familiar with grants, though not at all an expert in them, and it is completely different from my main job.)

Identify Collision Course. The biggest thing I learned from this experience was that when I am working with/for two departments that don't communicate and aren't aware of competing priorities, I need to make sure I am communicating my time limitations.

In other words, the department that needed grant support was viewing the deadline as the grant submission deadline. They did not know that I had an event coming up with my main department around the same time, so I would have preferred to work on the grant well before the event or after the event. When I asked for items in advance, they delayed in getting it back to me, and then I had to scramble to complete the grant items and the event To-Dos at the same time (which meant working some late nights that week). If I had told the grant people that I would be unavailable XYZ week, that would have encouraged them to send me the items needed sooner, and allowed me to balance out my workload more evenly.

HOW HAS TOGETHERNESS HELPED YOU COMMUNICATE AND WORK WITH OTHERS?

Close the Loops, Own the Outcome. As one faculty member in my office put it, "When I hand something off to you, I know I don't have to stress about it." Togetherness helps me keep track not just of what I have to do, but of what items I have passed off to other people and need to make sure get completed and/or passed along back to me. Ideally, my Togetherness helps alleviate others' stress because they know I'm there to manage the process and ensure no balls get dropped or forgotten. They also know I will give them only the information that they need, without overcomplicating it or getting into the weeds. People like working with me on complicated projects because they know I will cut through the near-endless paths that could be taken, narrow down the options, and get the project to "done."

HOW DO YOU BALANCE THE PROACTIVE FOCUSED PART OF YOUR JOB WITH THE REACTIVE TASKS THAT POP UP?

Typically, proactive work is either something that is a strategic initiative (e.g. improving workflows, revamping the website, etc.) or something that you are trying to get ahead of so you're not cramming everything into the last minute (e.g. prepping in advance for an event). What that means to me is that the biggest threat to proactive work is that no one will miss it if it doesn't get done right away, until somewhere down the line it's urgently needed and becomes reactive work.

My best way to balance the proactive with the reactive is to give the proactive items firm deadlines, much like the reactive items have. A deadline I set myself is not likely to be motivating enough, so I share these deadlines with my manager, and that helps motivate me to find time to prioritize them and also forces me to think realistically about when I will have time to complete them.

This way, when the reactive things occur, I am not stressing about the 20 proactive things that need to get done. Rather, I know that only XYZ items need to be done in the next one to two weeks, so I feel better punting those items if needed, and I know I can rework my schedule because I am setting the deadlines, instead of waiting for others to do it for me.

HOW DO YOU HANDLE WORKING WITH COLLEAGUES WHO ARE SLIGHTLY LESS THAN TOGETHER?

Stand in the Shoes of Others. The first and most important step, I think, is to understand those colleagues. What is their preferred communication style? What are they really good at doing and what are their weaknesses? Understanding those items helps me leverage and maximize their support. For example, I have a colleague who is great at documenting complicated processes, but not so great at pivoting when plans change.

Another thing that I'm still learning is how to establish boundaries. This might look like creating a specific agenda even for just a one-on-one meeting, to keep the conversation to a set time and keep it moving forward. This can also be requesting to move certain conversations to email to avoid one more meeting that may not be necessary. I have also reduced the stress that happens when I am pulled in to support at (literally) the last minute with events and projects, by making it known, early and often, that I am available to support, but setting a deadline that after a certain point (say, 12 p.m. the day before the event), I cannot take any requests for support.

WHY DOES TOGETHERNESS MATTER TO YOU AT WORK AND AT HOME?

My partner and I pride ourselves on having what you might call a semi-Together life. Sure, sometimes laundry doesn't get done on time or a dirty pot stays soaking for longer than we intended. But all in all, the things that matter to us and are most important get done. More than "getting things done," we don't have to stress about things that we see others commonly stressed over – we have food for every meal, we know where our money goes and what it has to do, bills get paid, we make it to all our doctor's appointments, keep track of family and friend birthdays and outings, and so on. We are known as the most Together couple in our friend/family group, and people know they can rely on us if we say we'll be there (even if we are a little late, ha-ha).

For example, just this weekend we helped one family member pick their health insurance plan and helped another form a game plan for buying a new car.

Both at work and at home, being Together means that I am not a burden on anyone else, and that I can help those I love and care about by alleviating a little bit of their stress.

Get the Team Together: Teammate Tricks to Move the Work Forward

CHAPTER 10

Craft Clear Communications to Move Others to Action

Ever send an email out into the world, only to get crickets back? Or draft a newsletter and watch your team miss the deadlines that you had included? Or text a colleague only to realize that this was a no-no? Been there, done that. This chapter focuses on clear written communication designed to get the outcome you need as Together Teammates. Because of your unique roles of frequently polling, gathering, compiling, and coordinating lots of information to get to clear outcomes and recommendations, the way in which you design even the smallest communications can be the difference between pushing a project forward or letting it get stuck.

In this chapter, you will learn to:

■ Observe your organization's environment and get clear on communications expectations

■ Produce clear outgoing communications that achieve results

■ Craft effective outgoing messages to convey information

This chapter includes helpful examples of various channels used for different types of communications, models of outgoing communication designed for folks to easily take action, and easy-to-read messages. I hope to find a healthy communications balance for you that juggles the needs of your organization with your own needs. Let's start with knowing your environment.

Whether you have worked at your organization for 2 months, 2 years, or 20 years, you are likely familiar with the communications expectations in one of two ways: they were explicitly named to you (less likely), or you observed them and jumped in. Let's start this journey by figuring out what the deal is at your current workplace.

WHAT METHODS DOES YOUR ORGANIZATION USE TO COMMUNICATE?

Let's start with the basics, such as which forms of communication your organization uses when, and why. Likely email is a given, but what else is used? Maybe you all picked up Slack during the pandemic when everyone was working exclusively from home? Maybe text groups or WhatsApp are used for particular teams? Maybe your walkie-talkies are back? Given that there are certainly a variety of forms of communication used, do you have clarity around what each method is specifically used for? If so, that's great! If not, you're probably not the only person at your organization who is confused.

Jordan's Communication Guidelines

Some teams and organizations try to set people up for success by defining which communications methods to use when. Jordan, an operations leader, took the time to articulate the channels for his team. By doing this, Jordan also created an expectation from his various audiences on what they would receive when. Let's check it out.

Operations Team Communication

Type of Communication	Purpose	Owner	Frequency	Format	Approval Process
Newsletter	Updates on ops, academics, and culture within the school	Director of Engagement	First Wednesday of every month	All items are posted online with a short version sent home via paper	Drafted by the third Friday of every month. Sent to MDO.
One off flyers and reminders from Adelante	Events, reminders, athletics	All	Wednesdays only	Paper	Draft sent to MDO by COB the Friday before
Flyers from External Partners		Director of Engagement	Wednesdays only	Paper only	Must be approved by DE
Text & Email Reminders	Event reminders, surveys, general housekeeping	Director of Engagement /MDO	As needed - No more than twice a week.	KinVolved: Text, Email	Ensure that there are no other scheduled messages. DE or MDO send.
Late Bus Notification	A text from KV about a late bus in the PM.	DOO	As needed	KinVolved	None
Emergency	School closing, mass emergency	MDO			

Figure 10.1   Jordan's Operations Team Communications.

Because communications can fly every which way, it makes sense to establish what will be sent by whom and when. In the absence of doing this, people may receive communications at various times and not pay necessary attention to them. Or a late bus notification may one day be sent from a teacher and the next day from an operations team member, adding unnecessary confusion. By establishing clear communications, you can ensure your outgoing work includes:

- **Predictable cadence of communications.** Choosing Wednesdays only for some key communications means parents and families are not bombarded by extra papers every day of the week. They know what to expect and when.

- **Same sender of information.** If a bus is late, it helps to know who will tell you so you can be on high alert for that message.

- **Plan for emergencies.** If there is a true emergency, the MDO (managing director of operations) will assume all communications. Knowing this in advance prevents confusion and provides clarity on communication channels in a high-stress moment.

Now let's review another example of how a team articulates expectations for various communication channels. As you look at these, keep your own organization, team, or even just yourself in mind.

Arthur Ashe Charter School's Communications Expectations

Arthur Ashe, a school in New Orleans, realized that communications had started flying in all directions. Been there, right?! The team there took time to get clear on when to use Google Hangouts versus text versus call. Hmm . . . I could use this idea with my children!

Similar to Jordan's example, this team took the time to get clear such that everyone could understand the guidelines. The goal here, of course, is not to police people's communications (no one wants *that* job), but more to help people feel successful in their main roles at the school site, reduce communications clutter, and let people focus on the heart of their jobs.

- **Person-to-Person or video call** (Google Hangouts, in their case). I love that this is first and it is spelled out that this is the way difficult conversations are handled.

- **Text.** Text is used for very quick requests, and even some shout-outs!

- **Phone calls.** No one has time for long phone calls. This document names when a phone call is appropriate – and that they should be quick!

Now let's look at a one-off example of other internal team communications, which may be well within your power or authority to set up within your own team.

20-21 STAFF COMMUNICATION NORMS

"Communication is one of the most important skills you require for a successful life." Catherine Pulsifer

During these unprecedented times, how we communicate and what we communicate will be crucial to our health as a school and team; therefore establishing a clear communication plan will be crucial. With that being said, please see the communication plan below and familiarize yourself as this is how we will interact as a team moving forward.

Form of Communication	Purpose or Typical Use
Person to Person (or Google Hangout)	1:1 meetings, Grade-level meetings, Team Huddles, Difficult Conversations or ugent student concerns
Text	Use for quick responses, shoutouts, or immediate needs, ie. Operational Needs, Send-Outs (Behavior Assistance other than fighting/crisis)
Phone Call	Use this for urgent matter (such as a crisis) and/or something that will take 3-5 minutes to discuss/resolve
Email	Use to follow-up on in-person conversations or meetings, 2nd Way to call off (after speaking with your supervisor; see Sick Day Protocol)

Email Norms:
★ We use our Firstline Schools email for all official school business. We adhere to the FLS Handbook when emailing about students (refer to the FLS Handbook about student privacy).
★ General Rules for using emails (adapted from MCD and TED's Chris Anderson)
  o Respect Recipients' Time- This is the fundamental rule. As the message sender, the onus is on YOU to minimize the time your email will take to process. Even if it means taking more time at your end before sending. **We respond to all emails within 24 hours.**
  o Make Subject Lines and Content Clearer- Start with a subject line that clearly labels the topic. Use crisp, muddle-free sentences. If the email has to be longer than five sentences, make sure the first provides the basic reason for writing. Avoid strange fonts and colours. We will use the following codes in our subject lines: **QQ- quick question, ACTION- This item requires an action from the receiver, Follow-Up-item requires follow-up, reminder or FYI**
  o Slash Surplus cc's- CC's are like mating bunnies. For every recipient you add, you are dramatically multiplying total response time. Not to be done lightly! When there are multiple recipients, please don't default to 'Reply All'. Maybe you only need to cc a couple of people on the original thread. Or none.
  o Cut Contentless Responses- You don't need to reply to every email, especially not those that are themselves clear responses. An email saying "Thanks for your note. I'm in." does not need you to reply "Great." That just cost someone another 30 seconds.

Figure 10.2   Arthur Ashe's Communication Guidelines.

AJ's Operations Team Slack Channel

AJ, in her former role as an operations director, worked on reducing her team's email load through encouraging shared utilization of Slack for quick messages throughout the day.

AJ says, "For my team, it has increased collaboration while reducing actual worktime interruptions. We also know email can take a full day to reply, Slack is same-day response,

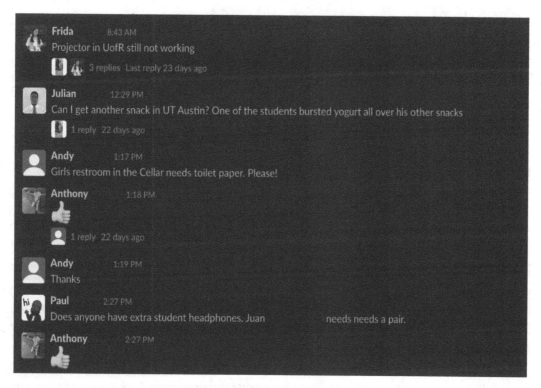

Figure 10.3   AJ's Operations Slack Channel.

and a phone call is *now*." As you see in the model, members of the school team can message the operations team for immediate support, such as toilet paper, student headphones, snacks, and projectors – all items that are needed quite soon (insert toilet paper jokes here). Anthony is charged with replying to the team so they know he is on it!

Slack or other messaging options can be helpful to:

■ Build camaraderie though memes, jokes, and other such bits of internet fun

■ Be more searchable than email (sometimes)

■ Keep threads around certain topics or projects separate, clear, and organized

 Reader Reflection: While you are likely not in charge of the overall communication landscape in your organization, it is helpful for you to reflect on which tools you use when and why. Take a look at all of your outgoing communications across your various channels for the past week. Do you have a bias for a certain type of communication? How does that play out? For example, maybe you send your manager detailed emails, but turns out she is faster on text messages. Or perhaps your team creates text messages that are ridiculously long and should instead be in email.

Now that we have determined which channels you use for what, let's look at crafting actual communications – designed to get the outcomes you want!

WRITE YOUR MESSAGES WITH A BIAS TOWARD RESULTS

As Together Teammates, you are often sending messages out into the world. They could be scheduling requests, newsletters, memos, or task assignments. On top of this, you are not just tossing the messages out in the world; you have to Close the Loops by ensuring the messages come back to you. And not only do you have to ensure the messages come back to you, but with the information you need in the manner and timeline you need it. No easy task, right? In this section, we will examine some outgoing messages and figure out what Keeps It One-Click and helps you Own the Outcomes.

As discussed in the previous part of this chapter, there are likely some internal spoken (hopefully) or unspoken communication agreements floating around your organization, and I hope you figured out what those are in your own situation. In this section, we will explore ensuring your own communications are crystal clear, such that you can make it easy for others to reply – and ultimately get your own work done with ease.

The first step is to be clear for yourself about the purpose of the communication. It could be a question, a task, or even just updating colleagues about something important. Think about what you want this communication to accomplish. You want to minimize words whenever you can and make sure things are very easy for the receiver. You also want to provide the context and information required for the message to be clear.

Kendra Makes It Multiple Choice

Kendra, a longtime member of the Together Team, is known for her incredibly clear communication; she is our gold standard. One of her key moves – to get the results she needs to do her own job well – is making emails multiple choice whenever possible. You know, like a test at school that gives options and you must choose one.

Let's see how she does this. The context for this sample is that Kendra had a question for me (her manager) around some new content for an upcoming class.

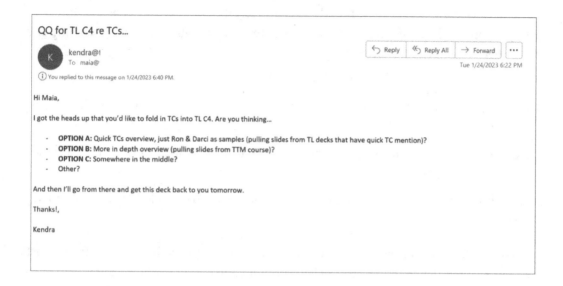

Figure 10.4   Kendra's Multiple Choice Email.

How easy was it for me to answer this? Very simply, I was able to write back "A." While that could seem abrupt, let's take apart why it was wildly effective and efficient for Kendra to make it multiple choice:

- **Written to Stand in Someone's Shoes.** Kendra knew I was incredibly busy with teaching and writing (this book, ahem), and yet she absolutely needed my reply to move her own work ahead. She put herself in my shoes to ask how she could get the quickest reply possible. She also knew I was likely to answer from my phone because my email was closed during writing and teaching.

- **Recommendation Ready!** Boy, was it! Kendra took the time to consider where I would want to add TCs (Thought Catchers, a Together Tool) into class instruction. By taking the time to give recommendations, I was more likely to give a response quickly. If she had just said, "What are you thinking?" I guarantee my reply would have been delayed. Remember, being a Together Teammate is not only about supporting someone else, but about operating so your own work can get done as effectively as possible!

Eryn Assigns Tasks to a Team

As an operations director for a nonprofit in DC, Eryn – a Together Teammate you met previously – sometimes uses clear and detailed calendar invites to assign tasks out to the team.

She sends a calendar invite for a month prior to recruitment with the steps it will take to make recruitment happen. This allows the entire team to see what tasks are upcoming and add to their own calendars accordingly.

This approach is effective for a few reasons:

■ **Clear subject line in the calendar invitation.** Eryn says <action required> with a specific assignment.

■ **Action required is well-planned.** Eryn asks the team to "block time on the calendar" for a key list of items.

■ **Keep It One-Click.** For the individual task assignments, Eryn added hyperlinks and key questions.

If you work on a team with Eryn, no matter what level, you will be successful because Eryn has enabled this with her clear delegation. Of course, this works because there is an agreement on Eryn's team that it is okay to send digital invites for task assignments. One cannot just run around throwing things on people's calendars and assuming that will translate into the tasks being completed!

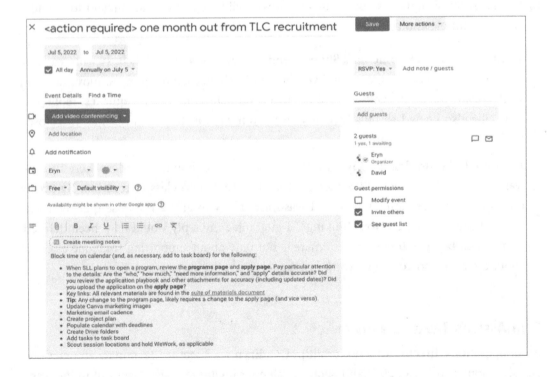

Figure 10.5   Eryn's Task Assignment Calendar Invite.

Kendra Creates Structured Replies

Ever crafted an email with *lots* of questions, only to get back "yes" as the response? Me too. Kendra, a member of the Together Team, ensures that cannot happen by locking her manager (yup, that's me!) into giving clear replies to each of her questions. Not only that, but as seen here, she sent her message to me at a time she knew I had work time to attack it on a train trip. She used the Try-It Stand in the Shoes of Others, and she made it so entirely One-Clickable that I could answer the email holding my luggage in one hand, my phone in the other, while boarding the train!

Give me a call if any of this is easier to answer over the phone!	
~Kendra	
Kendra's Question / FYI	**Maia's Notes**
RANDOM QUESTIONS	
Relay GSE – is there a particular session that I should flag for Shelby for the other deans? They're interested in "Align Your Time," right? Or is this something I should just ask you about in May or June? The other two assistant deans want to sign up for August when it's available, too. Best, Shelby	
Do you need a Prep Call draft for CMS now? Hi CMS folks, I hope you all are doing well! I wanted to check back on the email below as dates for fall are filing up quickly! See below for where we left off and some open questions. Expect a Prep Call request coming soon! Best,	
FYI: I asked Rachel to have her TG email set to forward emails to me. QQ: Do you want to pay for another account, or switch Rachel's to workshops@...? In prep for Rachel's role off, do you want to make sure you have access to her TG email account if residuals come in and then maybe we can make Maggie an workshops@thetogethergroup.com for her upcoming gig?	
The calendar icons on the website need to be updated to "2016" instead of "2015" (for the Resources pages). I tried to do one, but I couldn't figure out how to do it. - Want me to ask Vanessa to do it? - OR – do you want me to ask her to show me how to do it? (My preference, so I'll know for the future.)	
OPEN SESSIONS	
Open Sessions – do you still want to update the email template per your flagged email to Rachel? Should we do a quick review of all OS email templates and update before Maggie (hopefully) starts on Tues?	
Is the 6/21 Denver Open Session a go?	
PRODUCTION	
I'm a little confused about chart paper. What updates are needed? Is this something we can review easily in person on Tues?	

Figure 10.6 Kendra's Table-Formatted Email.

There is one story a teammate could tell: "My manager is busy and not getting back to me, so [tosses hands in the air and gives up]." But what a Together Teammate does is Own the Outcomes, Stand in the Shoes of Others, and Keep It One-Click and Recommendation Ready – all in a single communication.

Kendra did this by:

- **Careful categorization.** Kendra bucketed her questions and FYIs with Random Questions, Open Sessions, and Production. This offered me context per section and my own ability to batch.

- **Using tables to force answers.** As you can see, Kendra posed her questions and very clearly gave me a box to list my own answers. This ensured I could not skip any questions.

- **Pasting or linking items to give context.** Kendra reviewed outstanding emails (Closing those Loops) and pasted the context in her question boxes. This ensured I could respond without having to search for other messages or try to remember context.

How to Send One-Click Messages

- **Give full context.** For example, when sending a request, be sure to say what has happened already ("We have run the board agenda by Jill, but it still has to go in front of Danielle"), so the recipient has context for the request or question. If needed, link back to a more complete document or include additional data at the bottom of the email.

- **Make it multiple choice.** Instead of saying, "What should we order for the board breakfast?" you could say, "Here are three options, menus for each, and total cost. I recommend we do _____." Yes, it is more work for you up front, but when you get a quick email back with "Okay, great, I agree," it is also helping work not get stuck. It's also adding your value as a Recommendation Ready Together Teammate that you've taken on some of the work of doing research and making a proposal.

- **Consider the visual.** It may be bullets or tables, or certain emojis. But Stand in the Shoes of Others, think about the reader, what mindset they are in, and how they can best read the message.

- **Use clear subject lines or headlines.** Make sure people know what you are asking for and by when. On the Together Team, we do a lot of subject lines in the form of questions. Putting the question you want answered in the actual subject line makes it clear this email is prompting an answer, not just providing updates.

> ■ **Format for easy reply.** Make it very clear what response you are expecting from the recipient – whether it's a simple "yes, I approve" to sign off on something, a selection of one of the options you have proposed, or a longer response to a question you posed. And don't forget to let the recipient know the deadline for their response!

> **Reader Reflection:** Review past outgoing communications. What do you notice about your natural style? Where could you up your game? For example, I have a tendency to include many parentheticals, which is how I tend to speak, but it often doesn't serve my reader to write that way (well, except to make you laugh!).

SEND THE NEWSLETTERS, MEMOS, AND NOTES – OH, MY!

You likely play a role in communicating to groups of people, whether families, students, board members, associates, or whatever other groups of folks you work with regularly. You may play the role of overall coordinator of the communication, or you may gather the information and design, or be completely in charge. Whatever your specific role, let's look at a few methods that folks behind-the-scenes use to lead or support regular communications. We'll look at three together, and then debrief what we saw and what we can apply.

Erin's Weekly Email to Operations Directors

Erin helps keep her entire team of operations directors on track by sending an organized weekly email to help them track priorities and tiny To-Dos that come their way. Let's see what Erin included to help make this effective.

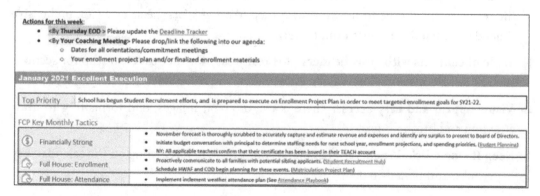

Figure 10.7   Erin's Weekly Email to Operations Directors.

Erin uses color and formatting wisely to make life easier for her readers. She also:

■ **Stays focused on priorities and has predictable formatting.** Key Monthly Tactics show up every month, as does the Top Priority. It's easy to get lost in the weeds in day-to-day work, but this helps pull back up to the big picture.

■ **Calls out action items loud and clear with deadlines, dates, and specificity.** "Please drop/link the following dates."

■ **Hyperlinks all relevant information**, such as Attendance Playbooks, Matriculation Project Plans, and Budget Planning. Yes, staff already have access to these, but it also makes it easier for people to have a one-stop shop.

If part of your role is to send any kind of regular communication, ask yourself the purpose of the communication. Is it to inform? Inspire? Assign action steps? Coordinate?

Let's look at a school-based weekly newsletter example in the following image. The newsletter is built as a website and the school sends out the link each week.

Shamrock Elementary's Weekly Newsletter

Shamrock Elementary, a school in Charlotte, North Carolina, produces a link-y (I just made that a word!) newsletter that is incredibly biased toward action for the recipient. Let's see what they did. The reason I'm showing you several newsletters is because the Together Teammate often plays a role in gathering, consolidating, curating, and distributing content for communications like these.

The purpose of the communication from Shamrock is to ensure their readers are informed, inspired, and can act on the information given. Let's look at what makes all of this possible. (And a reminder: if you want to review the entire samples, they can be found at www.wiley .com/go/togetherteammate).

■ **Predictable cadence.** Both newsletters come out weekly in a predictable fashion. This lets the recipients plan time to read it – with their Weekly Worksheets and Comprehensive Calendars in hand (see what I did there?).

■ **Table of contents with clear headers.** It is really easy for the reader to scan for sections such as Key Points and Core Values. As a reader, you feel guided through the process.

■ **Visual appeal and easy access.** There is use of color, images, and formatting to draw attention and break up text.

■ **Keep It One-Click.** Whenever possible, sections include forecasting on the calendar, key hyperlinks, and pasted-in data.

There Is Always Light, If Only We're Brave Enough To See It. If Only We're Brave Enough To Be It

UPCOMING WEEK

Monday, January 25, 2020

-

Tuesday, January 26, 2020

- 4th Grade Parent Night @ 5:30 p.m. (The 4th grade Parent Night will be using Christiansen's zoom information from the school zoom link document.)

Wednesday, January 27, 2020

- K-3 MAP Fluency Make-Ups

SGE COOKBOOK

For those of you who don't know, Shamrock will be creating its first ever cookbook! One School, Many Cultures. We are asking families (**AND STAFF**) to share a recipe that is special to them with the rest of the school. It could be a favorite holiday recipe, a traditional dish you always have on your birthday, a recipe passed down from a relative, etc. **Please see the link below for submissions.**

Please hype this up! In a year that we have so little to look forward to, this is something tangible that we all can share with each other! And who isn't spending all of their time in the kitchen at this time anyway??

CALL FOR SUBMISSIONS!

Figure 10.8 Shamrock's Weekly Newsletter.
Alexander Raths / Adobe Stock

UPCOMING DATES

- Monday, February 1 - Friday, February 5 - NO Meet Week
- Monday, February 1 - Black History Month Starts
- Monday, February 8 - Progress Reports Due for review by 5:00 p.m.
- Friday, February 12 - MAP Math Window Closes
- Monday, February 15 - Scholars Return to Building
- Wednesday, February 17 - Early Dismissal
- Week of February 22 - Love to Read Week

ACTION STEPS

- Submit recipe to support our school cookbook (if you submit a recipe, notify Ms. Potter through an email and your name will be put in a drawing for a gift card)
- Make plans for **NO MEET WEEK (week of February 1st - 5th)**

Figure 10.8   (*Continued*)

Reader Reflection: Who is your audience? How do they best read items? Digitally? Do they need a hard copy?

FAQ: What if I'm on the receiving end of one of these monster memos? (I'm not saying you're calling them monster memos; that's just a phrase I've heard.) If you're lucky enough to work with an organization or manager that consolidates communications, forecasts frequently, and helps name priorities clearly, hooray! However, that means you may need to block out time each week to "process" the memo, so to speak. What I don't want for you is to have you open the memo each day multiple times and use it as a pseudo-To-Do list because that won't help you juggle this work against your other work. If this mega-memo is released at a predictable time, I recommend blocking out time in your own calendar to read it and then move items to their rightful place. For example, if there is a deadline for the current week, you may want to put this task in your Long-Term List, or add it to your Weekly Worksheet. If there is a project that requires multiple hours and supplemental materials, you may want to give it its own time block in your calendar. If there is an item you need to discuss with a colleague, pop it on their agenda in Google Docs. Basically, you need time to deconstruct the memo and move items into your own system.

Another way to get information to people, instead of pushing out a communication, is to draw them in. That's where we're headed next.

Send People to a Centralized Hub

Shannon, a chief operating officer for Chicago Collegiate Charter School, built an operations hub to keep all information in one centralized location. Let's check out what that looks like.

This is *the* go-to spot for all items the operations team may need, from Calendar and Scheduling to Compliance and Legal to Facilities. Let's drill down into one of these pages. Picture being an operations team member with a question about Events & Trips. Rather than searching through your emails or Google Drive, let's come on over to the Internal Operations Hub.

As I reviewed this, a few items stood out:

- **The documents and resources section.** Imagine if you are brand new at planning college visits for your high school students, and you have no idea where to begin. You can come on over to the operations hub and look at past examples, and then build your own.

- **The navigation** makes it easy to find what you need. If you work in a large organization where questions come at you from a lot of directions, having a single-stop shop will help people access information more easily.

 Reader Reflection: Are there any top-of-mind resources that would be helpful to build into a centralized hub?

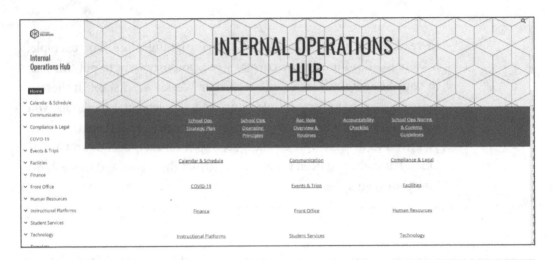

Internal
Operations Hub

Home

∨ Calendar & Schedule
∨ Communication
∨ Compliance & Legal
   COVID-19
∨ Events & Trips
∨ Facilities
∨ Finance
∨ Front Office
∨ Human Resources
∨ Instructional Platforms
∨ Student Services
∨ Technology

NETWORK GUIDELINES

Each year the network will share the following:

- List of students whose families signed the general permission slip - the ops team will need to ensure anyone who does not have this signed completes a separate permission slip for each field trip.
- A budget for field trips for the school year.
- Using the vision map, the network should oversee college field trips to ensure schools are returning to the same locations each year; if a change is made, it should be approved by the network first.

SCHOOL ROLE

Schools should determine what field trips they would like to plan for the school year based on incentives and academic needs. Ideally field trips would be repeated year after year to prevent an abundance of planning - e.g. every year the 5th grade goes to the beach.

For college trips, schools should align with the network to ensure students aren't visiting the same campus multiple times during their time at collegiate. Generally the college trips should remain in close proximity for younger scholars and branch out as they get older.

Schools are required to adhere to budgets set by the network and also ensure students have the correct permission to attend.

CONTACTS

- Stefanie Evans, Chicago Wolves
- Megan Burciaga, Event Coordinator, Fifth Third Arena,
- Venisha Johnson, Studio Movie Grill

DOCS & RESOURCES

- Field Trip Project Plan Template
- Field Trip Paycheck Tracker Template
- Past College Trips
- Sample Schedule and Logistics Memo
- Sample Field Trip Groups
- Student Scavenger Hunt Template
- Chaperone Sign Up Form
- Chaperone Confirmation Notice
- Past Trip Info
- Bus Request Template
- Incentive Trip Paycheck Tracker Template
- Sample Trip Expectations PPT
- Sample Flyer
- Sample Earned/Not Earned Letter

Figure 10.9   Chicago Collegiate's Internal Operations Hub.

Gem Prep's Link Sheets for Staff

If you need to have items frequently at your fingertips (and I could have just as easily plopped this into our Digital Organization chapter), you could do like the folks at Gem Prep in Idaho and make sure all staff members have a handy link sheet. When is testing? Oh, here is the link for the Assessment Schedule! Where is so-and-so's phone number? Ahh, let me click on the Master Staff Contact List.

Coaching Resources	Behavior	Academics	Data	Schedules	Misc.	Grading	Special Education	Assessments	Secondary
Coaching Website	Culture Guide	SOTW	IP/Data Dashboard	22-23 Secondary Schedule	Master Roster	Weekly GPA Teacher Tracker	Master Accommodati on List	SESTA	Graduation Requirements
CPF Rubric	Lunch Detention	GEM Academy	Unpacking standards	22-23 School Calendar		Report Card Timeline	SESTA		Middle School Requirements
5 Level of Leadership	Gem Service	Work Completion Tracker	Secondary Data Tracker	Wed PD Plan		Report Card Letter			College House Assignments
IM Commuity Hub	Secondary reflection sheet	Secondary RTI		22-23 Elementary Schedule					Secondary Padlet
TLAC Quick Reference	Academic Honesty	Secondary Data		College House Assignments					
TLAC Videos	Negative Dojo Points Flor Chart	TLAC Power of routines		Secondary Sped Schedule					

Figure 10.10 Gem Prep's Link Sheets.

You may want to set up a centralized source of information – rather than push out tons of notes – if you:

■ **Have forms that are frequently downloaded.** Let's say teachers are planning a field trip and need permission forms. Rather than emailing them, you could put them all right in the hub.

■ **Note that information changes frequently.** If you are on the receiving end of lots of policy changes, it's easier for you to go to the hub when you need it rather than track all the changes as they come.

■ **Want to share past context with the team.** If you have documents from past processes or events that would be a helpful reference, but you don't want it to get lost in the shuffle, this can be a way to make sure that information is available.

Phew, did this chapter make anyone want to blow up their phone or inboxes? Don't worry. With a bit of time and effort, we will get those communications back under control, I promise.

TURBO TOGETHERNESS

This chapter focused on crafting communications to get the replies, outcomes, and results you need in order to Own Your Outcomes. Through a variety of methods, frequencies, and audiences, a big focus of Together Teammate roles is communicating clearly. And not just in the sense of making your communications color-coded or fancy (though that can be fun too), but really to push the work forward in an efficient, user-friendly manner. Yes, pondering the right method, crafting careful assignments, and formatting the communications may take a bit more time, but I assure you it will be worth it because you will get back higher-quality responses, which will allow you to Own Your Outcomes more deeply. To get started:

- ■ Figure out if you are using the right communication mechanisms at the right times. If you're not sure, ask! If it is total communications chaos, propose something as simple as Jordan's.

- ■ Practice crafting your messages, especially those that are giving assignments to or asking for information from others, in ways that give context, Keep It One-Clickable, and are Recommendation Ready.

- ■ Compile, gather, curate, and distribute information in a way that is accessible, inspirational, and action-oriented. Keeping communications this clear ensures that the entire organization is moving along.

MANAGER MOMENT

Understanding how your team or organization communicates can be a source of confusion for your Together Teammate, who often stands in the center of incoming and outgoing communications. By taking the time up front to get clear on your own expectations – for yourself, your team or organization, and for the teammate, you will save lots of time and confusion. To that end, here are some ideas:

- Define which channels are used for what within your organization, preferably during onboarding. You can find more on this in my book *The Together Leader*.

- Get clear on your own expectations for response time on emails, calls, and messages.

- Articulate your *own* expectations for communications. For example, "I need incredibly clear emails from my team given the volume I receive on a daily basis."

- Name any organizational communication idiosyncrasies before your teammate encounters them.

- Consider how you could collaborate with your teammate to gather, consolidate, curate, and distribute any predictable communications.

CHAPTER 11

Make the Most of Your Meetings – Before, During, and After

Meetings. Just hearing the word is often enough to make everyone groan. Rarely are meetings met with excitement, but if you are thoughtful in your work as planner and participant, you can play a huge role in keeping your meetings Together (and maybe even a little more enjoyable!) before, during, and after the meeting. As with any job, but especially in your support roles, you are likely to participate in an assortment of meetings. These could be meetings you lead, join, staff, or even just listen in on to gather background information. In many cases, you will own the mechanics of a meeting – scheduling, food, video links, and such. But in some cases you will play a role in leading the meeting process from start to finish, such as preparing and distributing prework, setting up the agenda and contributions, and sending out notes and homework from the meetings – and maybe even ensuring meetings actually hit their targeted objectives. You may not be the person with the most content knowledge or subject area expertise out there, but you can be an expert on building a process to achieve the outcomes.

In this chapter, you will learn to:

■ Create thoughtful meeting agendas to drive toward meeting goals

■ Maximize meetings with your manager and colleagues

■ Track long-term meeting topics for future action items

■ Ensure meeting follow-up happens through tracking of next steps and accountability

Effective meetings can work wonders to move the work of the organization forward. If you are a skilled teammate you will see this fact, and you will help make any meetings of which you are a part do exactly that, because meetings are kind of awesome – they are what make the work happen. They allow for collaboration, celebration, brainstorms, decision-making, and question-asking. And they give you unique insight into how your organization realizes its mission. I see you as far more than agenda-senders or catering-orderers because of your unique Be the Bird's-eye view of the organization, your ability to understand how meetings can push toward results, and because you are often the person to push the work ahead when other colleagues or your manager are out in the field. Excited now? I thought so. Let's start with figuring out your role in various meetings. As with all chapters of this book, take what you need of my offerings and consider how they interact with your particular team or organizational culture.

GET CLEAR ON YOUR ROLE IN EACH MEETING YOU ATTEND

My guess is that you have a variety of meetings in your calendar. Likely you have some one-on-one meetings, some group meetings, and maybe even a conference or board meeting or two. Before we jump into the mechanics of all your meetings, it is important that you are clear on your role in each setting.

Here's what you might be thinking about as you review your calendar:

■ I see a weekly meeting with my manager. *I know the purpose is to both update and problem solve. I'm not sure if I am supposed to lead it (sounds scary!) or if my manager leads it. We have 45 minutes once a week, but we often run over time. I wonder if there are ways I can prepare for this meeting to make it more efficient.*

■ The executive team half-day meeting happens monthly. *I get a lot of last-minute requests for this one, in terms of both agenda formation and materials needed, and it's a frustrating, stressful scramble each month.*

■ I see bi-weekly team meeting with the entire development team. *I'm not entirely sure of my role in this meeting. Sometimes I take notes, but I never go back to them afterward, and*

I don't send them out to the team. I wonder if I should ask about this. It is valuable for me to be there and understand the big picture of what is happening in our fundraising world.

■ I see the monthly board meetings. *My role in this one is incredibly clear. I'm the project manager for the entire meeting cycle start to finish.*

As the list above reflects, you likely feel some level of clarity for some meetings, but not so much for others. So let's take stock. Pull up that calendar and look ahead for the next three months.

Reader Reflection: Role Clarity for Meetings

■ Which meetings do you own? Are you clear what ownership means? If not, how can you get there? (Don't worry if you don't know yet; this chapter will help you!)

■ Which meetings do you join as a participant? What is your role in this case? Note-taking? Food ordering? Invite sending?

■ Which meetings do you join as an observer or staffer? Are you clear why you are there? Are you responsible for any materials?

■ When there are staff meetings, what role do you play? Are you some combination of all of the above roles?

What learnings did you have about your meetings? What are your next steps?

MAKE THE MOST OF MEETINGS WITH YOUR MANAGER

In your role, you likely have meetings with your manager to move through the work for the week. While it can be tempting to just walk into the meeting and let your manager fumble to look for meeting topics or find work to delegate, you will likely achieve a better outcome if you own the preparation process and agenda. One-on-one meetings with your manager are crucial to your overall success in your role because they can help you prioritize for the coming week and months, clarify any tasks or projects that are unclear, and make recommendations and decisions to move the work ahead. They are also a tremendous opportunity to put your Together Try-Its to good use, especially Forecasting Forward (to prevent unnecessary last-minute scrambles), Close the Loops (to ensure your manager and others have shown proof of task completion), get Recommendation Ready (propose solutions and guide processes), and Be the Bird's-eye (naming implications of items across the organization). This will, of course, take preparation and follow-up, but we are here for that! What exactly can an effective manager check-in look like, you wonder? Let's explore this further by looking at several examples.

Venecia's Meeting Agenda with Her Manager

Venecia works at a national nonprofit organization, and she partners closely with her manager, the CEO, to prepare for meetings, schedule travel, and manage his calendar. Let's see how she prepares an agenda for a meeting with Chong-Hao each week.

Venecia & Chong-Hao O3 Agendas

Tasks to Complete	In Process	Complete

• Yakima Travel Oct 11 (2.5hr from Seattle) I will work with Sabrina on travel this week
   o   Jake
• New Profit Convening11/14 –16
   o   Registered
• Reschedule Marcia (Zoom)
• Confirm visits to Charleston & GR
• Meeting with Sarah
• Shawn HISD (in person)
• Ethan – School Kit
	• Gisele (OOO until 30 –sent availability)
	• Andrea Follow Up (sent availability on Tues 8/16)
	• Stacey at CCNY
	• GFE Austin
	   o Registration done
	   o Need vaccine verification
	• Todd w/ AK & LMM (sent availability)
	• Lisa (sent availability)
		• Tommy at CCNY

Items	Venecia	Chong-Hao

FYIs	• Agenda for Baltimore	• Baltimore 9/27-28 w LB
		• Carnegie NY 9/28-29
		• NY Funders 9/30 (Return to Houston 10/2)
		• HOLD: LT Retreat: 17-18, 24-25???
		• Austin 10/18-20 (Panel Day)(CHF DRIVING)
		• Charleston 10/20?
		• DC ASU / Coalition to Improve Teaching 10/27-28 (registered, flight booked, hotel?)
		• Philly: Schusterman CEO Dinner 11/1
		• Schusterman Convening –11/1 –11/3
		• Singapore PTO 11/ 11/12
		• New Profit Convening 11/14 –15 or 16
		
		ADD Chicago
		ADD Oakland
		
		Remaining Board 1:1s
		  1. SR: Before Board meeting
		  2. TM: Email sent
		  3. NB: 9/22
		  4. EH

Quick Questions & Tasks	1. When you leave **Inclusive Innovation in LA,** when do you plan to go to Austin? Directly or Thurs morning?
	2. **GFE**
	   a. Please review sessions
	   b. Verify vaccination status
	3. The **YVP** team is staying at this hotel. Are you OK to book there as well?
	   a. Sabrina was willing to carpool with you but she is arriving earlier in the afternoon.
	   b. Where is your return flight?
	4. How would you like for me to arrange your meetings for Board Day?	

Next Steps		

Figure 11.1   Venecia's One-on-One Meeting with Her Manager.

There is a lot to learn from this sample:

- **Status updates.** In the top table, you can see Venecia is proactively updating Chong-Hao on tasks in progress. A Together Try-It: Show Your Work! Why do this, you may wonder. This allows Chong-Hao to see at a glance the status of any given task and, in my experience, this can prevent your manager from worrying or having to ask a lot of follow-up questions about items that are still in progress.

- **FYIs for each other.** Venecia and Chong-Hao both have access to this agenda as a Google doc, and each person can add items for the other to see. These items may not be discussion worthy during the meeting, but this is a great way to reduce email and text communications by saving nonurgent items for this regular communication.

- **Quick Questions.** I love this section. If we dig deep into this example, you can see the Quick Questions were not just a few bulleted phrases, but they give complete information to take the task to completion with ease and efficiency. Venecia Made It One-Click! For example, in the Grantmakers for Education section, Venecia notes she tried to complete the vaccination status, but she was roadblocked. Rather than leave it there, she provided the hyperlink and password (which we have redacted), such that her manager can complete the task – possibly right in the meeting – without having to dig or ask for the information required. This can also help you Close the Loop on the task (more on that coming up).

- **Next steps.** What is a meeting without next steps? The instinct can often be to write the next steps in a notebook or an email only to oneself, but it is a strong practice to keep the next steps right here on the agenda for a few reasons. The first is it creates accountability for all parties, and the second is it allows you to bring the notes and next steps to open at the *next* meeting to ensure everything is done. Yes, you may need to transfer or copy your next steps into your own Weekly Worksheet or Long-Term List as they are also To-Dos for your own week, but it helps to have them all in this shared agenda.

 Reader Reflection: What sections do you need in a meeting agenda with your manager? Is there anything they want to include? If you don't know, can you propose or ask?

Let's review a few more samples. Keep in mind that not all manager meeting agendas need to be super detailed. In fact, some managers may cringe at seeing too much. But that doesn't mean you don't need to do the preparation to steer the meeting. Even if you don't show your manager all the preparation you have done, doing as much prework as possible on your end will make these meetings much more effective for you. You may want to make your own version of detailed agendas. Flesh this out further; even if you don't show your manager all the prep you've done, doing as much prep as possible on your end will make these meetings so much more effective. You may want to make your own version of some of these agendas – to force yourself to do the prep – even if you don't share all of it with your manager.

Emily's Meeting Agenda with Her Manager

Emily, a special assistant to Recy, a CEO in Brooklyn, keeps her meeting agenda with her manager in OneNote. Similar to Google Docs from the previous example, this allows both parties to contribute throughout the week and build the agenda together. And similar to Venecia's example, it's not just a laundry list of items. I love this agenda because it includes guideposts and structures, which allows them to maximize the time. Let's look at Emily's categories.

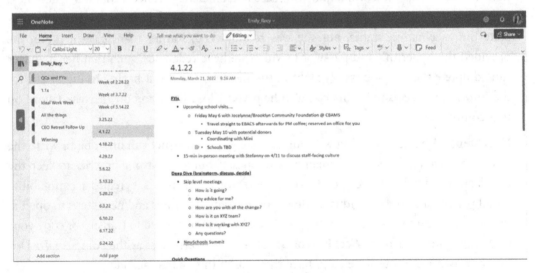

Figure 11.2   Emily's Meeting Agenda with Her Manager.

There are a few things I want to draw your attention to in this sample:

■ **For Your Information.** Similar to Venecia, Emily has an FYI (For-Your-Information) section. This is a place for her to jot items to keep Recy informed and, again, to reduce emails, texts, and chats. Recy can then know that Emily has reserved an office space on May 6 and he doesn't need to wonder or worry that it might not have been completed.

- **Deep Dives.** This is a chance for Emily to play a role in the strategy of the CEO's work. She is asking key questions about skip-level meetings (a common people leadership strategy where a manager meets with their direct reports' folks). Why would Emily have her hand in this? Well, it takes up Recy's time, she helps schedule them, and using their meeting to help Recy get headspace to create an agenda for these skip-levels gets some work done in the moment. She is able to Be the Bird's-eye in a way that her manager may not.

- **Quick Questions.** I love the placement of this section last. This means the meeting can stay focused on the biggest and most important stuff, and if they had to, Quick Questions could move to an email or a quick 10-minute phone conversation later. The reason to separate these Quick Questions from the Deep Dives has to do with prioritization and using your time – and your manager's time – wisely.

- **Overall Structure.** Because of the use of Microsoft OneNote, you can see that Emily has each agenda ordered chronologically. This is helpful because it allows her to look back and reference next steps and also neatly plop future agenda items as ideas or tasks emerge (Forecasting Forward!). Additionally, this prevents Emily from having to build an entirely new agenda each week. It is simple to cut and paste from an existing structure and fill in the blanks.

 Reader Reflection: What can you learn from this sample? Where will you store your meeting agendas?

What if your manager is not Together? Welcome to everyone's world. (Just kidding!) Rarely do we see a case where someone in a supporting role thinks their boss is Totally Together. In fact, that is why many teammates were hired in the first place – to help put things together.

In this case you will want to consider some of the following questions. These ask you to Stand in the Shoes of Others – namely your manager – to understand what their days are like and how you can play a role in making your collective work go more smoothly and effectively.

- **What are your expectations of that person and are they realistic?** For example, is it realistic to expect your manager to put holds in their calendar every time they schedule something? What kind of response time to your emails is realistic? Are there things you can do to assist in these areas?

(Continued)

> ■ **What is the impact of their lack of Togetherness on you and others?** How can you help? Do you get tons of last-minute requests for data right before a board meeting, resulting in you staying up until the wee hours pulling data and printing reports? If so, can you look ahead on the calendar (hello Forecasting Forward) and identify when the asks will be coming and then ask your manager to work backwards with you to design a reasonable workplan for your contribution?
>
> ■ **What are their greatest weak points and how can you assist?** Late to important calls? Not prepared for meetings? Think about it, and how you could assist. Maybe you create a folder with meeting agendas for each day and block time to review together.

Lola's Meeting Agenda for a Team

Lola, an operations leader at a school in Philadelphia (and who you will soon meet when she takes us on a Together Tour), has set up a check-in protocol to ensure the team is touching base on the right topics. Let's peek a bit more deeply at how she structures the time and why, as there may be items you can borrow as you work with your manager to most effectively structure your one-on-one time.

Similar to other samples, Lola has set up parameters of key items to discuss every single week. This prevents the meeting from turning into a laundry list of topics that are top of mind for both parties (while possibly missing some overall larger priorities). Of course, there is a time and place for the top-of-mind items as well. Let's discuss how Lola handles them as well as a few other takeaways from this agenda:

■ **Clear prework.** Lola can get a pulse on her teammates by having them complete some strategic prework before the meeting, around both the mood and the content.

■ **Quick hits.** Similar to Emily, Lola created a quick hits section, pointedly at the *end* of the agenda, so quickies can get covered, while being relegated to the end of the meeting so they do not dominate the agenda.

■ **Clear timing.** Lola includes ranges of times in her team agenda, and we can see the priority items get more time – as they should. It can be easy to create agendas that are laundry lists of items, but it is helpful to separate them into buckets so time can be used more efficiently and intentionally.

Obadina/Ops Manager 1:1 Meeting Agenda- 12/7

Section of Protocol	Topics	Ops Manager Pre-Work to be completed before Meeting
Opening (5 mins)	How was your weekend? What have been some of your roses (glows) and thorns (challenges) this week?	*Roses: Child came home from Harrisburg! Thorns: Not able to get much work done*

Roll-Out (15 mins)
 -Consists of the priority Alignment for the next couple of weeks
 -Consists of any new projects that Lola will introduce to Ops Manager during the weekly check in. These will include responsibilities Ops Manager will own for a certain period of time.
	• Review APO Blast
	 • Eschool Scheduling
	 • Upcoming winter events
	   ○ Winter Pop Up Event + Vaccine Clinic
	   ○ Winter Wonderland Event
	 • Offboarding Plan
	   ○ Create a google document/ spreadsheet with buckets of work you are responsible for by 12/20	

Progress-Monitoring/Follow Up (5-15 mins)
 - Projects/events that the Ops Manager owns that are not yet complete or that she is still working on
 - Any project milestones/key deliverables identified during the Roll-Out
	• Ops Metrics (99% alignment)
	   ○ SIS Alignment
	   ○ Ensure we are at least 99% alignment.
	 • Mailing out report cards
	 • Winter Coat Drive on 12/20
	 • Credit card reconciliation?
	 • Revised Inventory and Ordering System
	   ○ Updates on orders
	   ○ Headphone request tracker
	   ○ Boxes in cafeteria
	 • Household income survey collection	

Lola Quick Hits *-Items that need action/ follow-up and can be solved in 2 minutes or less*	• Link to Parent Clearances • 12/10 PD	
Ops Manager Quick Hits/Questions *-Any questions or concerns the Ops Manager has for Lola.*		

Figure 11.3   Lola's Team Meeting Agenda.

Reader Reflection: What needs more (or less) time on your agendas?

As you reflect on the previous samples and consider your own meetings with your manager, my hope is you keep in mind these key points:

■ **You own the meeting.** How can you get the most out of it in order to move the work forward? How can you make sure it works for your manager?

■ **Preparation takes time, but it is worth it.** It takes time to prepare like Venecia, Emily, and Lola, but this ensures you and your manager are using the time well to push the work forward. Specifically, think carefully about how to structure the meeting to make the most of the time – likely by recurring categories or sections. This is an investment of time up front that can help make preparing for the regular meetings much more efficient.

■ **Follow-up is key.** Don't assume your manager will follow up from the meeting, in spite of their very best intentions. Help them, make it simple for them, and exercise your Close the Loops muscle from the Together Try-Its.

Let's test your learning with a practice exercise.

Reader Reflection: It will take time to prepare thoughtfully for a meeting with your manager. This goes beyond just drafting an agenda, and even beyond you and your manager dumping items into a Google Doc or Calendar invite. You will want to think carefully about the purpose of each section, and how you can get to the outcome as efficiently as possible. Here are some examples of how you might craft a clear agenda item, and what steps you would take in order to prepare for the actual meeting with your manager. You are encouraged to build on this and make it even better!

Vague Agenda Item	Instead, Use Clear Agenda Item	Steps to Prepare for the Meeting
Board meeting	Review board meeting agenda	• Draft the agenda and put it in a format where you can note edits (or make revisions) as you discuss during your one-on-one.

Vague Agenda Item	Instead, Use Clear Agenda Item	Steps to Prepare for the Meeting
Holiday mailing	Sign off on proposed timeline for holiday mailing	• Draft a timeline that includes each task you, your manager, and anyone else will need to complete for the holiday mailing with clear deadline and owner for each task. (You might consider whether this needs a Project Plan!)
Copy machine	Select new vendor for copy machine lease	• Put together a table with three possible vendors and all the considerations that are relevant (price, ratings, reviews). • Determine which you think is the best choice (Recommendation Ready!). • Share with your manager ahead of time, letting them know you will push to make a decision during the one-on-one.

Now you try to improve these options:

Vague Agenda Items	Clear Agenda Item	Steps to Prepare for the Meeting
Office furniture		
Purchase order process		
Upcoming regional site visit		
Insert your own here		

The main takeaway here is that you want to carefully prepare for these meetings, feel empowered to propose solutions, and be crystal clear on the outcome you hope to accomplish. Note that the clear agenda items in the table above all start with verbs so that you and your manager both know what is the needed action step for this agenda item. Yes, this takes courage and it means entering the meeting fully prepared by knowing exactly what questions you want answered. This often means homing in on the question to make it as detailed and as specific as you can, proposing options when possible, and consolidating relevant information and context and having that at your fingertips. When possible, try to avoid asking an open-ended question such as "When should we send our next newsletter?" and say something like:

Today we need to decide when to send our next monthly newsletter. Last year in this month we sent it on X date with Y results. I saw two other big events on your calendar that may make it tricky for you to have time to draft it. Based on this, I propose we send it on X date to maximize the number of people who open it and also give you time to write it. As always, I will have a newsletter shell in your inbox one week prior for you to start filling in. What are your reactions?

Reader Reflection: Revise an agenda for an upcoming meeting with your manager and ensure you are as prepared as possible. Use the Together Try-Its, such as Keep It One-Clickable, Forecast Forward, and Stand in the Shoes of Others.

FAQ: What if I cannot get my manager to meet with me?

I have seen this happen, and it is often because the manager is too busy or deems some of your work "less important." Eventually it will catch up with them because if they don't align on the work, get feedback, and ensure things are delegated properly in all directions, the work will not be accomplished successfully. Here are a few ideas to get things started with a regular meeting time with your manager:

■ Figure out what the purpose of meeting is. To update? To get new work? To look ahead? To receive feedback?

■ Create a draft agenda, with pacing and objectives, for a regular meeting with your manager.

■ Share the draft with your manager and ask to meet regularly.

■ If they still say no, or unintentionally bump you, ask for a trial period for a certain length of time.

■ If they still say no, see if there is another willing thought-partner or manager in the organization who will regularly meet with you.

Now that you have some next steps for meetings with your manager, let's think about some team meetings with peers or colleagues.

MANAGE MEETINGS FOR A GROUP OR TEAM

Some of you are also managing your own teams of Together Teammates and you may be considering how and when to meet with them, and about what topics. Or you may coordinate or join other larger group meetings where the purpose may be different than your one-on-one agendas with your manager. As a reminder, if you are not clear on your particular role in the meeting, propose what you believe it is and seek alignment. Are you there to take notes? Are you there to contribute to decisions? Do you create the overall agenda?

Let's lean into a few models of team meeting agendas and see what we learn from the preparation, execution, and follow-up.

Kevin's Academic Operations Team Meeting Agenda

Kevin, an operations leader in Brooklyn, hosts a weekly meeting with his team. There is a collaborative agenda-building process (note the different initials by different items) and some guideposts to keep the meeting focused on priorities, running on time, and with efficient follow up. Whether you are leading a team meeting, participating, or somewhere in between, let's see what we learn from Kevin's agenda.

FY22 CIP Academic Ops Team Meeting Agenda

Wednesday: May 11, 2022

If any other AO has something they would like to talk through during the meeting, please add it at the bottom of the agenda before each meeting

Note Taker: Elizabeth

Upcoming AOM PS Duty:
- **PS Dump [Week of 05/09]:** TN
- **PS Dump [Week of 05/16]:** MF
- **PS Dump [Week of 05/23]:** RF
- **Next Week's Ice Breaker: HG**

1. **(KP) Quick Calendar Look Ahead:**

May
- 5/9 - 5/13: Q3 Conferences
- 5/16 - 5/20 : EOY Evaluations
- 5/16: Spring MAP NWEA Start Window
- 5/20: Spring MAP NWEA Window Closes
- 5/24: Gr 4 & 8 Science Performance Opens
- 5/27 - 5/30: No School; Memorial Break

June
- 5/3: Gr 4 & 8 Science Performance Closes
- 5/6 : Gr 4 & Gr 8 Science Written Exam
- 6/10: CIPHS Graduation
- 6/13 to 6/24: Regents at the HS
- 6/14: 9-12 Last Day of Instruction
- 6/17: K-8 Last Day of Instruction

Things to Add
- Stepping Ups
- ARFR or PID Final Decisions by 6/24
- Final Report Cards

Figure 11.4   Kevin's Operations Team Meeting Agenda.

- Yearbooks
- ATS Tasks (Graduation + grade-bumping)
- mClass Testing Window
- Technology Ordering (Staff Macbooks)

Action Item - TN will add these to the lookahead

2. **(KP) Q3 Family Conferences [5.9 to 5.13]**
   - **Timeline:**
     - o Conferences run from → 5.6 to 5.13
     - o Make-Ups will likely run for the week after until 5.20
   - **ARFR or PID:**
     - o Normally during this time AOMs run ARFR data and provide it to the SLTs so they can have these conversations with families.
     - o This will impact enrollment numbers → if you retain 5 kids in 3rd grade then 5 less seats in 3rd grade
     - o Notes
       - ▪ What are the things that are important to be data points
       - ▪ Create a tracker and they make a decision based on the tracker
       - ▪ Mail merge the letters and then the teachers share out the PDF.
   - **Next Steps [AOM role + responsibilities]:**
     - o Zoom Group Transition → Telicia: Zoom transition 05/05 EOD. Switch back on 05/23
     - o Email to Principal + DOO → KP
     - o Director IT will be super user
3. **(KP) Q4 Family Conferences [5.9 to 5.13]**
   - **Last Day of Instruction**
     - o 6/14: 9-12 Last Day of Instruction
     - o 6/17: K-8 Last Day of Instruction
   - **ARFR + PID Data :**
     - o At the LES + UES AOMs are in charge of putting together the data for ARFR Data.
     - o Radar that during this month the final retentions decisions are made.
   - **Report Cards**
     - o There are no FTC for Q4
     - o We should still plan to
       - ▪ Send secure docs
       - ▪ Email to teachers (download of the file and saved to the drive)
       - ▪ Publishing on SR parent portal
       - ▪ Send out 9am on 6/13 for LES/UES/MS
       - ▪ Save all report cards on drive
4. **(KP) MAP Testing**
   - MAP Testing Window → 5.16 to 5.20
   - Testing Grades: 3-10

- We all did the Fall Round → Time for the Spring Round
- Project Plan: Pulse Check
    1. UES Project Plan
    2. MS Project Plan
    3. HS Project Plan

Tip - you can roster students to fall and spring at the same time when you set up in the fall

Next Step - Ask Telicia for help if you need to add additional admin in MAP

Reminder to tell Warco when your testing is done so that she can pull the data

3. **(KP) Macbook Ordering:**
   - Circling back:
       - Have AOMs talk to their DOOs around new positions FY23.Need new position Macbook order count as soon as possible for our new Director of IT!
       - Did you talk to DOOs about purchasing cases + adapters for FY23 before the two-week shutdown.
       - Have AOMs + DOOs landed on a case for their campus?
   - **Next Steps:**
       - **Please begin to populate the** staff tech tracker for FY23. **by Wednesday, May 18**
           - **Please populate by next AOM team meeting.**
           - **Loop in LN**

Figure 11.4   (*Continued*)

Kevin has some interesting elements that could inform your own group meeting agenda process. Before we fully debrief, let's look at one more example.

Shannon's Operations Team Meeting Agenda

Shannon, a chief operating officer for a network of schools, leads regular meetings with the entire operations team to keep things moving along. Let's review the content and process of her agendas and see what we can learn.

As you can see, both Kevin and Shannon have live Google Documents that have main categories of Time, Topic, Notes, and Next Steps. All members of the team are making edits and additions in preparation for the meeting. (As a reminder, you can always view full models of our examples on the book's website at www.wiley.com/go/togetherteammate.)

So how do you create and use agendas like these? Ensure the following:

■ **Advance preparation.** I'm sure you see a theme here. This ensures everyone has an equal amount of time to prepare, which can lead to equity of airspace among participants.

CHICAGO COLLEGIATE | Operations Team Meeting
12/9/2021

Time	Topic	Notes	Next Steps
5 min	Whiparound	• *Shannon and Maddie will be joining at 10:15- please do whiparound and Tammy/Tricia topics while you wait for them to hop on • Shannon leads whiparound: Holiday baking only done this time of year/ tradition? • Pick someone for next week: Dolores	

15 min	General Updates from Shannon	• Big wins to celebrate!
		• Fails of the week!
		• Recurring topics:
		  ○ Hiring/HR
		    ■ Hoping to wrap up hiring process next week for open Network role
		  ○ Finance
		    ■ Shannon will alert Quatro we're closing for 2 weeks; make sure to have all regular monthly stuff for December submitted before break
			• Use these tools for student data tracking:
			  ○ Transfer In
			  ○ Student Mobility Tracker (for transfer out)
			
			PS: 5 | TLK: 6 | EP: 6
			ILC: 5 | DV: 6 | SD: 6
			MSB: 3

5 min	Attendance Updates	• Check in on where we are and what steps to take • Review the Tracker (see if we have anything to add and/or to close the loop on kiddos) • **Adrienne shares proposal on attendance incentives (Collegiate Bucks and gear?)**; talk through feasibility of those (Shannon thinks we can find some $$$ for them if we think they'll work to get kids in school)	Adrienne will create proposal/tier system for incentives and send to DSOs Reengagement tracker - needs more detailed notes in daily sheets and weekly attendance audit spreadsheet. Especially for home visits
5 min	Updates from Tammy & Tricia	• Tricia talks through Parent Pride Night - updated plan, schedule, assignments for ops team/all staff	
5 min	Closeout	• End with rose/thorn/gratitude!	

Future Topic

Time	Topic	Link	
	Strengths Finders		
15 min	Personality Tests	• Use the link to the left to access the personality types again • Read the sections on "Career Paths" and "Workplace Habits" - reflect on the following questions: ○ How does your current role align with the strengths of your personality?	Reminder: Here is the chart we filled out last time.

Figure 11.5 Shannon's Team Meeting Agenda.

- **Accessibility of the agenda.** Each participant can see exactly what is being discussed, link to key documents, and see next steps.

- **Rotating icebreakers.** All meetings need a warm-up, I think, and both Shannon and Kevin are sharing the workload and encouraging others to prepare.

- **Recurring topics each week.** This is to ensure the meeting stays focused on what matters, the recurring topics are in place for hiring, finance, and other must-talk topics.

- **Memorialization of next steps.** This is so all parties can review them and everyone signs off on their commitments.

- **Easily One-Clickable.** The last thing you want in a meeting is everyone stopping to fumble for various pieces of paper or a million digital bookmarks. Kevin and Shannon provide hyperlinks for easy access to various projects.

- **Calendar lookahead.** This plays into your role as Forward Forecasters for yourselves and others. This is helpful to scope out topics for the long-term, or to put a pin in something for the moment that could derail you.

Additionally both Kevin's and Shannon's versions are very visually appealing – or very Together, so to speak. As a participant in these meetings, I feel perked up and ready go to because of the care in agenda creation. Pay close attention to what works in your own organization, and don't fear spicing it up a little bit to engage others. Their agendas make it easy to prepare, participate, and follow up, and that is the goal of Together Teammates!

FAQ: If I receive or take notes on an agenda in a meeting, how do I ensure I go back to them? While looking at agendas like this can be a sigh of relief when you see that, "Okay, the next steps are captured," it is admittedly challenging to return to the next steps if they live here rather than your own Weekly Worksheet or Long-Term List. Multiply this by ten meetings per week, and you may have a lot of loose next steps lurking about. Be sure to copy or write the next steps you have coming out of a meeting into your own personal system designed in previous chapters (Weekly Worksheet, Long-Term List, Calendar, etc.) to ensure that all To-Dos live in their centralized location.

Reader Reflection: If you lead team meetings, what items can you build into your agendas?

TIGHTEN UP THOSE MEETING INVITES

Many organizations use digital calendar invitations to communicate key information about meetings. If you play the role of sending the actual invitations, keep in mind you are the key to setting up the meeting for success. Let's look at an example of being as thorough as possible in the premeeting communications.As you can see, all of the relevant details are included in this invitation:

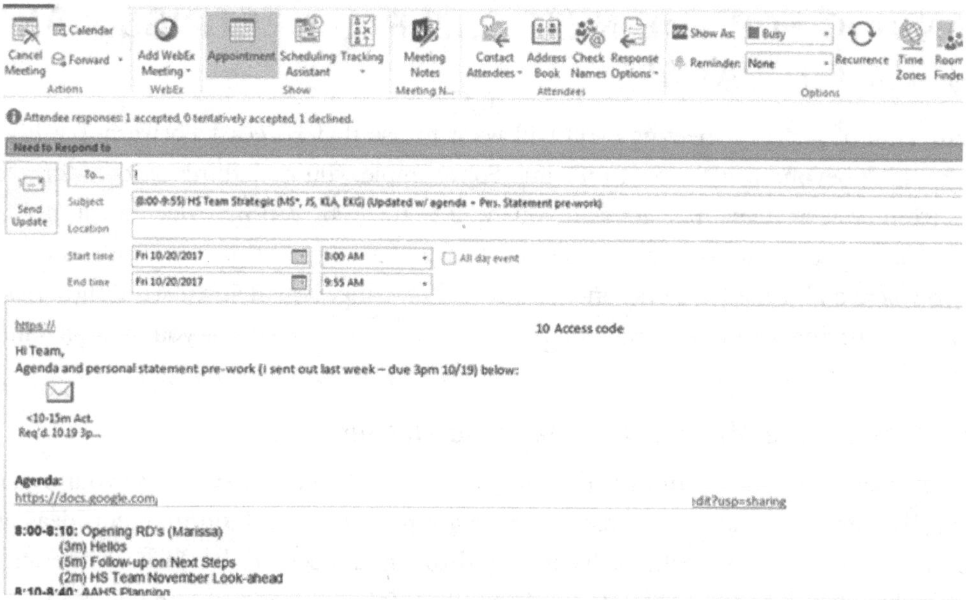

Figure 11.6   Marissa's Meeting Invite.

- **Times and locations are noted.** The exact time is highlighted in the actual subject. This is because the meeting ends at an "odd" time of 9:55 a.m. and Outlook doesn't reflect this as well.

- **Prework is clear.** The prework was sent previously, but it is also referenced in the invite.

- **Agenda is within the invite.** No one needs another email! The agenda is hyper-linked in the meeting invite and bulleted out for people as well.

Remember, you play a huge role in the success of the meeting. This is not "just send the invite." This is an opportunity for you to think critically about the purpose of the meeting, the participants, and their preparation start to finish. Make It One-Click and Stand in the Shoes of Others and you'll have the clearest meeting invites out there!

Reader Reflection: Is there anything you could shift about how you create meeting invites?

Now that we have reviewed individual meetings and group meetings, let's take our meeting prowess a step further and consider how to manage, track, and follow up on long-term meeting topics. This is a chance to put many of your Together Try-Its into practice.

PLANNING FOR THE NEXT SEVERAL MEETINGS – AND NOT JUST TODAY'S!

For any kind of series of meetings you will want to use that Forecast Forward Try-It and work to think beyond just the next meeting. For example, you may think of ideas for a few weeks from now, or items may get sent your way to track, or you may decide you need to pace out what you bring up when. Let's look at several models of this in action, depending on if you were collecting for a one-on-one internal meeting, organizing a standing series of meetings, preparing for a vendor meeting, or a variety of other situations you may encounter.

Josh's One-on-One Meeting Agenda Topic Tracker

You likely have standing meetings with individuals that are internal, or within your organization, that happen weekly or bi-weekly. There are probably a million different ideas and discussion topics for these meetings that pop up throughout the workday. Josh, an operations leader within a school, uses OneNote (a Microsoft digital notebook system you read about previously) to track discussion topics with his team members.

Figure 11.7   Josh's Meeting Agenda in OneNote.

As you can see, Josh keeps meeting agendas for each of the members of his team in OneNote, and then lists topics within each person's pages. In Andrew's example, Josh is planning items for the week of 6/24, then the week of 7/1, then the week of 7/15, and so on. This allows him to pace out what he discusses with team members when, which is considerate and prevents the overwhelm. If you don't capture the topics as they emerge, or if you try to cram them all into one meeting agenda, you risk important topics getting forgotten or delivered in a rush and not given their needed attention. Not everything needs to be discussed at one time! Phew.

As you consider this approach, you will likely find a set of proactive topics you can pre-identify with your colleagues. Here are a few ideas to get you started:

- For example, if you know a certain grant deadline is approaching in May, can you add this to your March–April meeting topics with the development team?

- If there is a date where data your organization uses gets released, can the data review prework be noted for people now? Bonus points for the Forecasting Forward and helping people block time for the work now!

- Are there upcoming shorter weeks where recurring meetings need to be canceled or rescheduled? For example, if you see a three-day work week coming, can you forecast a meeting cancellation months in advance? This will become second nature when you use your Meeting with Myself to look ahead on your Comprehensive Calendar.

You will also likely have some future agenda thoughts that emerge in the moment during a meeting, and this will give you a place to capture them as well.

 Reader Reflection: How will you record long-term agenda topics for individual meetings? Are there any proactive topics you can plot out now?

Jen's Topic Tracker for a Team

Sometimes in addition to your own tracking, you may want to plan and share with others a set of upcoming agenda items. The purpose of this is to keep the current meeting on track (the group can stay focused on today's agenda knowing there is time and space reserved for upcoming topics) and give placeholders to ideas that emerge. Let's look at how Jen did this – and subsequently communicated it to others.

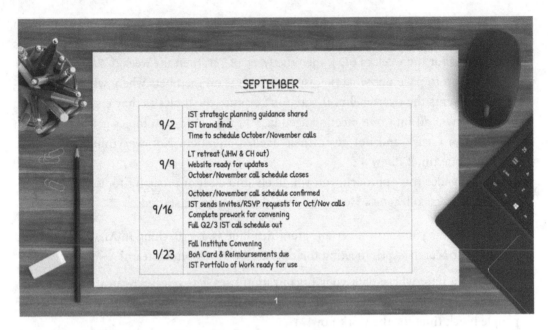

Figure 11.8 Jen's Meeting Topic Tracker.

Jen's slide was shown at the end of each weekly meeting to show the overall flow of meeting topics for the coming month. Participants can breathe easier knowing what is coming week over week. Of course, the topics can change if needed, but it helps the group stay on course if someone is looking out over the horizon and forecasting and tracking upcoming ideas – and leading the group to get there.

 Reader Reflection: Do you have any team-based meetings where you want to track longer-term topics? Does it make sense to structure a way to share these with the team?

Let's look at one more model of mapping out topics for an entire *year*!

Maya's Long-Term Topic Tracking

Maya, a director of strategy for a group of schools in New York, was charged with creating a long-term list of topics for the executive team of her organization. To do this, she had to think ahead, put herself in other people's shoes, and actively solicit topics from others. This is easier said than done! Maya had to Clear the Cobwebs and create a methodical process – and of course, Forecast Forward!

Month	Topics	Collaborators?
August	Finalize scope and sequence for 21-22 DOO PD Finalize DOL for Regional Ops Team	
September	Internal Audit w/MMB Onboard Director of HR	ED/Accounting Talent/Accounting
October	FY22 Q1 Budget Meetings Q1 DOO Dashboard Reviews Hire Director of HR	Finance/DOOs/Principals DOOs
November	Benefits Open Enrollment Hire Director of IT	HR/DOOs
December	22-23 Student Recruitment Kickoff	DC/DOOs
January	Return to school regional PD FY22 Q2 Budget Meetings PS Alignment Kickoff Strategic Planning/Project Planning for Accounting/HR Finalize ops strat plan for Jan to July	CSO/CAO Finance/DOOs/Principals Data Manager/IT AM, IT, HR
February	FY23 BDT Roll out Q2 DOO Dashboard Reviews Kickoff Intaact and UKG implementation IT Infrastructure upgrades - work starts with RICOH Ops Staffing - hire Finance Manager	Levelfield/DOOs DOOs/DC for data work

COO | CIO | CAO | ⊕

Figure 11.9 Maya's Meeting Topic Forecast.

In this case, Maya did the following to create an annual meeting forecast:

■ **Create the bucket.** She created a spreadsheet that had each executive team member's name and the month (as seen in the image), and then she considered proactive topics that may come up for that person. For example, she knew the COO would want to talk about finance, accounting updates, and compensation at certain times of the year because these were part of the organization's yearly cycle.

■ **Solicit the ideas.** Maya asked her colleagues to add to or edit the topics she had thought of so far. This likely required her to Make It One-Click and Close the Loops, as she may have needed to prompt the executive team members in creative and repetitive ways to get them to respond to her.

■ **Compile the topics.** After Maya gathered everyone's ideas, she then compiled them into a running document across the course of the year, noting other holidays and organizational events.

■ **Revise regularly.** A few weeks before each executive team meeting, she could prompt the group with a draft agenda, test it out, and modify accordingly.

By tracking topics for a long-term series of meetings, Maya was playing a few key Together Teammate roles:

■ *Gathering* the topics in one key place from all stakeholders

■ Supporting meeting participants and leaders in *forecasting* their possible meeting topics

■ *Compiling* into one location so the full group could see and name trade-offs

■ *Tracking* other changes along the way

■ *Collecting* all responses and summarizing back to the group (making sure you Close the Loops and get *all* the responses)

There is a chance you may be asked to play this particular role, or ideally you will spot the need for this role and can offer to play it. This is a case of Systems Spotting (more on that coming up), but also playing the role of coordinator, forecaster, and compiler for the group – an essential role to moving any group ahead.

 Reader Reflection: Are there any series of meetings (think executive team, leadership teams, cohort gatherings, board meetings, etc.) where you could play the role of meeting forecaster?

MANAGE THE MEETING MATERIALS

Whether as simple as a one-on-one meeting with your manager and having hyperlinks ready or as complex as a large group convening where the technology should be triple-checked, you may play a role in gathering physical or digital materials for meetings. I think this is worth calling out as a separate section in this chapter because having the right materials can make or break the meeting. I like to put myself in the shoes of

(Continued)

the attendees and think through the entire meeting start to finish. This comes in the form of asking and answering the following questions:

- ■ Do participants know the meeting is coming?

- ■ Is there prework? How long will it take? Does it need to be submitted in advance?

- ■ Is the meeting in person, video, audio, or a combination?

- ■ If in person, what location will be used? Has it been reserved?

- ■ Will there be food or drink needed? Does it need to be picked up?

- ■ Do participants need a copy of the agenda and/or note-taking materials?

- ■ Are any supplies needed, such as chart paper or sticky notes?

- ■ Is the technology in place, such as power cords, Wi-Fi passwords, and screens?

TAKE NOTES IN MEETINGS – AND OWN THE FOLLOW-UP

There are some cases, in meetings you are attending or leading or staffing, where you will want to or be asked to take notes. Together Teammates play a crucial role in meeting follow-up because you are often the person to keep things moving behind the scenes while other work is happening. If notes are clear and steps are taken, you are often playing a role in advancing some of the more strategic work in the organization. In this case, let's return to our list of meetings from the beginning of the chapter and ask ourselves some questions about each type of meeting:

- ■ What is the purpose of note-taking? Compliance? Tracking next steps? Decision-making? Share out as FYI?

- ■ What is the best mechanism? Of course, it is most efficient to take notes digitally, but there may be cases where that is not appropriate. Do you want to take notes right into a space on the agenda or in a separate location?

- ■ How are notes distributed after, if at all? Is there a shared drive space where they live? Email with a link?

- ■ How are next steps revisited? Circulated at the next meeting? Emailed out to task owners or the group?

Once you know the answers, you can devise a plan for yourself and others. And, in true Systems Spotting form, there may be some templates you can create for yourself or others. Let's examine a few note-taking templates to see what you need.

Note-Taking for Accountability and Follow-Up

In this case, you will likely need a table with a Who, What, and By When that is easily distributed and followed up on. Most likely, if this is part of a series of meetings about the same topic, you will want to create an ongoing document in a format that allows easy revisiting, such as a shared Google Doc or some kind of project management tool. For starter templates, you can look at our offerings over at www.wiley.com/go/togetherteammate.

Note-Taking for Memorialization and Communication

In some cases, you will want to take notes to record which decisions or outcomes were determined and why. These kinds of notes can be a useful reference point when you are in future decision-making, or when someone wants a justification of why a decision was made. In these situations, you will want to make sure you have a clear format for notes that allows you to "stamp" each section of the agenda – meaning getting crystal clear on next steps.

"I heard many suggestions for the location of our gala venue in this meeting. To be absolutely clear on next steps, I think we determined Staci will call these three locations for quotes, Rolando will make these two site visits, and I will compile all of the data in a chart for our next meeting where we will make the final decision. Is that right?"

Note-Taking for Scripting

While less common, there are going to be some instances where you will want a word-for-word version of everything people said. This will involve you scripting each person's words. This may be more likely in a board meeting or a meeting where other people may want to review the exact notes publicly.

Reader Reflection: Which types of notes do you need to take for which type of meeting in your world? Are there any specific templates you need to create?

THE TOGETHER TEAMMATE® | MEETING NOTES

Meeting Topic: ______________________________ **Date:** __________
Participants: ____

NEXT STEPS

Action	By Whom?	By When?	Notes

DECISIONS MADE

Decision Made	Rationales

OTHER MEETING NOTES

RESOURCES: template

Figure 11.10 Meeting Notes Template.

Regardless of how the notes are taken, and whether by you or someone else, it matters most that you have a method to follow up on those notes. That could look like:

■ Being responsible for reviewing the next steps prior to or during the meeting

■ Circulating all next steps out to others and gently having them complete status updates

■ Assigning next steps or getting to clarity on fuzzy ownership

■ Placing your own next steps onto your Weekly Worksheet, Long-Term List, or other place that leads to action

At one level, the direction of "take notes at the meeting" might feel like a basic task, but I want you to think deeply about the purpose of the note-taking using the mechanisms listed previously. At the most basic level, you could simply write some stuff down in a document and distribute it and dust your hands off. But that isn't a Together Teammate move! I want you to feel empowered to determine what type of notes need to be taken, why, what happens to them, and how to close the loops to move the next steps ahead. As Together Teammates, you are at your best when constantly moving things forward behind-the-scenes so that others can focus on the instructional program or direct service to the mission. Keeping the trains running on time is invaluable and driving the work of meetings forward is an important part of your contributions.

Now, as we advance in this chapter, I want to point out the possible advanced power of your role in meetings. I covered detailed preparation, crafting clear questions, creating agendas, taking notes, sending invites, and other important mechanics of making the most of meetings, but there may be some cases where you really *own* the entire meeting – start to finish. Don't let it sound intimidating. The next section discusses how to be a Meeting Manager – not just owning individual tasks – but taking charge of the full process.

BE THE MEETING MANAGER – OWN THE MEETING START TO FINISH

There may be some meetings when you truly oversee all the aspects of the meeting; I'll call that Meeting Manager. This may include not just securing the venue, but doing the research of possible venues, proposing options, and providing a recommendation. Or creating a Project Plan for the entire board meeting, start to finish, including managing others to complete the agenda, following up on all next steps captured, and leading the charge to schedule the next one.

As the overall Meeting Manager, your role may include taking on any of the following tasks:

- Propose the people who need to be in the meeting and why

- Get clear on purpose of the meeting

- Identify decisions to be made and research needed to make these decisions

- Create an agenda to hit the objectives

- Lead the actual meeting to achieve the outcomes

- Summarize the next steps and follow up on the meeting to ensure loops are closed

Let's say you are the Meeting Manager to determine the development's annual gala date, location, and programming, a topic that has no shortage of opinions, options, and factors playing into it. This is very different than just scheduling a meeting or taking notes on the meeting or even staffing the meeting. It requires you to think through a process start to finish and lead others to get there. Let's do some thinking aloud to practice how this could work.

- Who should be in the meeting and why? *I will need to have the president, her assistant, development vice president, director of events, and chief of staff in the meeting. I will need to have surveyed the regional executive directors in advance of this meeting, and have their recommendations at my fingertips because I know the president will want that info.*

- Who are the decision-makers and why? *I think the president makes the very final call because of her knowledge of the funding landscape, but I need to check that with her. My guess is she will want to know the opinions of others in advance of the meeting. I could survey the others and have the research ready to present.*

- What kind of agenda will meet these objectives? *I think it could be helpful if I reviewed all regional and organizational calendars in advance, got a sense of who would be the most important players to be there, and then proposed some actual dates.*

- What is the right time of day and mode for the meeting? *Since everyone has different schedules and worksites, I don't think we all need to travel to one place for this meeting. However, screen sharing will be helpful, so I want to make sure we can be on a video call together.*

As you can start to see, this goes beyond scheduling and preparation; this is bringing you to the position of driving process ahead and pushing decisions forward in your organization. And honestly, even if you are not the "official" Meeting Manager for a specific meeting, you can look for opportunities to do any of the items in the previous list to help a meeting achieve the desired results.

Reader Reflection: As you scan your upcoming meetings, are there opportunities for you to be a Meeting Manager? What would you need to learn and why?

TURBO TOGETHERNESS

Meetings make the world go 'round, and for the most part, they are a useful way to keep your organizations informed, collaborating, and acting on decisions. You will be asked to "take notes for the meeting," "order lunch for the retreat," and "schedule dinner with this donor." But these tasks alone don't signal the value you can add to your organizations. There is time and space for you to step in and fill a common organizational void, which is seeing the bigger-picture purpose of the meeting, how preparation plays into achieving the outcomes, and how follow-through leads to results. When the people leading the program or doing direct-service are pulled into the day-to-day-frenzy, you can elevate yourself as a leader to ensure the trains run on time or even ahead of schedule. You play important roles in setting up agendas for success, preparing thoughtfully, and tracking follow-through. If you want the speed version of this chapter, here we go:

- Clarify your role in each of your meetings, i.e. staffing, owning, managing

- Create a manager one-on-one agenda template and strategy for building the agenda for each meeting

- Track ideas for meeting topics for the long term

- Decide which note-taking and follow-up methods are most suited to the meetings you are part of

- Decide where you are a Meeting Manager and see how you can amplify your role

MANAGER MOMENT

As you read this chapter. you may notice that I deliberately tried to "flip the script" in terms of meeting preparation. You may have previously felt that it was your role as a manager to create the agenda and track every next step, and at some level, I am asking you to cede control of the meeting. I want to acknowledge up front that, if this is new to you, it could feel uncomfortable at first. But we are in the business of people development – always – and this is one of the most empowering moves you can do for your teammate.

But this doesn't mean you will just say, "What's on your mind today?" and hope the meetings turn out well. A successful meeting will involve some co-creation. You may want to make sure you are preserving time and headspace for a regularly scheduled meeting with your teammate. It may be helpful to co-create an agenda template together to make sure it meets both of your needs. You may also need to say – several times – to your teammate, "You are truly in charge of this meeting, and if I jump in too quickly, remind me that you are leading the way."

I encourage you to lean on your teammate more as it comes to tracking topics, follow-ups, and helping you forecast. I want you to feel freed up to say, "Can you make sure this topic lands on our executive team agenda next March?" and feel truly confident it will land. This is to free you up to focus on the big-picture goals of your work and to step out of process management.

Lastly, I challenge you to empower your teammates to be Meeting Managers. Rather than a situation in which you assign them individual tasks for a large meeting, instead work with them to own the entire cycle of meeting preparation from start to finish. This could look like working alongside your teammate to create a Project Plan for an upcoming board or staff meeting, including dates, times, and deliverables. This could look like having your teammate propose the meeting topics and structure, and you filling in the blanks during a meeting together. This isn't "putting your work on others," but I'm trying to keep your hands and brain out of process management – because you have hired outstanding Together Teammates for this! – so you can be freed up to think about how to achieve the broader goals of the mission of your organization.

CHAPTER 12

Peek Around the Bend – Forecasting into the Future

You likely picked up this book because you are already an excellent planner – or you wish to be. Well, once you have mastered the art of planning ahead for yourself (as mentioned previously in many chapters of this text), you may wish to utilize your planning prowess to assist your colleagues and organization even more! Because now that your *own* planning game is strong, you have the headspace to support others in their planning efforts.

In this chapter, you will learn to:

- Support your manager(s) in forecasting for their own calendars and tasks

- Assist a team in planning ahead by identifying events, projects, and tasks in the future

- Create systems to support stakeholders in planning ahead by laying out the asks for future

What exactly do I mean by forecasting? By Forecasting Forward into the Future (a Together Try-It), I mean picking your heads up from the immediate day-to-day and identifying events in the near and far future that require preparation, spotting calendar collisions or efficiencies, and backwards planning to meet outcomes or goals. As a Together Teammate, you are often uniquely qualified to be the person looking into the future, the one noticing conflicts and forecasting the preparation needed. This is because many people you work with may be out in the field all day, the first responder for crises, or busy dealing with staffing and management situations. (To be clear, depending on your role, you may have some of that going on too.) Your overall aim is to be the person who identifies items coming around the curve, and helps others get ahead of them.

SUPPORTING OTHERS TO FORECAST

Ever been struck by a very last-minute manager request that could have been predicted? Or perhaps watched a colleague work down to the wire on something that could have gotten a head start? Me too! This is where your unique position as a Together Teammate just may be able to help someone else – and maybe make your life a bit easier too. In my experience, it isn't that other people don't *want* to look ahead. It is often that their day-to-day Work Whirlwind is just too heavy for them to pick their heads up to Pause to Plan. Enter you, The Together Teammate (superhero cape optional). Let's look at a few examples of how this can work in practice.

Jenny and Jennie's Forecasting Meeting

I had an opportunity to spend time with a chief of schools (Jenny) and her talented chief of staff (Jennie) during the course of writing this book. They set up a system called Forecasting Meetings where they partnered to look ahead on various organizational calendars to see what was coming and what Jenny could plan for. Let's look at the agenda Jennie created as a forcing function each week. These questions of her manager helped her see how she could be most effective as a behind-the-scenes teammate.

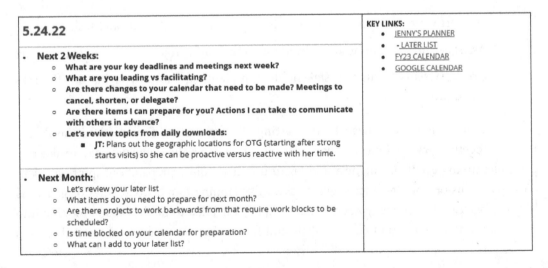

Figure 12.1   Jennie's Forecaster for a Manager Meeting.

Jennie created some key questions to ask her manager as they forecasted into the future. Here are a few that really jumped out at me:

- **"What are you leading versus facilitating?"** is a great question for Jennie to understand because she can play a role in the preparation. This is also a direct connection to helping your manager with their energy levels and cognitive loads. This also means Jennie may get last-minute requests to format slides or make copies.

- **"Meetings to cancel, shorten, or delegate?"** This is a great question for Jennie to ask her manager because it helps clear time to focus on priorities. Now you may wonder, couldn't Jennie's manager figure that out for herself? Certainly, but she is often out in the field all day and doesn't have as much time to look ahead. Jennie, as a Together Teammate, plays a unique role in looking ahead on her manager's calendar. Jenny needs a forcing function to consider this question as it relates to her calendar – and Jennie will likely be the one communicating about the shifts.

- **"Are there items I can prepare for you?"** Let's say Jennie spotted an upcoming interview on her manager's calendar. Jennie could offer to pull together interview materials, consolidate and summarize them, and insert them right into her manager's Google Calendar – thus playing a huge role in Keeping It One-Click, an important Together Try-It.

Jennie, the chief of staff, identified some benefits to this regular Forecasting Meeting with her manager.

- We caught scheduling conflicts.
- It prompted my manager to remember steps she needs to take to be prepared for the week(s) ahead.
- It prompted her to take time to prepare for meetings.
- It gave me immediate action items I could do to support my manager.
- It allowed me to identify opportunities for her to delegate to the rest of the team.

One added benefit here is if your manager is more Together, it can make your life as a teammate much, much easier. If Jennie hadn't created this forcing function in advance with Jenny, things might have gone off the rails quickly. (This is not to say they *would* have, but who wants to risk it?) By forecasting *together*, with someone like Jennie leading the way, you can reduce crises and last-minute requests in your *own* week. How's that for a win-win?!

 Reader Reflection: Whether or not you manage a calendar for your manager, how could you play a role in forecasting with or for them?

Lauren Helps Her Colleagues Forecast

Part of your job as forecasters is looking very far down the horizon, and one way of doing this is to ensure you have carefully prepared for meetings – and helped others prepare for them. In the following example, Lauren, charged with supporting school coordinators across an organization, helped the team plan ahead by segmenting the seasons, and planning proactive questions to get ahead, preventing at least some last-minute stress. Lauren created questions to help those in Teammate roles work with their managers on forecasting. Let's peek at them in more detail.

Coordinators

Recommended Meeting	Recommended Date
Spring Priorities	Upcoming Check-In
Summer Priorities P1	Between 4/30 – 5/11
Summer Priorities P2	Between 5/28 – 6/8
18-19 Schedule	Between 6/11 – 6/22

Spring (Upcoming Check-in)
1. What are your priorities between now and the end of the year?
2. What meetings do you need help with scheduling in order to support those priorities?
3. What ways aside from scheduling could I be supportive of those priorities?
4. Are you going to visit each of your schools during state testing?
5. Are you going to be out of the office during spring break?
6. Do you need any readiness meetings scheduled with Principals?
7. Do you need any close-out meetings scheduled with Principals before the last week of school?
8. Are you going to be visiting schools during the last week of school?
9. Is there anyone that you will need to meet with before going on vacation?
10. What are the big buckets of work that I support you on, and what are my monthly responsibilities through August on them?

Summer Priorities Part 1 (Between 4/30 – 5/11):
1. What are your summer priorities, by month? What is your ideal summer schedule, including meetings with direct reports, readiness review, facilitation prep, onboarding, TLL management?
2. What are summer PD facilitation and design/review responsibilities, and what structures and time blocked in your calendar do you need to fulfill them?
3. Is there any session that you think you're going to need on site support for in addition to what the ops team provides?
4. State test results come out in late July/August – what will you and I need to be doing to prepare and act on these?
5. What are the big buckets of work that I support you on, and what are my monthly responsibilities through August on them?

Figure 12.2   Lauren's Team Forecaster.

As you can see, this example is full of ways Lauren is helping her team forecast with their managers. I want to call out a few things:

- **Very specific questions.** Lauren prepared very detailed questions for the coordinators to ask their managers. Ultimately, getting to this level of specificity will help you support your manager and teammates better by understanding exactly what their needs are, right down to "Is there anyone you need to meet with before going on vacation?" Getting the answers to these questions right now in this check-in meeting prevents you from having to write those multiple-choice emails later when you realize you still need a little more info from your manager in order to proceed.

- **Prompt thinking for "weird weeks."** We see Weird Weeks scramble people all the time – for example, the four-day week, the off-site-training week, the people-on-vacation week. By looking ahead at upcoming items, such as the last day of school, your Forecasting Flag should go off in your brain to ask: What may need to be different about this week? Do any standard items move? Does an extra scheduling need to happen?

- **Overall organizational awareness of other happenings.** For example, state test results land in late July or August, and this prompts the coordinators to ask managers early on the role they may play in preparation and follow-up. The impact of not asking in advance is what may feel like a lot of very last-minute requests, like "Create a deck of slides with a summary of our results," or "Comb through this data and look for trends."

What this requires is a Together Teammate not only to have a keen sense of your own Year-at-a-Glance, but also to have a pulse on organizational happenings that can have an impact on the workload, mood, and activities of the organization. How do you gain this knowledge? We spoke about it earlier in the book with regard to learning your organization up front, and then you will benefit from continuing to be aware of the primary organizational calendar, any reports that come out – whether directly related to you or not – and anything else that may impact overall priorities.

You may be thinking, "Why on earth would anyone listen to me about these types of long-term or big-picture plans?" I want to reassure you in the most non-woo-woo of ways: You *do* have the power to do this. It will take some time and some learning, but remember, you have incredible expertise around how to help your organization run more smoothly. Once you start this kind of forecasting, your colleagues will realize how immensely valuable it is that someone can help them pick their heads up from the day-to-day. This could be added on to your Meeting with Myself checklist once a month to look three to six months out by:

- Clicking through the entire set of calendars (whatever those may be) for the next few months (Look for published events, meetings, and other happenings.)

- Asking other people items they have seen happen during particular seasons or months

- Noting any other Project Plans that are underway, and asking how you may plug into those

- Paying attention to moments of stress for yourself or your manager, and thinking through how those could have been avoided by checking in earlier

 Reader Reflection: How can you help your manager and other senior leaders forecast? What steps do you need to take?

 FAQ: Can I support someone else's Meeting with Myself as a Forecaster?
In some cases, you may be asked to play a role to help someone else conduct their meetings with themselves. This is not because they cannot handle it; it may be because you are uniquely equipped with control of their calendar and the ability to forecast, and you may function in a gatekeeping capacity. In these specific cases, it makes sense to create a checklist for that person and pick a standing time and place to lead them through their meeting. You may ask some specific questions, such as:

- How aligned do the next two weeks look with your priorities?

- Are there any meetings that could be longer, shorter, moved, or canceled?

- What preparation is needed for particular meetings?

- How do you best want to use your work time?

- Have any To-Dos come up recently that we need to incorporate into your upcoming week?

- Are there any delegated items you want to check back on with team members?

- Is there any information you need to communicate out?

The ability to help someone else clean up their own week and prep for the week ahead adds unique value to organizations, and you are in the position to offer this support.

Kendra's Pre-Vacation Forecast

Not only can you help others forecast, but you will of course need to forecast for yourself. Kendra, a member of the Together Team, was preparing to go on vacation and she forecast for a colleague, Heidi, who was helping cover some of Kendra's work during her time away. Imagine how good it feels to go on vacation, prepare another team member to cover you, and know you will not return to a mess! Let's see how Kendra did that.

Kendra carefully created a step-by-step guide for Heidi to execute those tasks. She made it very easy for Heidi to plug and play by making it One-Click and Standing in the Shoes of Others:

- **Sequenced chronologically.** This way Heidi can insert those dates right into her own Comprehensive Calendar and Weekly Worksheet.

- **Spelled out the task in painstaking detail and made it easy on her.** Check out how Kendra said, "Send book tracking details to Catie and Danielle *(draft emails set up for you)."*

- **Included Plan B.** Kendra's forecast even anticipated if something went wrong and built in an escalation clause. Positive Pessimism!

Even if you aren't about to be out of the office, if you work with multiple people, it may make sense to communicate to them proactively about your next few weeks on a regular basis. The purpose of doing this could be to:

- Align with the people around you on priorities

- Communicate your overall capacity and whereabouts

- Make critical choices about overall tasks

- Proactively seek out last-minute asks that may come your way (Soliciting them allows you to start working on them earlier!)

FAQ: What if my forecasting is not welcomed? You may quietly be thinking, "Well, that is all fine and good, Maia, but no one wants me forecasting around here." Hmm, I would say. This is the one time I would ask you to trust me and try it. In over 20 years and thousands of folks, I have never seen forecasting be unwelcomed. It may feel hard or intimidating to be the person looking ahead, but it will keep things on track – and make your own work life a bit easier too.

From: Kendra
To: Heidi
Cc: Maia
Subject: Overview of tasks while I'm OOO

Hi Heidi, (FYI Maia, to keep you in the loop)

Thanks again for covering these tasks while I'm out of office! Below is a list of tasks by day. All emails are saved in the workshops@ Drafts folder for you.

Please reach out with any questions!

~Kendra

Date	Task	Notes
Wed, 7/27	- By 1:00 PM CDT → send "post-class" email for HISD 7/28	
Thurs, 7/28	- By 1:00 PM CDT → send "post-class" email for HISD 7/29 - By EOD → Circle back to Vendor if we haven't received tracking information for Crescent City Schools & Einstein Charter Schools' book orders (per the email I sent you 7/25)** o Send book tracking details to Catie & Danielle once we have them *[draft emails set up for you]*	**Escalate to Maia on Fri if nothing back re tracking
Fri, 7/29	- By 1:00 PM CDT → send BES Trainer C4 pre-class email - By EOD, once BES C4 Nearpod available → o Save BES C4 Nearpod PDF to class website & publish the updated page *Save Nearpod in the Together Trainer / BES folder:* My Drive > Documents - Together Trainer Classes ▾ Name ↑ 📁 20220628_0801 BES *Class website is "20220628_0801 BES":* My Drive > _Online Class Google Sites ▾ Name ↑ 📄 20220616_0621 DeKalb 📄 20220628_0801 BES o Save BES C4 Nearpod to co-host folder 0-Co-Host Files > 20220628_0801 BES - The Together Trainer 's TG Files / Name cordings - Cornelius / Class 1 orkshop & Coaching Material / Class 2 orkshop & Coaching Material / Class 3 Files / ☑ Class 4 Files ARCHIVE / Roster - BES Trainer - By EOD → I ordered Legacy College Prep books on 7/26; if we haven't seen the invoice come through, please check in with Aaron to make sure it was ordered; no need to track the book shipment (I'll do that when I get back) – I just want to make sure it gets into their ordering system	
Mon, 8/1	- By 1:00 PM CDT → send CFA + YMCA C2 pre-class email - By 1:00 PM CDT → send KIPP Pueblo Unido pre-class email - By 1:00 PM CDT → send BES C4 post-class email++ - By EOD → attach any HW emails received for CFA + YMCA C1 in Maia's 8/2 "Prep for class" calendar hold, so Maia has easy reference to them [screenshot of emails] - By EOD → confirm CCS & Einstein received their books & materials *(flag for me if anything doesn't show as delivered)* o CCS TL books – 1Z5859020397610998 o CCS TT books – *WF Aaron* o CCS materials – 1Z8VT92Z0300021411 o Einstein books – *WF Aaron* o Einstein materials – 1Z8VU3T70320018612	++ Draft sent to Maia 7/25, please send after Maia has edited // Maia may decide to send herself
Tues, 8/2	- By 1:30 PM CDT → send CFA + YMCA C2 post-class email - By 4:45 PM CDT → send KIPP Pueblo Unido post-class email - By EOD → send KIPP CO "final reminders" email	NOTE: I'll plan to upload the BES C4, CFA + YMCA C2 & KIPP PU class recordings on Wed morning.

Figure 12.3   Kendra's Pre-Vacation Forecast.

Kendra's Staffing Forecast

Over here in the Together-verse, our talented colleague Kendra is responsible for ensuring that our online and in-person classes are staffed. Each class happens on different days, at different times, and in different cities and a few of our team members are better suited to some classes than others. Long story short, staffing our classes is complex. Because it requires my input and involves waiting to hear back from others once we invite them to support, it is necessary to have forecasting strongly in place.

At regular intervals, Kendra sends along a proposed staffing email for the next four to six months. Let's look at it in this image.

As a Together Teammate, Kendra did a few enormously helpful things here:

■ **Created a chart** in a Google Doc with upcoming classes so we could look ahead together

■ **Proposed staffing** for each class based on her past knowledge and availability of trainers

■ **Followed through** on the staffing proposals once I signed off, and brought it back to me if a trainer wasn't available (Closing the Loop!)

Sometimes I like to do a thought experiment and imagine what would happen if Kendra *didn't* do forecasting. Quickly an alarming scenario comes to mind that involves last-minute requests and unavailable trainers and possibly not being staffed to set our classes up for success. Not good!

Now, how does Kendra "remember" to forecast staffing for the team? A few trusty Together Tools help her do this:

■ During her Meeting with Myself, Kendra looks ahead several months to see which courses are coming.

■ Kendra's Comprehensive Calendar/Weekly Worksheet has regular reminders to check in on staffing.

■ A table for staffing is set up with every class listed so Kendra has a built-in mechanism to plan and record staffing.

 Reader Reflection: What recurring events or tasks do you have where forecasting could be useful?

HOST	DATE(S)	TYPE	# Participants	CO-HOST / TA	WHO TO ASK?
CO DOE	Tues, 2/21/2023 Tues, 2/28/2023	The Together Leader: Plan, Prioritize & Protect Your Time	~40-60	Co-Host: Tammie TA: Cornelius	All set (pending final count) KRS to monitor final # of participants / if tips 50+, need to secure 1 additional co-host
The Together Leader - Online Course [Leader 101 Series 20]	Mar 7 - Mar 28, 2023 Four-week series on Tuesdays	The Together Leader: Plan, Prioritize & Protect Your Time	~75	Co-Host: Ana TA: Cornelius	All set Maia – since the registrations #s are over 50, would you like to add a 2nd co-host now? If yes, would you like to ask Chrystie for this one?
Martin Luther King, Jr. Middle School @ Charlotte-Mecklenburg Schools	Wed, 3/8/2023 Mon, 3/27/23	The Together Teacher: Create a Personal Organization System	~50	Co-Host: ____ TA: ____	1/23 → KRS asked Ana & Cornelius KRS will re-ping if haven't heard back by 1/27
The Together Teacher (Evening Edition) - Online Class [TT PS]	Wed, 3/8/2023	The Together Teacher: Create a Personal Organization System	~50	Co-Host: ____ TA: Cornelius	Maia – would you like to ask Bri to co-host this class?
The Together Leader - Online Course [Leader 101 Series 21]	April 18 - May 9, 2023 Four-week series on Tuesdays	The Together Leader: Plan, Prioritize & Protect Your Time	~75	Co-Host: Ana TA: Cornelius	All set KRS to monitor final # of participants / if tips 50+, need to secure 1 additional co-host
The Together Teammate - Online Course [Teammate Series 7]	May 1 - May 22, 2023 Four-week series on Mondays	The Together Teammate: Plan, Prioritize & Protect Your Time	~50	Co-Host: ____ TA: ____	Once these dates are 100% confirmed → ask Ana & Cornelius?

Figure 12.4 Kendra's Staffing Forecast.

FAQ: Is forecasting even in my job description? Maybe and maybe not. I would argue that, no matter what your exact role, forecasting and planning are necessary for any organization – and especially mission-driven organizations with fewer resources. Together Teammates are often poised to be forecasters because they see all of the moving pieces, look ahead on calendars regularly, and often interact with many teams within the organization. I guarantee if you start doing this consistently, you will become an invaluable resource to your organization, gain even more interesting work, and be a trusted member of the team.

SUPPORT STAKEHOLDERS WITH FORECASTING

Now that you have thought about helping individual colleagues and managers forecast (and even entire teams), you may want to think about how you can support any other stakeholders, such as vendors you may interact with frequently.

Kendra's Book Order Forecast

For example, my team regularly orders bulk shipments of our books to be shipped to various conference sites and locations. Granted, it is very easy for us to just email our distributor each time we need a shipment and leave it at that. However, we can help them help us by forecasting our needs farther out. The email seen here demonstrates Kendra forecasting our next quarter's book orders.

Now why would Kendra take time to do this when she already has to email the distributor each time we have an order? There are a few reasons:

■ **Gets results.** It ensures we can get what we need from our vendor. If we blindsided them with lots of last-minute orders, they might not be able to meet our needs.

■ **Saves money.** It allows us to save money by bulk purchasing and ensures they can keep enough in stock.

■ **Shows strong partnership.** It helps us be a great partner to our vendor and help *them* plan ahead with their own work.

In order to do this, it means Kendra is looking ahead during her Meeting with Herself to see which trainings are coming up and what materials are needed. She is forecasting to help other people do their jobs well – and ensuring she meets her own goals as well.

Host Site	Date	Type of book needed	~Quantity
Chicago Open Session	3/17/2016	Teacher	15
NYC DOE Office of Student Enrollment	3/24/2016	Leader	20
Endeavor College Prep	4/8/2016	Leader	10
NYCDOE High School Science Research Pathways	4/13/2016	Teacher	26
NYCDOE Division of Early Childhood Education	4/13/2016	Leader	20
DC Open Session	4/21/2016	Leader	20
NYC DOE Office of Student Enrollment	4/27/2016	Leader	20
Acelero Learning	5/11/2016	Leader	14

Figure 12.5   Kendra's Book Order Forecasting Email.

Heidi's Summer Closure Previews

Heidi, previously a program director in a university setting, oversaw summer interns in her program. To help the internship supervisors prepare for their summer tasks, she sent a forecasting email to help ensure they did their work – and were kept abreast of various dates and deadlines.

Rather than just sending out one deadline at the last minute and hoping for the best, Heidi did some forecasting to assist the internship supervisors in completing their tasks. Let's notice:

■ **Sequence of deadlines for the entire summer.** Heidi didn't just send each date as a one-off, thus risking getting lost in the shuffle of everyone's deluge. She forecasted and looked ahead for an entire six-week period. This allows the supervisors to plan out their work on their own calendar. Bonus points if she also sent along digital invitations for the events listed!

■ **Clear communication.** As you learned in the Clear Communications chapter, formatting matters. It is worth the time to craft bullets, and use various text features such as bolding and short clear sentences.

 Reader Reflection: Look ahead on your Comprehensive Calendar. Do you see opportunities to forecast with any audiences?

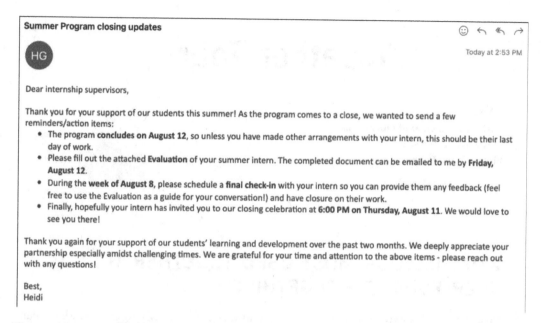

Summer Program closing updates

HG

Today at 2:53 PM

Dear internship supervisors,

Thank you for your support of our students this summer! As the program comes to a close, we wanted to send a few reminders/action items:

- The program **concludes on August 12**, so unless you have made other arrangements with your intern, this should be their last day of work.
- Please fill out the attached **Evaluation** of your summer intern. The completed document can be emailed to me by **Friday, August 12**.
- During the **week of August 8**, please schedule a **final check-in** with your intern so you can provide them any feedback (feel free to use the Evaluation as a guide for your conversation!) and have closure on their work.
- Finally, hopefully your intern has invited you to our closing celebration at **6:00 PM on Thursday, August 11**. We would love to see you there!

Thank you again for your support of our students' learning and development over the past two months. We deeply appreciate your partnership especially amidst challenging times. We are grateful for your time and attention to the above items - please reach out with any questions!

Best,
Heidi

Figure 12.6   Heidi's Summer Closure Preview Email.

TURBO TOGETHERNESS

My overall goal for this chapter is for you to feel empowered to play a unique – and often missing – role in your organizations: the person who can see around the bend into the next few months, anticipate upcoming events that require planning, and spot places in projects where you need others to block time to do work and meet deadlines. Some of your roles formally entail this, and some of you may play this role informally. Ways to be a Forecast Forward Together Teammate include:

- Look ahead two to six months into the future each time you Meet with Yourself, and see if any events, projects, or tasks warrant reminders, time blocks, or preparation.

- Identify any other impacts on your organization in the future that could require people to prepare, such as a data release, grantees named, or other external deadlines.

- Notice moments when things feel stressful or messy, and think about how previous forecasting could have prevented it, and then build the forecasting process you wish had been in place!

- Look ahead for any tripwires or places where things might get "stuck" and see if you can figure out a clear path forward (a combination of Clear the Cobwebs and Forecast Forward).

Together Tour

Lola
Assistant Principal of Operations
Mastery Charter Schools
Philadelphia, Pennsylvania

WHAT IS YOUR MOST USED TOGETHER TOOL TO KEEP *YOURSELF* TOGETHER?

I use my Weekly Worksheet as well as my Outlook calendar. My weekly huddles, team meetings, weekly team one-on-ones, and other meetings are all on my calendar. I even schedule work time, breaks, and block out other time blocks for important projects on my calendar, so I am maximizing my time at work! My Weekly Worksheet divides each day up into action items that are "big rocks, tasks, and quick hits."

Pause to Plan. I try to be intentional about what goes into each category each day so I am setting myself up for success each week in terms of keeping myself organized and completing action items/projects.

HOW DO YOU RE-TOGETHER YOURSELF WHEN UNEXPECTED THINGS POP UP?

I try to leave some wiggle room in my schedule (Outlook calendar) when possible to address emergencies or any unexpected things that happen. This means, when possible, I don't schedule back-to-back meetings, which gives me time to address any unexpected things that may come up. My weekly action plan lays outs big rocks, tasks, and quick hits for each day; however, I usually try to plan for my Thursdays and Fridays to be less task heavy to allow for some wiggle room in the event I have to move things around from earlier in the week. So when things do pop up, I may have to prioritize some tasks over others, which may mean I may need to clear my schedule for one day and move those tasks to another day during the week (usually my more flexible days – Thursday or Fridays if the deadlines allow for that).

WHEN IS A TIME YOU HAD TO ADJUST YOUR TOGETHERNESS PRACTICES AND WHY?

During the pandemic, I had to adjust my schedule when my school leadership team had to plan for an unexpected school closure. There were several pieces of communication that had to go out to families, staff, and even students that needed to be planned for/created in addition to planning for a transition to virtual learning. This changed my Togetherness plan, and I had to quickly add on my new priorities to my weekly action plan as well as reschedule a few meetings to ensure I was maximizing my time. Many of my in-person team meetings and one-on-one meetings with my team members also had to be adjusted on my calendar to become virtual Zoom meetings.

HOW HAS TOGETHERNESS HELPED YOU COMMUNICATE AND WORK WITH OTHERS?

Forecast Forward Frequently. Togetherness has helped me to be a very proactive leader who is able to forecast and plan ahead for projects. Togetherness has also allowed for me to be a better planner and get feedback from key stakeholders in projects, which has been helpful with the rollout and execution of those projects.

Be the Birdseye. For instance, I have a scope and sequence document that outlines all the events, projects, and upcoming key actions for Operations for my school for the year, broken down by month. This is a planning tool I use to delegate projects to my team members, identify key stakeholders involved, and identify key action items.

Clear the Cobwebs, Show Your Work. One project where Togetherness really helped was with the rollout of a new laptop plan for students in my school. My scope and sequence listed items like when the Project Plan was due, when the presentation to staff was due, and when execution of the laptop plan needed to happen. My actual technology Project Plan outlined the granular details like when the draft plan needed to be shared with the rest of my school's leadership team for feedback as well as when the presentation for teachers needed to be created and delivered to teachers. Ultimately, by being Together, I have been able to make sure my communication is planned, timely, and relevant.

HOW DO YOU BALANCE THE PROACTIVE FOCUSED PART OF YOUR JOB WITH THE REACTIVE TASKS THAT POP UP?

I think knowing that there will be things that just "pop up" and actually planning for that to happen is important. No matter how proactive you are, unexpected things come up, especially in school operations. I think being okay with flexibility is key! As long as I am not always spending all my time on reactive tasks and I am still able to adjust my schedule and plans to allow for time for the proactive focused part of my job, I still feel on top of things.

Own the Outcome. Generally, I'm always thinking of what my contingency plan is if my original plan doesn't go as expected because of a last-minute emergency or just something that may pop up. I've learned that togetherness is not about being perfect but being organized, proactive, flexible, and a quick problem solver.

HOW DO YOU HANDLE WORKING WITH COLLEAGUES WHO ARE SLIGHTLY LESS THAN TOGETHER?

Stand in the Shoes of Others. I think it's important to recognize that not everyone will have the same workstyle as you. While it would be ideal for everyone to be *super* Together, that is just not realistic. I think that as long as there is alignment on the goal and criteria for success, we have a common ground to work on regardless of our Togetherness styles. I am also always happy to share Togetherness tips or resources if my colleagues are open to it. Nonetheless, if a lack of Togetherness does get in the way of the actual work, I will give the direct feedback so that the colleague knows the importance of improving in their Togetherness to ultimately be able to meet goals.

WHY DOES TOGETHERNESS MATTER TO YOU AT WORK AND AT HOME?

Togetherness matters to me because it helps create balance and organization in my life! I cannot function in chaos, and I do not like missing deadlines or important events either. I am a busy professional who likes to travel, work out, hike, and plan other fun family activities. There isn't a way for me to accomplish all of that successfully without Togetherness. All the things I need to do on a monthly, weekly, or daily basis can't just live in my head; I'll forget them and won't be able to do any of the things that are important to me! That's exactly why Togetherness matters to me both at home and work.

CHAPTER 13

Systems Spotting – If You See Something, Say Something!

Ever felt like you were playing whack-a-mole all day with one emergency after another? Or perhaps in a recurring dream with the same crisis over and over? Or rewriting an instruction guide you know full well you wrote up last year? Well, it turns out a lot of disasters may be a little more predictable than it first seems – something I hope you learned in my chapter on the Daily Deluge. What you need here is an instinct for Systems Spotting and a drive to codify. In other words, hunting for patterns that can be turned into checklists, creating routines for cyclical events, and designing templates to avoid doing all the same work over again each year. Of all of my preparation for this book, this particular concept of identifying the need for a system and then putting said system into place (which I call Systems Spotting) was one of my favorites to identify in The Together Teammates I interviewed. It stands out because it is where your support roles can add the most value to your organizations.

In this chapter, you will learn to:

◼ Fine-tune your systems sense to see when something can benefit from a system

◼ Develop routines to turn pain points into smooth systems

◼ Codify processes so they can be replicated in the future

So what is Systems Spotting? For example, let's say you frequently get a last-minute request from your manager to secure a retreat location, a common task that could come through in the Daily Deluge. As a Together Teammate, you may spot this pattern of last-minute requests and build a proactive system that might look like a table created with all retreat dates, the date by which you anticipate the venue should be booked, and possible locations. Then you'd bring this blank table to your one-on-one and ask your manager to work with you to complete it. This allows you and your manager to Forecast the Future, but also turn a one-off request into a system. Or let's say you lead the Girl Scout troop for one of your kids (#togethertroopleader) and you find yourself handwriting the same camping packing checklist twice a year. If you took the time to step back and create a shared Google Doc you can simply update for each trip, you have saved yourself some time and likely improved the process to boot. (This only took me four camping trips to figure out!) The beauty of this process is that it can often reduce stress, automate decision-making, and allow for batch processing. It also allows you to codify the process for the future so another teammate doesn't have to start from scratch. This process involves seeing your tasks within categories and as part of a larger ecosystem. Let's start with figuring out how to tune in our systems antennae, or be aware when the need for a system surfaces.

TURN UP YOUR SYSTEMS ANTENNAE

I'm guessing your day might include some combination of the following, on repeat: Answer this email! Fix this copier! Call this vendor! And yes, your job *is* to do all of these things. However, if you can train your mind to step back, you will likely observe patterns that would benefit from a clear system. It could come from observing a repeated request, noticing timing for work at a certain time of day or year, or looking around to see what is a pain point and considering creative ways to achieve it. It could be noticing that this is the fifth time this week you've cleared a copier jam, and realizing it's time to post a sign above the copier reminding people not to overfill the paper tray! In this section, my goal is to train your sensors for when a repeated task or request can suggest the need to build, propose, or create a system, thus reducing pain points in the future, allowing for stronger choices, and leaving time and space for real emergencies. Bonus points: This can even work in your own home, and I bet you have tried it already. No more starting from scratch!

Push yourself to step out of your day-to-day task mode. I encourage you to:

■ Keep track of all requests or other unexpected problems from the Daily Deluge to solve for a month. You could download one of our trackers here www.wiley.com/go/togetherteammate or just keep track in a notebook.

■ Now scan them and look for data. Are the tasks coming about a certain topic? From a particular person? At a certain time of year?

■ Let's say you spot a pattern regarding a particular topic. Now go deeper. Is your boss always asking for data right before a board meeting? Are you often scrambling for an icebreaker before a gathering? Are you hunting for one-off event space over and over?

 Reader Reflection: Consider your past month of work. Can you identify any repeated requests or unexpected challenges that you can turn into systems or routines to be more proactive?

A few examples could include:

■ Schedule a donor meeting turns to . . . . Make a list of all donors and create a proposed schedule of which ones to meet with over the course of the year.

■ Find a vendor to supply food for the staff picnic turns to . . . . Create a menu of vendors the entire team can use in the future.

■ Request and print these staff photos for the employee guide turns into . . . . Save photos on shared drive and create a system to have staff update annually.

Now that you have considered any repeated requests you can turn into systems, we'll see how to go ahead with creating those systems.

TURN PAIN POINTS INTO SMOOTH SYSTEMS

Once you have a clear sense of patterns and the ability to identify spots where systems are needed, the next step is to create routines for yourself and others. The system may be for you, or it may be for others. It could be anything from an email template to an FAQ system for staff to repeated meeting requests for the year. There is likely some set of tasks you conduct often where having a system would lead to more efficiency. I'll start with sharing one of my own, and then share a few examples from others.

Maia's Teaching Pain Point (Times Two!)

Back in the early years of the Together Group, I noticed that I often scrambled to scribble down a pacing guide before I would teach a class. I keenly remember being in a women's restroom in New Orleans writing down a pacing guide on an index card minutes before the start of a training! And this would happen to me every single time. Talk about a pain point. It made me feel stressed, and *not* Together. It impacted my mood, and it hindered my ability to connect with participants prior to instruction. What could I do to avoid this scramble? Eventually, I created a few things that helped me.

The first was a standard pacing guide. It's not actually the product that matters here, but the process by which I noticed a repeated stressful moment – scribbling out my pacing guide – and realized there could be a product that I could keep 50 copies at my desk for the year and have them ready to go when I was heading to the airport. Boom – no more scrambling when I was getting ready to teach. Grab my pacing guide, and I'm ready to rock. And just in case some of you are like, "Scramble, whatever, Maia, it's no big deal," I want you to convince yourself of the need for this by picturing the outcome here. A calm teacher is a present one. I was setting myself up for success.

Let's peek at another example, a frequent packing exercise for professional development seminars I was teaching. Similar to the previous personal example, I also observed myself rapidly packing, occasionally forgetting things, and then scrambling to get to the airport before a work trip. Besides keeping a packed suitcase, what else could I do? I was spotting the need for a system! And so I built a checklist.

Does this take time to Pause to Plan – a key Together Try-It? Yes, it does. But let's chat about how the benefits of pausing make it worth it:

- **Lowers stress.** No more running around at the last minute (#nottogethertraveler) gathering items the morning of a trip. I could efficiently and calmly pack myself up. Given that this list is very long, I could also make sure I blocked 30–45 minutes on my Weekly Worksheet to pack up. If I just listed "pack" without any sense of what was really behind it, I could severely underestimate.

- **Allows you to ask for help.** If I was running behind or late, I could nicely ask one of my children to gather my markers, fanny pack, and other materials. Or I could ask the Together Team to help review the Pre-Workshop Questionnaires for me.

Maia Personal Packing List (suitcase, backpack and grey nylon bag)	Packed?	Notes
Print boarding pass		
Travel Outfit (Leggings, flats, sweater)		
Pajamas/Flipflops/Bathrobe/underwear/bra		
Exercise Outfit (bra, sneakers, shorts, shirt, flip belt)		
Presentation Outfit (Outfit, undergarment, bra, shoes, stockings)		
Toiletries Bag (hair products, deodorant, razor, chap stick, moisturizer, toothbrush/toothpaste)—check each for supply		
Nightguard/Clip/Eye Mask/Ear Plugs into green bag in backpack		
Snacks (nuts, Wasa crackers, oatmeal, Cliff Bars, fruit)		
Water bottle		
Stationery and pen		
Fun magazines and decompression activities		
Travel pillow/blanket, if needed		
Driver's license		

Maia Workshop Packing	Completed	Notes
Clipboard/Pacing Guide		
Gadgets (iPad, Kindle) + Power Cords + Air card pouch		
Fanny pack with jump drive / 2 clickers and batteries / WATCH		
Markers		

En Route	Completed	Notes
Pacing Guide filled out and on clipboard		
Review PreWorkshop Questionnaire		
Review PDF of Togetherness Self-Assessment and adjust quotes, as needed		
Review Client Notes		
Update deck and check for all page numbers		
AT HOTEL: Set out all materials/save to Dropbox and jump drive/repack suitcase		

Figure 13.1   Maia's Work Trip Packing System.

■ **Reduces forgotten items.** As someone who frequently got on a 7 p.m. flight (at the end of a daylong workshop) and landed at 1 a.m., you can bet I love a travel pillow. However, I would often forget to pack one because I wasn't thinking about the trip home. My checklist ensured I'd be able to get at least a little rest on the trip home.

Teresa Checklists Up the Supplies

Teresa, a senior manager of event and design operations for a network of schools, was responsible for the participant experience and operations for multiple leadership cohorts per year. This also included her own travel, as well as setup and takedown of each event.

The mental load of needing to consider for each trip exactly what to pack, let alone sorting and replacing supplies, could take hours of extra time – and leave room for extra mistakes. Teresa describes the initial situation: "We had sets of materials; one set lives in Chicago and one set lives in Houston. There are a total of six supply boxes, and a set of printers, standing banners, and extra Post-its." Sounds like a lot to travel with, right? So what did Teresa and her entire team at KIPP do? A checklist, of course.

Teresa's checklist is simple, yet detailed. It doesn't just say stapler, it specifies two staplers. It doesn't just say batteries, it says which type and how many. Teresa describes, "At the event,

---

Supply Box Checklist

- Tech Supplies
    - USB drive
    - Power strip (1)
    - 3-Prong Extension cord (1)
    - Speakers (1)
    - Projector & Cords
        - Clickers (2)
        - AAA Batteries (5)
        - Mac adaptor (USBc (new) & Mini Display (old))
        - HDMI cord
        - VGA cord

- Office Supplies

    - Paper clips (100)
    - Binder clips (10)
    - Scissors (2)
    - 3-hole punch (1)
    - Stapler (2)
    - Thank you cards and envelopes (30)
    - Clipboard (1)
    - Blue tape (3)
    - Shipping gun and tape (2 rolls, 1 gun)

- Room Setup Items
    - Index cards (3-4 stacks)
    - Post-it notes (variety : at least 10-15 pads)
    - Flip chart markers (2 bags)

Figure 13.2   Teresa and the KIPP Team's Conference Supply System.

when we were packing up, we would make lists of what needed to be replenished or was missing, put a note on top of the box so I could replenish, and ship to the next event. It was so hard to do because I would be exhausted, but it was worth it because it is worse to get to the new site and be missing things!"

Let's take apart what Teresa and her team did here:

■ Identified a recurring event that required many details, too many to keep in one's head (leadership cohort gatherings)

■ Figured out and built the right tool to support that event (a checklist for packing)

■ Set up a routine for operationalizing the system (reviewing the boxes after each event and putting a Post-it on them for interns to replenish)

 Reader Reflection: What are any recurring events in your world that would benefit from a routine or checklist to prevent pain points?

Kat's Tracker for Purchase Orders

Much like Teresa and me, Kat, a business clerk in the external affairs office at a large school district, has a lot of projects to juggle. For example, she is responsible for all purchase orders, and clearly that system cannot be handled with sticky notes. Kat would also get additional inquiries throughout the day requesting updates for the status of various POs. Kat had to create a detailed tracker for all of the purchase orders, and where they were in process. She even got fancy and added filters and such to keep track of things.

Kat's instinct, like Teresa's, is awesome:

■ **Spot the Need for a System.** Kat and her manager noticed the inundation of purchase order requests coming from all directions and at all hours of the day. She and her manager decided to ask all requestors to load the requests into Wrike (software) so they could be more carefully tracked.

■ **Make It Multiple Choice.** Because the requests were sometimes coming in with only some of the information needed, thus forcing Kat to double back and ask questions, she set up fields so information could be collected completely – the first time!

■ **Show the Work.** Now at any point in time, Kat is able to show the status of purchase orders by region, by budget code, and by team. This helps build trust with the team *and* makes Kat's life easier.

That was a fun foray into Spotting the Need for Systems to support ourselves in the deluge – what about supporting *others* with systems?

FUND	OBJ	SUB-OBJ	FUNC	REGION	LOCAL 1	LOCAL 2	OWNER
5723 (FOUNDATION SCHOOL PROG)	9941 (OBJ CONTRL SERV)	4500 (TEAM AO)	51 (FUNDRAISING)	0000	DISC (DISCRETIONARY)	DOPS (TEAM AO)	Kat
5723 (FOUNDATION SCHOOL PROG)	6472 (GEN SUPPLIES)	9300 (REG DEV)	51 (FUNDRAISING)	0000	DISC (DISCRETIONARY)	000 (AVAILABLE)	Kat
5723 (FOUNDATION SCHOOL PROG)	8572 (MISC)	4500 (TEAM AO)	51 (FUNDRAISING)	RGVR	DISC (DISCRETIONARY)	DOPS (TEAM AO)	Kat
5723 (FOUNDATION SCHOOL PROG)	1216 (DUES)	9300 (REG DEV)	51 (FUNDRAISING)	RGVR	DISC (DISCRETIONARY)	000 (AVAILABLE)	Kat
8712 (MISC PROG)	6718	9300 (REG DEV)	51 (FUNDRAISING)	RGVR	DISC (DISCRETIONARY)	000 (AVAILABLE)	Kat
5723 (FOUNDATION SCHOOL PROG)	1216 (DUES)	4500 (TEAM AO)	51 (FUNDRAISING)	0000	DISC (DISCRETIONARY)	DOPS (TEAM AO)	Kat

Figure 13.3   Kat's Purchase Order System.

CREATE SYSTEMS TO SUPPORT OTHER HUMANS

Setting up systems for others is helpful for them, but will also make *your* life easier when it cuts down on others' day-to-day requests of you. This skill comes with pattern recognition, and a willingness to take time, step back from the larger task, and create a way to make things smoother in the future. In many ways this encapsulates many of our Together Try-Its: Pausing to Plan, Forecasting Forward, and Keeping It One-Click.

Kendra's Icebreaker System

Because much of my own work gets examined through a Together lens (it can be painful, I tell you), let's turn a mirror back on me. One of my favorite things to do when I teach is to have fun icebreakers, but I would often change them up depending on my mood, who was joining me from the team, and the vibe of the group. This created a lot of unnecessary design work for my team who was building the slide decks, but *I didn't know that*. Until Kendra, our longtime senior director of operations, pointed it out to me. Kendra is one of the most Together humans I know – and has incredibly high systems antennae. Let's look at her note.

Hi Maia,

You've started adding the "what's your favorite…" questions in the decks.

Per your email about making sure we have them in for TPM, will you let me know what you'd like for the following class types so I can standardize this across the board? Not locking you in forever, but anything I can make plug and play right now is <u>extremely</u> helpful!

Thanks,

Kendra

Course Type	Prompts	Maia's Notes
TL Ext Ed Course (8 classes)	1. Togetherness intention 2. Favorite kids' book 3. Favorite song 4. Favorite Zoom snack 5. What you wanted to be as a kid 6. Favorite kitchen appliance 7. Favorite scent 8. _____ (TBD)	

Figure 13.4 Kendra's System Spotting.

Kendra *could* have gone on just having me ask for icebreakers every single time she helped me prep for a class – which is sometimes upwards of eight training decks per week – but that gets old fast. So how was she able to identify the need for and then create a system?

■ She noticed that I had started adding icebreaker slides with fun questions and I was requesting images in certain decks.

■ She took notes on the patterns of questions I asked. (Sidenote: I love asking people their favorite kitchen appliance. Kendra noted that.)

■ She created an email (with a chart!) to let me know what I was doing, and asked for my input to make this standardized. This is making it One-Clickable!

SHANNON'S SUPPLY ORDER FORM

Now that your systems-spotting antennae are very high, you can constantly be on the lookout for how to help yourself and others streamline systems so as not to overtax roles that often are hit with requests all day long. Take a classic example in any school or office setting: supply orders. Pity the office person tasked with supply ordering, but no longer! Once you realize you are frequently ambushed for colored cardstock for a class project, emailed requests for special coffee pods for the employee lounge, or texted last-minute needs for nametags, you may realize you need . . . a *system*. Let's look at what a COO put in place across a network of schools.

Shannon created this supply request Google Form to streamline purchasing across multiple campuses in Chicago. In a less Together world, each school could have created their own supply-ordering system, but since Shannon is responsible for operations across an entire network, she ensured there was a singular way to request supplies. When is enterprise-level uniformity useful? I urge it:

■ When individuals are relying on a shared set of service providers (No one wants to use multiple forms.)

■ When you want to carefully track budget and spending (You can categorize and sort across the network.)

■ When you want to be able to batch your own work (for example, doing a bulk order on Tuesdays)

■ When you want to track the asks, such as when they came in, who is spending what, and so on

Campus *

☐ High School

☐ Middle School

☐ Network

Items *

Your answer

Reason for request: *
Ex: "Student incentives for 4th grade, math materials for Module 2)

Your answer

Link/Web address *
(Amazon/Staples link preferred)

Your answer

Quantity *

Your answer

Unit Price *

Your answer

Figure 13.5 Shannon's Supply Request Form.

But often systems like that may use software that you don't have access to, or that are designed for huge corporations. My hope is to empower you to create your own system with easy tools like Google Forms, SurveyMonkey, and other simple technology solutions.

 FAQ: What if I create a system and no one uses it? Admittedly, this is hard. As a person who used to try to email IT directly for help and avoid Trouble Tickets altogether, I get that people often want to bypass the system. There are a few questions you can ask yourself if your system is getting bypassed:

- What is the purpose of the system? Does the situation require a system? In the case of supply ordering earlier, if only three people order supplies a year, you may not need a system.

- Do people know about the system? Is it communicated in onboarding and training, and refreshed at regular intervals? Is it posted in every available area – both physically and electronically?

- Is the system readily accessible? Hopefully it doesn't require someone to fill out a form in triplicate each and every time. Can people access the system on the go?

- Is the system overly complex? If so, people may avoid it because it is too much work. Now, to be clear, I don't mind if the system causes people to do a little bit of work. Finding out the unit price of a certain type of supply is the work that the requestor should be doing.

No one wants to be passed around like they're at the Department of Motor Vehicles when they are just trying to get materials to do their job. That said, if you create simple, clear, and purposeful systems – where you tell people the why – they are more likely to use these systems to get their jobs done. Ultimately, your roles serve as enablers to help others achieve mission-driven work and you want to create efficient and effective systems to get them there.

Emily's Meeting Tracking System

Emily, whom you met previously when I shared her meeting agenda with her manager, was asked to schedule meetings for her district leadership to be on site at each school over the period of a few spring months. At one level, Emily could jump in and just attack the meeting requests, but she Paused to Plan and created a system! Now, how did Emily's system antennae pop up? She spotted:

■ **Series of connected tasks.** She observed that the project was not one task, but a series of meetings to be scheduled that are interconnected. They needed to be tackled as a group and in sequence.

■ **Increased complexity due to number of people and locations.** Emily noted multiple people and locations were involved, thus increasing complexity.

■ **Communications were required.** Emily didn't want to send a lot of one-off emails explaining these meetings. By realizing they could exist as a group, she could design one large communication introducing purpose and process.

School	Exec 1	Exec 2	Date	Invite sent	Room	Added school list serv	Ordered coffee and donuts
CAMS	J.R.	M.S.	4/26 10:00-11:30	✓	✓	✓	✓
CALS	C.C.	D.B.	4/26 3:00-4:30	✓	✓	✓	✓
BVMS	J.P.	G.L.	4/29 8:00-9:30	✓	✓	✓	✓
CBACS	P.C.	A.A.	5/2 9:30-11:00	✓	✓	✓	☐
BWMS	T.N.	M.N.	5/3 2:00-3:30	✓	✓	✓	☐
CHACS	D.C.	T.S.	5/4 1:30-3:00	✓	✓	✓	✓
LGACS	A.S.	E.O.	5/5 2:00-3:30	✓	✓	✓	✓
EBACS	N.M.	A.M.	5/6 1:30-3:00	✓	✓	✓	☐
EFACS	K.H.	A.G.	5/11 3:00-4:30	✓	☐	✓	☐

Figure 13.6   Emily's System for Tracking Meetings.

She created this tracker to do a few things:

■ **Be the Bird's-eye.** If Emily had just scheduled each meeting individually via email or digital invite, she would have lost sight of the total ecosystem of meetings. This tracker helps her envision the entire series of meetings, noting issues such as too many in a week or her manager running all over town instead of grouping them efficiently by neighborhood.

■ **Close all Loops.** By adding headers such as "Invite Sent" and "Ordered Coffee and Donuts," Emily made sure the small steps were completed for each visit.

■ **Show the Work.** This tracker let her check in with her manager and show the status of each of the upcoming meetings. Emily can hyperlink to this tracker in her one-on-ones with her manager, and give a quick voiceover of what is on track or what is tricky.

Shannon's Staff Exit Checklist

Shannon, a COO at a small network of schools in Chicago, is one of the best Systems Spotters I know. When she realized that staff were entering and exiting their roles over time and noticed each process happening individually – thus taking up a lot of people's time – she immediately knew it was time for (you got it) a *system*. Enter Shannon's Staff Exit Checklist.

Category	Step	Deadline	Notes/Links
Admin	Notify your manager of your intent to depart and your last day	ASAP	
Admin	Email operations@chicagocollegiate.org with your confirmed departure date, once you and your manager have agreed upon it	ASAP	
Admin	Fill out the Departing Staff Info form with how we can reach you if necessary after your departure (e.g. to send you your W-2 next year - make sure to keep us updated if you move in the next 12 months), as well as with all your account and password information	Last Day	Departing Staff Info
Finance	Complete and submit any final receipts for reimbursement	Last Day	
Finance	If you hold a Collegiate credit card, turn in the card to the Admin Asst along with any unsubmitted receipts and a reconciliation form	Last Day	
Technology	Transfer any personal information off of your Collegiate laptop	Last Day	
Technology	Organize/archive all of your work files on your laptop that you want to pass on to your peers/manager/successor and get them to the appropriate people	Last Day	
Technology	Upload any curricular materials to your grade level folder in our shared Google Drive	Last Day	Google Drive
Technology	Transfer any personal information off your Collegiate cell phone and do a factory reset of it, turn off "Find My iPhone"	Last Day	Check with the COO first - if your phone is going to be given to another staff member, it may be helpful to keep some info within it but turn off/delete specific data

Figure 13.7   Shannon's Staff Exit Checklist.

Shannon she did a few things to keep this user-friendly, so it can easily be activated each time she has staff leaving.

■ **Created clear categories.** Shannon broke the steps involved in staff departures into clear categories, such as "finance" and "technology." This can be helpful for seeing which departments handle what, especially when projects are cross-functional.

■ **Gave clear instructions.** She listed each step sequentially, with a high level of detail. She didn't just instruct "turn off your phone." Instead, her guidance is "transfer personal information, do a factory reset." Giving this level of detail ensures that the team handling the phones doesn't have to do a lot of back-end work.

■ **Kept It One-Click.** Because you want to be sure people can follow the checklist without bouncing between multiple documents, Shannon included "Notes and Links." If there are forms or documents associated with a process, they can be easily linked and used. If you want people to do the work, you have to Stand in their Shoes and see how to make it easy on them.

When you find yourself repeatedly typing out the same answers to questions or processes, pick up your head, perk up your antennae, and be all, "I smell the need for a system!" And then take a moment, open a new document, and ask yourself if you had to make this streamlined, simplified, and sustainable for 100 people, how would you do it? Review all of the messages or documents you have sent with instructions, pull out details you may have added one time, and make sure you create a primary checklist that can be used again and again and again!

 Reader Reflection: Do you see any opportunities to create a system and support others?

Now that you have Spotted the Need for Systems for Self, and Systems for Others, let's make sure your systems live in infamy (okay, fine, I took it too far) – or at least last some years – through codification.

THE CALL TO CODIFY – WHY?

Indeed, you might feel that codification – or documenting procedures for future use by yourself and others – is just another thing that takes up time and creates a product that no one will ever look at. But I would argue that codification benefits others, shares knowledge, and reduces the number of questions you get asked (hello!). Yes, it absolutely takes time to codify items, and my assertion here is that the up-front time will ultimately *save* you time in the long run. Picture the next time you are asked to book a venue and you can call upon a list of already researched sites in a particular location. Or, if you want to really Forecast Forward, picture someone else in your role in the future, and think of what a leg up you are giving them in their role.

Eryn's Recruitment Codification

Eryn, a director of operations and communications at a nonprofit in Washington, DC, frequently puts together one-pagers to orient people toward particular happenings or events. Let's peek at one. And a reminder, you can look at the full image over at www.wiley.com/go/togetherteammate.

Eryn has taken the time to clearly name:

- **Roles and responsibilities.** She actually hyperlinks to these, knowing they may change year over year, and this keeps her codification current.

- **Cadence of the recruitment cycle.** This is helpful if someone is picking up this project for the first time and needs to understand the big picture.

- **Documents to create.** A document creation list is useful so that nothing is forgotten!

Why do this? Eryn's creation of this easy-to-manage guide helps her align with her peers and manager, backwards plan, and share work with others. In the event she is no longer in her role, it becomes easy for someone else to pick up the plan!

Recruitment Launch

Communications Roles + Responsibilities
- See here

Communications Cadence + Content
- One Month Prior to Recruitment Launch
    - Update website (after updating appropriate docs, see below)
- **[SLC/Business Development only]** PL and/or ED will send out initial emails to LEAs to set up meetings, as well as one follow-up 2 weeks after initial send.
- **[SLC/Business Development only]** PL and/or ED will track confirmation of meeting dates in business development Excel spreadsheet. EC will do a third follow-up email for those who have yet to reply and schedule.
- Marketing Emails
    - Canva is used for all SLL recruitment marketing emails outside of business development. Make sure to update appropriately and space out marketing images not tied to a deadline (eg apps due in one week), based on how many weeks recruitment is open, any holidays, etc
- Weekly
    - Ask 'EdWorld' orgs to include our blurbs in their newsletters
        - See specific programs for which orgs to work with
- Every Two Weeks
    - LinkedIn
    - Twitter
    - Facebook
- Ongoing
    - Nomination email
    - Invite to interview
    - Acceptance/rejection

Application Process

Documents to Create Before Recruitment Launch**
- Applicant Playbook (PL)
- Interest Form

Figure 13.8 Eryn's Recruitment One-Pager.

FAQ: What if I'm in an organization that never codifies anything? Well, there's no time like the present to begin, right? In some ways, this frees you up to think about the right templates, storage containers, and processes to codify recent processes – essentially giving you a blank slate to have fun with! It will be on you to determine what could most use codification, to carve out time, and to invest others in the process.

Lola's Report Card Codification

Lola, the assistant principal of operations introduced previously, oversees many events and processes at her school that occur year-over-year. Rather than begin by scratch each year, Lola takes the time to make a "Show Flow" for items that happen annually (callback to the Year-at-a-Glance!). Take a glance at this image, and then we can deconstruct the how and the why of this kind of codification.

Wister RP3 Report Card Conference Event Show Flow

Overview of Event:

Event Name	Date	Location	Time
RP3 Report Card Conferences	4/20	In Person at Wister	3-6 pm
	4/27	Virtual	3-6 pm

Event Description and Objective:

The purpose of Parent Conferences is for teachers and families to have the opportunity and space to discuss student's achievements and areas of growth. Conferences should be about 10-15 minutes long. If teachers sense the parent needs more time, a second conference time should be scheduled.

Homeroom teachers are responsible for ensuring that all parents receive conference information and sign up for an appointment time/timeslot. Homeroom teachers should continue to follow-up with parents who do not sign up for an appointment/time slot.

Pre-Event Action Items

Item	Who is responsible?	Deadline
Create Parent Sign Up Form through Parent Square (for virtual and in person)	Ops (Ms. Walker)	4/5
Order Folders	Ops (Ms. Walker)	4/5
Create labels for folders (student name, grade and cohort)	Ops (Ms. Walker)	4/8
Create and send out hard copy report card conference	Ops (Ms. Hackney)	4/4

Figure 13.9 Lola's Report Card Codification.

Lola writes up the following to ensure report card time can run smoothly this year, and in the future. A few things I noticed:

- **Event description and objective.** Have you ever been handed a new project and been like, "So what is the purpose of this?" Me too! Lola took the time to write out the basic description and objective so everyone is on the same page.

- **Pre-event action items.** Lola lists everything that needs to happen before report card night, and then in future years she can simply swap out the dates. No need to write out all of those steps each year. And bonus points for updating this document *after* the event, if anything changes.

- **Detailed timelines.** This is useful for Lola to have laid out so the team can follow it throughout the actual day, but also to see who is responsible for which tasks during report card time.

The point of the past few examples is if you do it once, you will likely be doing it again – and let's let your future self thank your past self. I know that once I created that Girl Scout trip packing checklist in a Google Doc instead of my notebook, it sure made each trip a lot easier to get ready for! Once you have determined what to codify, it then will take some time to determine the best container for that codification.

Consider your codification container:

- **Author.** Who knows the most about the material to be codified? Is it one person or several people?

- **Timing.** Is the form of codification to be read up front once, or referenced regularly?

- **Editability.** No doubt whatever you codify will likely get adjusted over time. Once you "publish" your codification, how often do you edit it? In what format?

- **Home base.** Once you publish it, where is the best "home" for it to live? Does it need to land in an old-fashioned binder? Be put in the employee handbook? On a shared drive? Preloaded on all staff computers?

While it can feel tempting to write an entire book (trust me, I get this instinct) with every single detail, keep in mind that the simpler the codification is, the more people will be able to internalize the message overall. If you can format it in such that it has a high-level table of contents, and materials are loaded in a chronological way, you will find people will take the time to reference it much more often.

TURBO TOGETHERNESS

So what does it take to spot systems to help yourself and others?

■ A willingness to pause, slow down, and observe. What happens repeatedly that could be automated? What are little thorns in your side where a little help could be useful?

■ Courage to share observations and ideas with others. Kendra felt comfortable sending the email requesting a system for icebreakers because we have a partnership where it is encouraged. I love being able to say, "This was a great place you added a system!"

■ Being able to articulate the need for a system and present a concrete idea. Being a Systems Spotter is a bit misleading, I suppose, because I want you to be a Needs-a-System Spotter and Solution Bringer. Let's change the name of the chapter!

Becoming a Systems Spotter will take some practice, some time, and some refining. I find it to be a skill that sets apart a lot of Together Teammates. Rather than just simply reacting to the task placed in front of you, you can take headspace to step back, identify categories or buckets, and then create a system to make things run more smoothly – for yourself and for others. Here is how you can consider yourself on track to identifying and building necessary systems:

■ Identify repeated asks or patterns in your role that create stress-inducing moments.

■ Build systems to make these situations more efficient or effective.

■ Codify as much as possible for ease of use by you and others.

MANAGER MOMENT

Spotting the Need for Systems is an area where your Together Teammate can add a high level of value to your organization – and advance the work efficiently. Add to this some codification of the systems and think how happy you will be when the instructions, guides, or documents are built and codified for a new person to take over in the event your current teammate leaves their position.

■ Encourage your teammate to be a Systems Spotter; when they name something and propose building a process or routine, support them!

■ If you see your colleague in a Total Task mode, observe their work with them and see if there are any patterns where systems could help.

■ Look for opportunities for your teammate to codify their work or the work of the organization, and encourage them to do so.

CHAPTER 14

Own the Outcomes: Take Charge, Especially When You Are Not the Boss!

In some ways, this particular chapter is what inspired this entire book – and this is why it is my last chapter to close out the tools and mindsets offered here. While my hope is the theme of "Owning the Outcomes" comes through strongly throughout this entire text, I also want to use this next chapter to define, inspire, and lay out a process for truly, deeply owning outcomes from start to finish. Granted, this process is closely connected to project management (and yup, in addition to the chapter in this book I wrote a whole entire book on that!), and at the same time I will pull out some nuances and opportunities to deepen this skill as it relates to mindset, outcomes, and creative problem-solving. Whether you are planning a high-stakes fundraising gala, are charged with laying out a complicated decision-making process to select a benefits provider, or are creating welcome bags for new employees, this chapter will assist you with owning the outcomes through to the very end.

In this chapter, you will learn to:

■ Define what deep Outcome Ownership looks like

■ Practice asking specific questions to define the outcome

■ Creatively monitor progress toward the outcome

■ Manage other people as needed to achieve the outcome

The bottom line with deep ownership like this is that I want to empower you to stop and think before just diving in to *do*. With fast-paced, customer-service-oriented roles, the instinct can be to just jump in and start *doing* – because the work is piling up, everyone is hot-potatoing projects left and right, and people want it *right now*. So the call to action in this chapter is to pause and develop deeper ownership over the task. Now, I love crossing things off a list as much as anyone does, but that habit can often lead to less powerful outcomes, costly mistakes, or lack of satisfaction with one's work. When you deeply own the outcome from start to finish, you can likely spot duplications in the work, find more ways to creatively get results, and be more flexible in how goals are met – while feeling confident that you are advancing your organization's mission and work.

Sounds great, right? But how to actually do this in practice is much more challenging. Let's break apart the mindsets, questions, and practices to help you more deeply own outcomes. Some of this is just good project management, but as mentioned earlier, my intention is to push you to go deeper into ownership. Whether you are owning tasks, such as "Get this meeting scheduled," or entire events, such as "Create and run a recruitment event for teacher hiring," or even entire processes, such as "Figure out if our school district should teach cursive," my hope is you will feel deep ownership – and pride – in your results.

The reason I am focused on Outcome Ownership is because it results in you, as a Together Teammate:

■ Achieving stronger results for the organization or team

■ Having deeper job satisfaction through more creative employment of tasks

■ Spotting off-track moments and course correcting along the way

■ Asking for help from others when your own course correction hasn't been enough

WHAT IS OWNING THE OUTCOME AND WHY DOES IT MATTER?

Good question. The definition of this is something I've been pondering for over a decade, and an unhelpful answer is "I know it when I see it." However, to get crystal clear on ownership, I think examples can be illustrative. And let's take an example of a specific assignment that could land in your lap: **"Recruit 50 people to attend the school board forum."**

Owning the outcome start to finish here looks like you taking the time to ask questions to define the task, execute the task, monitor progress toward the goal, and employ other people as needed. Here are some examples of steps an Outcomes Owner would take:

- Gain an understanding of how the recruitment process has (or hasn't) worked in the past. What has driven higher levels of attendance and what has fallen short?

- Build knowledge about the actual possible participants and their preferences for how they best respond and commit to RSVPs.

- Understand stumbling blocks in previous recruitment processes. Where have we lost participants in the past? Do RVSPs need a reminder the night before the event?

- Seek clarity on resources you have to help recruit attendees, such as mailing lists and databases. Is there a budget?

- Send out the invitations and closely monitor progress toward achieving 50 RSVPs – or more!

- Set a timeline to progress monitor how RSVPs are doing. If behind, propose or try another set of outreach strategies.

- Check the progress on the new strategies a few days later by reviewing RSVPs again. Still below what you need?

- Schedule a meeting with colleagues or manager to share data to date, summarize what you have tried, and ask for additional tactics.

- Try those additional tactics and report back on progress toward the 50 RSVPs.

Not owning the outcome looks like designing really cool evites for the event, sending them out, ticking it off your list, and letting the chips fall as they may. If you do this, you will lose sight of the outcome you ultimately own and get stuck in just executing a task.

Deep Outcomes Owners:

- Internalize the absolute goal they are trying to hit (e.g. "50 people *will* be at this school board event.")

- Exhibit confidence they can lead a group to an outcome or recommendation (e.g. "Here are my ideas and tactics to get us to these 50 people.")

- Shepherd every next step along the process (e.g. "Here is my plan to achieve this outcome, and PS I've assigned you all tasks.")

- Close every open loop, question, or task (e.g. "I'm tracking back on each task I assigned, not only for completion, but for efficacy.")

- Can be flexible enough to adjust the plan because of deep understanding of the full process (e.g. "I'm not on track to hit 50, so I need to pause, reassess, and re-execute.")

I want to dive deeper into how to set yourself up, both philosophically and practically, to Own the Outcome.

ASK QUESTIONS TO CLEAR THE COBWEBS (AKA GET CLEAR ON THE OUTCOME)

Sometimes when you are tapped to own a problem or process, it can be easy to just jump into the swirl with everyone else. But trust me, it is a necessary skill to be able to step back, take a moment, and actually make sure the problem or question you are trying to solve is crisp, clear, and aligned with what others think. Yes, Pause to Plan can be applied everywhere.

At its very worst, *shallow* ownership can look like executing tasks and not thinking critically if they are even moving toward the intended outcome. And before you know it, you may spend time, money, and effort on To-Dos that don't build the outcomes you want.

Sometimes you may get asked to Own the Outcome for something that is deeply murky without any obvious answers. It may be a decision that needs to be made, a process that needs to be cleaned up, or a plain old tough question that needs to be answered. These are cases where just answering questions won't equate deep Outcome Ownership, and you have to get in the weeds of process design to lead others to the best outcome. Let's read about a few examples of how Together Teammates have Owned the Outcomes of a murky project or process – remembering a Together Try-It of Clear the Cobwebs.

Lauren Asks Questions to Own the Project

Lauren, a member of The Together Team, was charged with figuring out when and how we can resume our in-person open enrollment Together Leader trainings. My delegation sentence was "Can you please research DC venues and send me options to make the decision of where we host the training?" Fuzzy at best, right? Lauren put on her Together Teammate hat and came back to ask questions.

Lauren did a lot of beautiful things in reaction to my fuzzy request, "Please research venues." Let's see what we can learn:

- **Recommendation Ready.** For each question Lauren asked me, she proposed answers that reflected past research (such as what time we held the sessions) or AV needs (which Kendra briefed her on).

- **Process and context laid out.** Lauren noted she had already reached out to a member of our team, Kendra, for a pre-conversation and she closed her email with when the result could come back to me (middle of the week). This builds trust because Lauren is Closing the Loops and Showing Her Work.

> **From:** Lauren
> **Date:** Wednesday, January 18, 2023 at 12:47 PM
> **To:** maia, kendra
>
> **Subject:** Venue planning parameters for in-person PS in DC
>
> Hi Maia, (FYI Kendra)
>
> As Kendra and I begin to plan for the in-person Together Leader public session on May 11, the first step would be for us to secure a venue. As we start this process, we have a couple of questions to help guide our venue research:
>
> - What time would you like to hold the session? Would it be 8:30 AM – 4:30 PM as it has been in the past?
> - Would you like for us to set up the space 2 hours prior (~6:30 AM)? Or the night before, if the venue allowed it?
> - How big is your target audience? Should we be looking for space for 50-75? 75-100?
> - Do you have any guidance on price? From what I can see, in the past we've spent between $5k (without catering) and $9k (including catering) for event spaces, but prices might have increased due to COVID.
> - Aside from the Management Center, Convene, and the National Union Building, all of which we've used in the past, are there any other venues that you'd like for us to look into?
> - Is there anything we're not thinking of regarding venue? Kendra has debriefed me on AV needs (projector, 1-2 large screens, speakers, high speed internet, lavalier/headphone mic, etc.) but let me know if there's more that we need.
>
> After we look into venues to see if we're able to secure a space in the current time frame, we can move on to next steps. Our goal is to get you at least 3 venue options by the middle of next week.
>
> Best,
>
> LFL

Figure 14.1   Lauren's Clarifying Questions.

■ **Narrow parameters.** There is a world when someone is asked to locate a venue and they enter in a Google search "DC Event Space," and forward a bunch of links. That is the opposite of Outcome Ownership. Lauren's questions show her narrowing the task so she can deeply own the research.

Let's look at an even more complex situation, Jen's determination of whether a summer training should move online.

Jen's In-Person versus Remote Training Decision

Jen, a nonprofit operations leader, described a pandemic decision that needed to be made about in-person teacher training. Jen and a small team of people were tasked with figuring out the answer to this question in a very compressed timeline, and without much information about COVID-19 at the time.

In this case, Jen stepped back and asked herself:

■ What is the real question we are trying to answer? *In this case, it was how to best train teachers in the midst of an unknown pandemic.*

■ What are the key problems we are trying to solve for? *In this case, it was asking: What can we let go of? What parts of our training are negotiable versus non-negotiable?*

■ What are the parameters to guide the decision? *Jenn's manager was clear about a certain timeline by which the decision needed to be made, in order to communicate to others.*

■ Who else needs to be involved in the process? *Jenn's manager identified someone with instructional knowledge, someone who understands the board and executive directors. This gave Jen a team of content experts to help Clear the Cobwebs.*

■ What is the best "container" for the information? In other words, how do we package it for others? *Jen had to figure out if this should be a PowerPoint, a memo, or a chart. Does she send it before the decision-making meeting or give it in real time?*

■ What is our working process to get there? *Are we co-working? Brainstorming independently?*

■ Where does a recommendation get shared? *Jenn knew her manager would take her team's work to the board on a certain date.*

Granted, Clearing the Cobwebs by asking clarifying questions for this kind of murk is not easy, but it is deeply necessary and incredibly rewarding. You may be wondering how on earth could you lead a process like this when you are not the content or subject-matter expert, but Together Teammates possess skills to ask the right questions to educate themselves as needed and stay process-oriented to ensure the process leads to a clear outcome. Jen's job was not to make the actual decision, but she was charged with coordinating the various people who had the content knowledge. Jen's real job – and value add – was to lead the *process* of bringing the decision to the finish line. She did this by assembling the people, creating the time, asking the questions, and ultimately presenting the recommendation.

 Reader Reflection: Consider your current task. What questions can you ask to get clear on the absolute outcome?

Got it? Your job is to ask questions to deeply understand and internalize the absolute outcome. Tracking progress toward the outcome comes next.

TRACK PROGRESS TOWARD THE OUTCOME

It can be very, very easy to just toss an email out in the world ("Hey boss, here is what I noticed when reviewing the surveys") and then it falls into the vortex of others' very busy schedules . . . and gets stuck there. And then two weeks later, your manager is like "Where is the survey situation?" Oops.

Now I understand the instinct to just lob a task out there and expect it to come back, but the truth is that you have to track each open loop. By that I mean that every item you toss out there must have some sort of deadline, tracker, or reminder so you can follow up if it doesn't come back.

Let's look at a few examples of tracking progress and closing loops when you Own the Outcomes. Oh yeah, why is this important again? Because you are not simply box-checking robots, but rather you are carefully overseeing important processes and projects start to finish. Let's review several examples. (Sidenote: All of these next examples are from our internal Together Group operations. Imagine working for me and the pressure of having to demonstrate all of these Together Try-Its *all the time*.)

Heidi Closes a Loop – with a Bow!

Heidi was charged with owning The Together Group's entire website redesign process, start to finish, and of course, bumps come up along the way. When there was an unexpected recent error, Heidi didn't just send an email to the vendor to fix it; she Owned the Outcome. Let's see what she did.

While this looks like a simple email, it demonstrates a lot of Together Try-Its all at once:

- **Showed the Work.** Rather than her manager (me) wondering about the status of the urgent website fix, Heidi Showed the Work by letting us know, "I'll keep pinging them today until I get the assurance they will fix it ASAP." This also builds trust with the team because we all know we can count on Heidi.

- **Closed the Loop.** Heidi also quickly let us know she had handled replies directly to people who hadn't been able to find what they needed on the website, so we knew those emails were not outstanding.

- **Tied that loop with a bow!** And one step further here: Heidi says she will let us both know when the website is fixed.

As the recipient of this email on a very busy day, I breathed a huge sigh of relief. To recap, there was a big website issue, and Heidi jumped in, Owned the Outcome, and communicated about her plan to track progress until the issue was solved.

From: Heidi
Sent: Thursday, January 26, 2023 9:30 AM
To: Maia
Subject: Toolkit / website update!

Hi Maia and Lauren,

I am still waiting for Alter to respond, but I'll keep pinging them today until I get assurance that they will fix it asap.

Meanwhile, all 4 people who Maia forwarded yesterday have received the toolkit they wanted (some only responded to me and I wrote back directly).

From now on, Lauren can handle any other requests – she has all four pdfs. I'll follow up with both of you when the website is fixed!

Thanks,

Heidi

Figure 14.2 Heidi Owns the Outcome.

Heidi Requests Others Show the Work

There may be other times when you toss a task to someone and think it is off your plate, but it is not. You may want or need complete and absolute evidence that the task is completed – not because you are trying to micromanage people, but because you are committed to Owning the Outcome, no matter what the level of task. Here is an example that happens in my world often: I get asked to do some kind of administrative task – something only I can do, as the CEO – but it is not *my* top priority, and then it gets delayed.

Heidi needed me to issue a refund. Peek on the next page to see what happened.

Heidi didn't just lob the task at me and cross it off her own Weekly Worksheet. She did a few things to ensure she was tracking the outcome to the end:

- **Provided the context.** This ensured I didn't have to write her back and say, "What on earth is this about?" Heidi anticipated my questions and provided context, and this enabled her to get an action from me more quickly.

- **Gave details to take the task to completion.** I didn't have to say, "Which address?" "Where do I send this?" Heidi provided all details for me to finish the work.

- **Tracked it carefully on her Weekly Worksheet.** There are many ways you can keep track of your progress, but often Weekly Worksheets or Comprehensive Calendars do the trick quite nicely! (Full disclosure, she did have to email me twice before I actually sent the check. If I hadn't sent her this evidence, she would have kept pinging me on a regular basis until it was done!)

FAQ: What do you mean by Closing Loops? You have seen this before, on the Together Try-It List. One of the most Together Teammate Try-Its I have seen over the past two decades is the ability to ensure Loops are Closed – in other words, seeing them through to the bitter end. Closing the Loop is a term borrowed from the business world, and it basically means following up to ensure the task is done. I think of it as an essential part of Owning the Outcome. Consider it an essential part of your job to Track the Loops to the finish line (mixing metaphors here!), but what I mean is that if you delegate or request an item to be done, be sure you have a way to check that it is finished. This may mean a way to track an email you sent out to make sure it was responded to and then a system for following up with people until the Loop is Closed.

From: Maia

Date: Monday, November 1, 2021 at 3:32 PM

To: Heidi

Subject: evidence! RE: TASK: Issue refund to STEM Charter School

---

STEM CHARTER SCHOOL – Vendor

Pay from	Amount	Send on	Deliver by	Status
CHK (...1234)	S1,475.00	Nov 1, 2021	Nov 8, 2021	Funded

Memo	Transaction number
Invoice (TG-3270)	123456789

From: Heidi

Date: Wednesday, October 27, 2021 1:10 PM

To: Maia

Subject: RE: TASK: Issue refund to STEM Charter School

Hello, Maia!

Please issue a refund to STEM Charter School (details below).

Context:

■ They paid twice for the same invoice. This refunds one of the two payments.

Reach out with any questions.

Thank you!

Heidi

Check amount: $1,425

Make check out to: STEM Charter School

Memo: Invoice TG-3270

Address:

314 North 15th Street
Lansdale, OH 12345

Figure 14.3 Heid's Task Assignment to Close the Loops.

Kendra Assigns a Contract Signature

It is likely you will end up assigning tasks to others to execute because it is something only they can do. Let's look at an example of something I was required to get notarized for a school district. Of course, the members of my team could have just sent me an email with the attachment and said, "Please sign this."

But Kendra knows my days are full of teaching and writing, and my inbox is out of control, so a one-off message like this is, sadly, likely to be ignored. And since she is striving to Close the Loops of all of her stuff and to deeply Own the Outcome, she knows she needs to make sure it gets signed, while still being protective of my time. So she did the exercise of Standing in Someone's Shoes – fully recognizing that my priority wouldn't be this task. But she got it done anyway. Let's see how this happened.

What magic did Kendra use to get me to do this task? Let's take her email apart and see what we can learn:

- **Complete any prework.** Kendra pre-completed as much of the vendor form as possible, only leaving items she was unsure about.

- **Specifically assign tasks.** She named the exact tasks I was supposed to do, right down to the signing locations. There is zero ambiguity.

Hi Maia,

For the DeKalb form, here are your steps:

1. Please print the attached PDF. You can just print pages 3-6, if you prefer.
2. Please double check the answers I checked off for you, specifically:
    a. On Page 3 of the PDF: For #2, I think 2b is the best choice to check off. Does that look right?
    b. On Page 4 of the PDF: Are you OK with initialing #5? I have no idea what this is.
3. Please have the forms signed and notarized. You'll see two signing locations – on pages 4 and 6 of the PDF.
4. Please scan the signed and notarized form back to me.
5. Please also send me a scanned copy of your driver's license.

Additional notes:

- I will send the completed form to them.
- They want it back ASAP but I think your deadline of Wed or Thurs is fine, especially with the date change.

Thanks,

Kendra

Figure 14.4   Kendra Assigns a Task.

- **Include timelines and dates.** Kendra included a timeline, and bonus points that she helped me find space on my calendar to do so.

- **Add supplemental information.** Kendra flagged that she needed a copy of my driver's license! And knowing Kendra, she'll store that so she never needs to ask again.

Now, I'm going to be honest. I had a busy week, and this task involved me finding a notary. Plain and simple, I didn't want to complete this, but Kendra made it so much easier on me to do so. And that resulted in it actually happening, rather than me putting it off until later, thereby frustrating the vendor and leaving Kendra with this task still undone.

TOOLS AND MINDSETS FOR ASSIGNING SOMEONE A TASK TO EXECUTE

It doesn't matter if this is your boss, a direct report, a colleague, or a volunteer (or heck, even a spouse or partner), our job is to ensure the job gets done because we are Outcomes Owners – not just Task Tossers. So let's make sure we can help someone play their role in achieving the outcome.

- **Get in the person's head.** Will they find this task annoying? Exciting? Last minute? Frustrating? Be aware of the mood it could bring up for someone. For me, it is tough to fit in an errand with only a few days' notice, as in the previous example.

- **Figure out the preferred mode of delegation.** Does the person do better if items are hard copy and paperclipped or is it better to email or text them? Consider your audience each time, and use your knowledge of how they are most likely to respond to figure out the best method of assigning the task.

- **Do any pre-work to move the process along.** Is there a form you can complete or even half-complete to reduce the time needed from the other person? An email you can draft or ghost-write for the person and all they have to do is copy-paste-send?

- **List out all the steps to complete the task.** I would even say make this a numbered list rather than a bulleted list. Every single step counts. I sometimes call this "dummy proofing the task." This ensures they are easier to reference (e.g. Did you complete item 3?).

- **Consider any materials or supplies needed to complete the task**, otherwise known as One-Clickable in our Together Try-Its. For example, does the task require a printer? A scanner? Stamps? A certain kind of envelope? Rather than ask someone to send a sympathy card, have the card ready, the address researched, and just have them write the note in real time with you.

(Continued)

> ■ **Make note of any deadlines.** You might even offer to help the person find times in their calendar, if they prefer. A very real example of this for me recently was when a member of my team was the Outcomes Owner of getting our new website launched. I was struggling to make time to review some key content, and Heidi helped me identify time on my calendar and co-worked beside me.
>
> ■ **Follow-up, follow-up, follow-up.** Never assume that just because the task is assigned, it is done. You toss a task into the world, and you bet you have to chase it back. You may email your manager and think, "Phew, that is crossed off my list," but it isn't truly off your list until you see evidence that your manager has completed the task.

Let's peek at an even more complex example – managing a group of people to prepare for a board meeting.

Sophie's Board Meeting Prep Assignments

Sophie was the Outcomes Owner of board meeting preparation, and it involved a lot of people! Her charge was to solidify the agenda and prepare the slides. This goes beyond the task-like examples you saw previously. Keep in mind that, like many of you, Sophie was not the decision-maker for the board agenda, but in her Together Teammate role as chief of staff, she played a key role in gathering, summarizing, curating, and preparing the information – and leading the team through the process! Let's peek at what she did in the following image.

Moving something as complex as a board presentation forward is certainly a challenge, especially when you may lack "formal authority." One may be thinking, "This is so complicated, we better schedule a meeting to talk it through!" That is an option, but the challenge may be in actually securing the meeting – especially if it is a one-off for team members with some very busy schedules – or perhaps the work actually needs to be accomplished individually and wouldn't happen during a meeting anyhow.

So, what did Sophie do in this situation?

■ **Name the product to accomplish** (board deck) **and by when** (April 8). Even though this may be one of your most important projects, it could be easy to let it fall by the wayside of other people's lists because they have their *own* priorities.

From: Sophie
Sent: Tuesday, March 22, 2022 10:08 AM
To: Executive Team, Janet, Jordan
Subject: April Board meeting

Hi everyone,

Attached is the draft agenda for the April 13 board meeting, please take a look and share any feedback. And please add your slides to the deck by Friday, April 8.

A few questions –

DH	Because you'll be on PTO that day, who will you be designating to respond to the public comment?
AR	Can you and the academic committee share out on the curriculum, schedule and calendar changes? Is there also new data to share, along with a reminder that we're in testing season now and any information to be shared about that?
CM & AP	We should update the board on our new approach to scheduling and where we are in the calendaring project. By the board meeting, will we have shared with school leaders, or will that be after spring break?

Thank you!

Figure 14.5 Sophie's Board Prep with the Executive Team.

■ **Flag any issues with roles and responsibilities early.** Forecast Forward Frequently! Here Sophie noted a member of the executive team would be out of office on the actual board day. If Sophie hadn't previewed that, it might not have been on anyone's radar until too late.

■ **Know who is responsible for which sections of the process.** Even though Sophie is not intimately familiar with all content of the board conversations, she knows enough to know who is responsible and the experts on each section.

■ **State exactly what she needs the group to do and make it easy for them to do so.** In Sophie's case, she prebuilt a set of slides, and gave everyone guidance on how to add their version to the actual deck.

- **Keep everyone informed on where everyone else is within the process.** Sophie was the Bird's-eye for the team. For example, rather than Sophie sending individual emails to each person, it is helpful for them to all observe each other's roles in the process.

- **Give multiple options.** In the cases where Sophie is not sure of the exact information, she is offering up other options, such as bumping topics to executive committee sessions and so on.

Owning the Outcome with multiple people is never easy, but it is possible – and it is a unique value add to your organization. Think about it. There is likely no one else positioned to shepherd an important product, project, or process to the finish line while making it as easy as possible on those involved, and it is helpful to remember this is a tremendous asset to your place of work.

FAQ: What if I do all of this, and I *still* don't get the results I need? Oh, you mean people missing the deadlines, not engaging, and the like? Sure thing, and this happens all the time. A few things to keep in mind:

- **Stand in the Shoes of Others.** Hold a meeting or write some sort of kickoff email to get everyone bought into the process. In the case of recurring events, such as a board meeting, or a regular process, such as receipt processing, it may help to review once per year and get feedback from others on the approach.

- **Make it Multiple Choice.** Give recommendations, options, or limited choices to force a decision.

- **Offer to co-work with the individuals** (or enlist their assistants, if they have them) to help create a situation where they can tell you how to fill in the blanks, while not taking over total ownership for the content.

- **Name the impact of them not engaging early and often enough**, such as that their information won't make it to the board, and so on.

HOW TO MECHANICALLY TRACK OPEN LOOPS

If your role requires you to manage multiple projects, push various people to action, and ensure things are tied up neatly, you may find you need to maintain a larger tracker of open loops. I recently asked Kendra, a Together Teammate you have heard a lot about, to share how she tracks all of these on a weekly or daily basis.

Waiting For (Work)
☐ TL S19 C4 PPT deck back from Maia?
☐ TL S10 C4 PPT deck back from Maia?
☐ Rec'd final counts & pre-work for classes taking place the week of 2/6?

Figure 14.6   Kendra's Open Loop Tracker.

Kendra is charged with keeping a lot of trains moving on time behind-the-scenes at The Together Group. I recently got a glance at her magic, and she said, "Once I assign someone something to work on, I add it to my 'Work Waiting Fors' section in OneNote (where I keep my Weekly Worksheet) to check back if I haven't seen it come through. In other words, if I haven't gotten the materials I'm waiting for by 3 p.m., I re-ping the person to remind them I need a response to continue to move my work forward." Boom! Now I see the behind-the-scenes of those gentle reminders she sends when she hasn't yet gotten what she needs from me!

 Reader Reflection: How will you track all open loops – both in communication with others and for yourself?

TURBO TOGETHERNESS

This chapter focused on a slightly less tangible part of Togetherness, but a portion I see as invaluable in moving important work ahead. Building your muscles to move from Task Ownership to Outcome Ownership takes more work, sure, but it also positions you as an invaluable member of the team. Anyone (well, not quite anyone) can get things done, but driving ahead an entire process – especially murky-never-been-solved-processes – is a whole other level.

■ When assigned a task or process, ask clarifying questions so you can deeply understand the outcome desired. Keep in mind that the Pause to Plan will always save you time and pain later.

■ Once you are clear on the outcome, carefully map out in detailed steps how you believe you will achieve that outcome.

■ Pause to check along the way and monitor your progress – for yourself or to share with others – to see if you are on track to hit the outcome.

■ When you are charged with leading a group to an outcome, consider how they best give and receive information, and don't be scared to pitch in with co-work or getting Recommendation Ready.

■ And lastly, Close those Loops and tee up recommendations.

The beauty of Outcome Ownership is it often gives you deeper understanding into the overall mission of the organization, allows creative solutions to hit goals, and is an area where I'm utterly convinced Together Teammates can shine in supporting their organizations.

MANAGER MOMENT

How can you help a teammate cultivate a mindset of Owning Outcomes? This is a very, very hard question, but indeed I have thoughts on the topic. I see Owning Outcomes as a two-way street, and while hiring someone who thinks deeply and critically about all tasks and projects is part of it, I also think these are muscles we can build and enable as managers. Here are a few ways to do this:

- From the beginning, share examples of Task Ownership and Outcome Ownership and name what you expect for all tasks.

- Model thinking aloud with an example of Task Ownership (schedule meeting) to Outcome Ownership. (What is the purpose of the meeting? Who is it with?)

- Help your teammate put themselves in someone's shoes and ask themselves questions from that person's perspective. Job shadowing works well to build this.

- Encourage your teammate to think critically about every single task or project that comes their way. "Why do we do it this way? Is there a better way to get this done? What are we really trying to accomplish?"

- Delegate items with the task or goal in mind. Resist the urge to hand over one-off tasks, and really think about the project or goal. Instead of "Find a location for the staff holiday party," you may have your team member *own* the outcome for the entire holiday party. This doesn't mean they get license to make all decisions; they should work with you to figure out how you want to lean in and why.

Together Test

So you made it. Step by step, chapter by chapter, you have prioritized, planned, forecasted, communicated, categorized, and more. But to what end? Your Total Together System – whatever that looks like – should ultimately serve to ensure you are successful in your role and you can sustain it over time. So I know I didn't warn you that there would be a test, but what kind of teacher would I be if I didn't do a little check for understanding? Get your pen or keyboard ready, and let's test your Together Tools. I'm looking to see how you would think about each situation and how you would process the information.

Together Test Reader Reflection

1. You receive an email full of action items related to the budget planning process, and it looks like two or three hours of work. It is all due in about five days. What do you do next?

2. You are in the middle of creating new slides for the upcoming board meeting (the slides are due by end of day), and your manager drops by with a "fabulous idea" for staff training next year. How do you respond?

3. You are two months into your new role, and you realize that you don't have any idea what's coming in the next few months. How do you resolve this issue?

4. You are walking down the hall on the way to lead a professional development session for the new hires on HR policies, and a senior leader stops you to get your advice on a hiring situation. What do you say?

5. About a year into your role, you realize that a system for supply purchasing is already in place. But no one uses it and instead everyone just sends one-off emails and texts and Slacks. What do you do?

6. At the end of the day, you realize you spent the entire day answering quick emails to people – which were important – but you made no progress on updating the marketing materials for the scholarship program, a key priority for the week. What do you do for the next day?

7) You are handed a very big project with a tight timeline: rebuild the organization's website. Where do you start?

8) It is up to you to draft the internal organization's newsletter, for which everyone can send in contributions. How do you set up this process?

9) You see an upcoming meeting on your calendar for next week, and you are not sure what role you are supposed to play in preparation. How do you clarify?

10) You are expected to clear out the training inbox on a weekly basis. How do you make sure this gets done?

There are not necessarily exact right answers to these questions. What I care about is that *you*, dear reader, have the confidence to be able to tackle these situations or your own real-life set like them. I want you to have clarity on your Togetherness, tools to support your work, and mindsets to make it manageable and meaningful. You can even design your own Together Test questions with a role-alike colleague and explore how *they* keep it Together. There's always more to learn about Togetherness – take it from someone who learns something new in each class I teach!

CHAPTER 15

Togetherness Is a Journey, Not a Destination

Well, I saved this chapter for the end. It is called the conclusion, after all. But I did wait to draft it until I completed the rest of the text. I am sitting here by candlelight at 4:30 a.m., surrounded by 100-plus boxes of Girl Scout cookies that need to get delivered or eaten, four sleeping children (including two in the same bed because another child has COVID, so she has the basement to herself), four cats chasing each other loudly, a pile of both clean and dirty laundry, and a likely sleeping husband (he gets a huge shoutout in the Acknowledgments). On the flip, there is challah French toast waiting to be cooked in a few short hours (hot breakfast Wednesdays are a thing in my house), my Outlook Calendar is set with details for the week, backpacks and homework have been laid out at the door (by the kids, not me!), and I presume each child has clean (likely unmatched) socks to wear to school today. I paint this picture because it is illustrative of how I view Togetherness. Choose where it matters to you – in work and life – and dial it down where it doesn't (helloooo, massive sock bin full of singles in my house). I am not, I repeat *not*, asking you to be uber-Together in every single move you make, but rather to assess where it has the most impact and don't worry where it doesn't. Perfection is not a thing around here (#recovering).

317

In this chapter, you will learn to:

■ Reconnect to the why of your work (if you wish)

■ Integrate this text in your ongoing work

■ Sequence your learning in a way that works for you

■ Have a process for resetting days (or weeks!) that go off the rails

I waited to write this section last because I truly wanted to create a wrap-up that could take you to the finish line and help you experience your work as manageable and meaningful. Maybe you read this entire book in one sitting (in which case, I humbly offer you a power nap), or maybe you enjoyed it chapter by chapter on an as-needed basis, or maybe (no shade), this text has been sitting on your office shelf for a year and you just turned to it in a moment of Together 911 (this happens). Regardless of how you read it, you did it, and here we are at the end-ish Together. Let's close with recalling why your work matters, how you could use this text or practices in your ongoing work, ways to sequence the learning, and how you can reset when your day goes off the rails – because it will! (Of course, that is okay because you are well equipped to Powerfully Pivot – one of my favorite Together Try-its!).

RECALL THE MEANING OF YOUR WORK

Inevitably, even though your work is mostly mission-driven, there will be times when a day still feels composed entirely of monotonous meetings, endless emails, and work that doesn't feel fun or connected. We have all been there. If this happens, consider recalling your why. I remember that in my years working in the back office of a large charter management organization, if I hit a wall, I would try to find fifteen minutes to sit in a kindergarten classroom. That charged me up real fast.

Perhaps you have been in your organization for a long time, or maybe you are new. If you feel like you know everything there is to know about your place of work, then by all means, skip this section! But, if you feel like you could use a refresher, or that things may have changed underneath you without you even being aware (this has happened to me!), it may be helpful to build or rebuild your sense of the organization.

What initially attracted you to your organization? I'm asking this question because it can be helpful to recall your thoughts here. If you were attracted to the mission of preserving the natural world, or registering voters, or college access, then it could be helpful to consider a way to remain connected to the core of the mission – even if you are working behind the scenes. This may look like carving out time once per week to tutor students directly, register voters during voter drives, or clean up trails. A word of warning that you will never, ever, ever feel like you have time to do this, but by making the time to do it, you will ensure you stay connected and feel like your work matters. For example, if you play a behind-the-scenes role in voter registration efforts, say by building databases, you will likely start to feel particularly removed from your mission if you don't have a few times in your calendar to do door-to-door voter registration or work at the polls yourself. This is completely optional, of course, but seeing the impact of your work can do wonders for your daily morale. I recommend working to build it into your actual job description so it is not an after-hours kind of thing.

Consider ways you can reconnect with the mission when things feel dreary or monotonous. Having a plan in place will help you quickly get re-connected.

- **Observe or participate directly within your mission.** Join a book sorting day for your literacy nonprofit? Or supervise a school field trip to see kids in action? Or talk with recipients of your organization's mission? Even better than doing any of these things reactively is to build them into your schedule on an ongoing basis.

- **Re-read anything you wrote before you worked at this particular location.** Maybe you had a compelling cover letter of what attracted you to the organization? Or a personal story of the mission mattered to you?

- **Create visual reminders.** This one sounds cheesy, but do you need photos on your bulletin board of your organization's impact? Actual numbers of people served? Pictures of the houses built? Books distributed? I know keeping framed pictures at my desk of my first few classes of fourth and fifth grade students sure motivated me one year I was buried in reviewing school leader applications!

- **Save those kudos.** If people have ever sent you thank-yous or appreciations, save them in one location. One of the best pieces of advice from a former boss of mine was to create a Kudos folder (I still have one!) to scroll through on the days when you could use a little boost.

After finding a way to remain directly connected to your organization's mission, you may also find it helpful to remain connected to what is happening overall within your organization. This could look like reading board notes, attending student performances, or glancing through the annual report. Even in a support role, you have the opportunity to represent your organization and its mission – and staying current is helpful. You may even want to set up Google alerts for any media mentions of your organization and follow it on all social media.

Yes, this will take you extra time (and should be built into your Weekly Worksheet), but it will be worth it when you have the ease of familiarity with all your organization's initiatives and projects, and a sense of the big picture of the organization's work. You know, Be the Bird's-eye and all!

FAQ: What if no opportunities are readily available to connect to the mission? They may not be, especially if your organization is small. I recall a former executive assistant of mine in a large charter school district – who eventually ended up becoming a teacher – being interested in tutoring in a classroom while she handled her administrative and project-based role. No options were readily available for her, so she took it upon herself to create an opportunity to remain directly connected to the mission. Yes, it took her some extra work, and yes, she had to fit it into her schedule, but she communicated about it to me – her manager – and we made it happen. And if you want your job to be your job, and you don't feel the need to see the mission at hand, that is completely okay too.

Reader Reflection: If you choose, how will you stay connected with your organization's work?

WALK THE TOGETHERNESS PATH WITH OTHERS

There are lots of ways people read my books, and I want to offer you a few follow-ups to deepen your Togetherness Takeaways. Let's think about self-studies, peer cohorts, show and tells, and group learning.

Complete a Self-Study Through Individual Reflection

If you didn't take time to answer the Reader Reflections on your first pass through the book, go back and read them again (it ages well, I promise!) with the space to complete the answers. You can either jot your responses in the text as you go or print out a copy of the questions from the book's website at www.wiley.com/go/togetherteammate. I find it helpful to refer back to answers I've written over time, and my answers evolve based on my job or my life at the moment. Another way to do this is to set a timeline with a peer, and swap examples and Try-Its at the end of each chapter.

Read and Practice with Others

Maybe you want some accountability and you want to discuss what you learned? Consider reading along for a second time with a trusted group of peers. I have seen from my in-person and online classes that having people to chat with along the way is a powerful way to practice your learning. I have seen people set a reading schedule over a semester and commit to two or three lunches to discuss. Or you could go systematically chapter by chapter. It's up to you, but the point is to try to achieve accountability for yourself and to learn from others. There are so many ways you can be Together, and I'm always blown away by what people create and share with each other – hence why I have included so many samples in this text!

Share Learnings with Your Manager or Mentor

As you think through your own learning and development – no matter where you are in your career path – it can be powerful to share observations, show off your tools ("Well, let me check my Weekly Worksheet about that new request and get back to you!"), practice your Together Try-Its ("I'm Pausing to Plan my week, but I can share more about my capacity after that process"), and generally make sure your Togetherness supports your overall work. I use the term "manager" throughout the book, but maybe that individual doesn't have time to engage with you, so you may process with a trusted mentor instead.

 Reader Reflection: Are there others in your world who could support your learnings around Togetherness?

A BONUS FOR YOU! CREATE A PEER COHORT FOR YOURSELF

Unless you work in a very large organization with a lot of people in similar roles, it is unlikely you have a formal cohort of peers. In most cases, you will need to establish this yourself. But, Maia, isn't that more work? At one level yes, but I believe you will see more satisfaction in your role – and stronger results – if you take the time to do this up front. Emily, a special assistant with a charter school network in Brooklyn, describes how she and the other special assistants meet to help figure out upcoming projects, schedule meetings, or give updates. Another former assistant of mine set up regular lunches with folks in similar roles once per month, and I once even saw a chief of staff take the lead in organizing these for operations team members.

- Grab a weekly working session to review Project Plans and scheduling requests
- Have a monthly off-site lunch to recharge and rejuvenate
- Create a brown bag lunch series with each person presenting on a different best practice
- Daily huddle to review existing Project Plans for fast-moving projects

YOU ARE NOW A TOGETHER TEAMMATE! (YOU PROBABLY ALREADY WERE)

You've graduated! We did it! You are a Together Teammate! You have:

- A clear description of your role and measurable goals to define your work

- A Year-at-a-Glance to build your understanding of cyclical events and tasks

- A Comprehensive Calendar with all of your deadlines and due dates in a single location

- Project Plans that break down complex outcomes into bite-size steps

- A Long-Term List to track *all* of those action steps

- A Weekly Worksheet that has your priorities, schedule, and little list for the week

- A weekly Meeting with Myself checklist to clean up the week behind you and prepare for the week ahead

- Orderly inboxes that let you handle messages with ease and efficiency

- Methods to handle the inevitable Daily Deluge of requests, messages, and changes

- Carefully crafted outgoing messages that make it easy for others to reply

- Meetings designed with thoughtful preparation and detailed questions

- Forecasted into the future for yourself, and for your organization

- Spotted the need for systems, and designed them for future use

- Deeply owned outcomes for projects you own and across the organization

I hope you feel great! Empowered! Excited! Like the work is manageable! Like you understand your connection and importance to the mission!

But (and I feel a bit like a Dr. Suess book), when the dark Un-Togetherness Times come – and oh, they will – you are now prepared to use your Together Teammate moves. This *will* happen. Let's start with expecting that no day will go as planned. You work in dynamic environments with real-life humans, *and* you may have days when the dog gets sick, a kid needs to get picked up at school early, or the car needs immediate servicing. This is when your Together Tools matter the most. They help you anticipate the challenges and react well in the moment. At the same time, you should also not assume the entire day will blow up on you every minute all day long. Hopefully the Together Tools in this book have helped you emerge from that level of daily chaos.

And when things do get Un-Together, don't be too hard on yourself. We all have those days, trust me! Sometimes I have to take a few hours to Re-Together myself. It helps to do the following:

■ **Build in some buffer.** Build some buffer into your calendar for when you know things may be scrambled. If you often get pulled into preparation for board meetings at the last minute, let's add some buffers so you can be ready for this.

■ **Prioritize carefully – and communicate accordingly.** Before you jump into problem-solving mode, take a minute to look at your calendar. What might get delayed or bumped? Take a few minutes to communicate the changes.

■ **Make a mental reset.** Have a plan to mentally reset yourself and regroup back to regularly scheduled programming. Some of the things that pull our days off track are emotional or taxing or both. Have a plan to "re-Together" yourself. Maybe it's a quick walk outside or some deep breaths. It doesn't have to be a go-to-the-mountaintops retreat plan, but just five minutes of how to return to center.

TOTAL TOGETHER TOURS

While each chapter spotlights one individual Together Tool, I don't want you to lose sight of the fact that each is part of a greater whole. Ultimately, I want to ensure you have a Totally Together System to get you cruising through the day, forecasting out months, and showing the shape of the entire year. One challenge I see is people have a tendency to add systems without thinking through the time and effort it may take to keep all these systems maintained. So I have a few guidelines as you think about your very own Totally Together System.

1. **Streamline your Together Tools.** It can be easy to have a Project Plan in one tool, a digital Comprehensive Calendar in another place, and two notebooks for two different kinds of meetings. Look for opportunities to streamline and consolidate. This may look like you deciding to exist in Outlook and OneNote or Google and Asana or a homemade paper planner. Try to select just two things and seek to land your system within that. We have several great videos on the accompanying book website with more ideas on this.

2. **Everything in its place – the first time.** This is the same idea as the common advice that everything in your house should have a spot. So should everything in your system! Short-term action steps? Boom! Passwords? Check! Meeting Prep time blocks?

You got it! Look, no one has the time to be flipping through a notebook trying to dig up action steps. As you are taking notes in meetings, ask yourself, "How could I get this in my calendar or on my weekly To-Do list immediately?" And if that doesn't work for you, make sure you have an airtight "catching tool" (like Dr. Together's notebook in his back pocket at all times!) and then you can sort them back into the appropriate Together Tool later.

3. **Make the priorities pop.** Your system should highlight your priorities, primarily to keep yourself focused *and* to allow you to share them with others as needed. You may have to hack up some existing tools to make this happen. For example, nothing in your Outlook calendar forces you to prioritize, so you have to do that heavy lifting yourself. Show your priorities in your calendar by making them all-day appointments across the top of a week or highlight them in your paper planner. On any given day, there are likely a million things you could be doing. Carve out the time to do your deeper work.

4. **Keep your eye on the prize.** Your work likely requires you to be a zoom-out Systems Spotter and also to make sure you have the exact amount of swag for the annual gala. It can be easy to go into Check-the-Box mode because of so many different tasks on your plate, but pause and ask yourself if the actual task is leading into the outcome you want. It can be easy to get into the details of planning an event, but if the event is not actually achieving its goal (whether that is raising money, finding board members, enrolling students, or something else), then you want to rise out of the weeds and reassess what steps you should actually be taking.

5. **Forecasting is your friend.** Many people around you are likely immersed in the day-to-day of their own roles, and it is essential that you are the person who can pause, look ahead, and forecast what is coming. If your executive director is constantly in fundraising meetings trying to hustle in the cash, they are likely not going to be looking ahead on the calendar to preplan the board meeting.

GOODBYE, BE WELL, AND BE TOGETHER

I sit here a little sad to see you go. Each time I write a book (this was number five!), I swear I will never do it again. I'm a teacher at heart, not a writer, and sitting alone (even when I have a great thought partner/editor/reviser extraordinaire, Heidi, and wonderfully organized project manager, Maggie) is truly tough for me. This particular book is very important to me because of the many wonderful, talented, and thoughtful Together Teammates I have worked with, taught, or partnered with over the past two decades (more on them in the Acknowledgments). I am thrilled to amplify your work, highlight your tools and routines, and ensure that you are collectively supported, developed, and trained to operate at a high level to keep our organizations running well, on time, and effectively.

If you need to find me, there are a few ways you can reach out:

■ Pop over to the Together Group's website at www.thetogethergroup.com. You will find blog posts, resources, and opportunities to register for online and in-person Together Trainings.

■ Poke around The Together Teammate website over at www.wiley.com/go/togetherteammate. We included full-color images of all figures in this book, photos, and a few things that just didn't quite fit in!

■ Sign up for my monthly newsletter called Together Tips at https://www.thetogethergroup. com/contact/newsletter/. Each month, a link-y newsletter with some personal reflections, Together highlights, and connects to others' work will land in your inbox.

■ Follow me on my (limited) social media channels. I'm fading quickly from most social media, so check our website for the latest on where I still remain. My kids keep pushing me towards TikTok, but I'm not there yet! I'll still take your hashtags though (#togeth-erteammate).

■ Write me directly at maia@thetogethergroup.com. Due to volume, I cannot personally reply to each email (this pains me, but I must finally admit it), but I read each and every communication. And I love hearing from you.

#togetherforever

CONTRIBUTORS

This book would not be possible without the contributions of the following Together Team-mates. Their interviews, artifacts, and quotes make this book come alive, and I deeply appreciate each of these humans!

Emily Acuna	Jordan Habayeb	Kevin Pesantez
Josh Alfred	Venecia Harris	Waltrina Potter
Colleen Bolton	Eliana Hernandez	Sara-Kate Roberts
AJ Bute	Kat Hernandez	Fiama Romero
Katie Carpenter	Jen Hykes Wilson	Ana Rosales
Eryn Cochran	Dominique James	Kendra Rowe Salas
Erin Crespi	Molly Joyce	Elizabeth Saari
Hannah Curry	Clara Kang	Jazmin Sanders
Lauren Cutuli	Liz Kohler	Marissa Siefkes
Shannon Donnelly	Sophie Kramer	Maggie Sorby
Jennie Dougherty	Brett Leghorn	Maya Tucci
Amanda Frazier	Ashley Lynch	Teresa Velasquez
Lauren Fryer-Lewis	Stacia Mills	Lauren Voelker
Shanda Gentry	Lola Obadina	Priscilla Zamora
Heidi Gross	Teresita Okayawa	

ACKNOWLEDGMENTS

This particular book has been a long time coming, and it was written entirely during the COVID-19 pandemic, which admittedly was no easy task for the team and me. However, it wraps up the Together Trilogy, and is based on the hundreds of talented folks I have worked with over the past 20 years. It was an honor to reconnect with many of these individuals, interview dozens of them, and pore through their samples to identify themes, curate artifacts, and share their stories with you. I first dreamt of this Together title over a decade ago as I spent time in schools, nonprofits, and other organizations and found that the Together Teammates were consistently a bit less supported, developed, and celebrated than some other roles. Well, I hope we changed that a bit here.

To the folks who contributed to this book (our full list is in Contributors), I thank you for your time, generosity, and patience with my gazillions of questions and requests throughout such a busy time for you all. Almost all of you were involved in or leading the COVID-19 response for your nonprofits, schools, or districts, and you found time to share your tools, your mindsets, and your examples. I'm so excited to showcase your work. To those folks who specifically shared their Together Tour replies with us – Ashley, Kevin, Fiama, Brett, and Lola – thank you for so generously and expansively thinking about your work and your own Togetherness trajectory.

To my two writing partners-in-crime . . . first of all, Maggie Sorby, this is our second or third book together (I've lost count) and without your memes, project management prowess, and gentle threats to "put my pencil down," this book would not have hit deadline. Second of all, Heidi Gross, you are an introvert who makes writing as an extrovert fun, you are scary in the comments section, and your structural assists, wording revisions, and push to clarity make this my best book yet. May there be many lattes in both of your futures.

To the core Together Team – namely Kendra Rowe Salas, Ana Gutierrez, Lauren Fryer-Lewis, and Cornelius Arther – thank you for cheering me on when I set bizarre word count goals, keeping every single train running on time for our courses and core operations, and chatting on Zooms galore, and also ensuring every day that the hundreds of people who come through our classes have the best possible experience. To my trusted Together Trainers and editors – Chrystie Edwards, Erica Beal, Emily Reynolds, Tammie Holt, Marin Smith, and Briannon McLoughlin – thanks for your perspective, class feedback, and contributions to the culture and spirit of our work. I'm not the easiest person to give feedback to, but I can take it from you all. Your comments, cards, and brainstorms strengthened this book immensely. An additional thank you to Kendra for cool graphics, and to Ana and Lauren for their investigative skills.

To my Together support team and those who help me keep this entire thing running – Josh Lowitz, Nicole Garner, Chad Spader, the folks at Alter Design, Lee Kirby, Kim Berger, and Lee Weiner – I appreciate you helping keep my dream up and running with all the behind-the-scenes legal stuff, accounting work, and design prowess. To the WoMos (Emily, Mary Claire, Lindsay) for the WhatsApp, HoPas, and VaPas, and the Wolfpack (Analisa, Anne, Amy, Karn, Melinda), thanks for the cheerleading and encouragement along the way.

To Amy Fandrei, Pete Gaughan, and Mary Beth Rosswurm – and the entire Jossey-Bass team – thank you for joining my trainings, extending my deadlines, and being generous with your time and expertise to get this book to press!

And lastly, to the Together Family (!). First of all, is that a thing? Well, it is now. Four kids (hi Indigo, Ada, Reed, and Neala!) in four different schools and four cats and two full-time working parents in a blended family is no easy feat. And yet it remains joyfully chaotic or chaotically joyful, depending on the day. We have too many calendars to count, Tidy Time checklists galore, and I love you all. Dr. Together (Keith O'Doherty), I love that you discovered Workflowy, send me calendar invites for your work travel, and cheer me on as I work through word count. You shouldered a large load for me to take this book to the finish line, including (but not limited to) somehow taking four kids skiing entirely solo to give me weekends to write, sending me to a hotel three miles away or to the woods of Pennsylvania when you caught me procrastinating by consolidating Band-Aids and tossing expired spices, and keeping our very busy household afloat. Your performance review definitely exceeds expectations.

ABOUT THE AUTHORS

MAIA HEYCK-MERLIN

Maia Heyck-Merlin has over two decades of experience juggling high-volume roles in results-oriented organizations. For the past 20 years, she has dedicated her life to supporting teachers, school leaders, central offices, and nonprofits to prioritize, plan ahead, and execute efficiently – while maintaining flexibility, empathy, and humor. Her past four publications have helped thousands of educators, school leaders, operations team members, and nonprofit staffers across the country. She has worked closely with large traditional school districts, such as Houston Independent Schools, NYC Department of Education, San Antonio Independent School District, and Oakland Unified Schools, as well as big and small charter school networks, like KIPP, Success Academies, Aspire Public Schools, YES Prep, and IDEA Public Schools. Maia's work has also expanded to include many nonprofits and other mission-driven organizations, like Martha's Table, Act Blue, Elev8, and other organizations seeking to make the world a better place. Lastly, Maia has taken great pride in her decade-plus of work with leadership cohorts, such KIPP's Fisher Fellows, Boston College's Lynch Leadership Program, BES Fellows, and the School Leader Lab.

Prior to founding The Together Group, she served as chief talent officer and chief operating officer for Achievement First. Previously, she worked at Teach For America in a variety of capacities, including executive director and institute director. Maia began her career as a TFA corps member in South Louisiana, where she taught fourth grade and was named Teacher of the Year at Delmont Elementary and selected as a Fulbright Memorial Fund recipient. She was then a founding fifth grade teacher at Children's Charter School in Baton Rouge, where her largest claim to fame may have been a weeklong trip to Atlanta with all of her students.

Maia holds a BA in child development from Tufts University, and served as president of the Leonard Carmichael Society while an undergraduate. She was born and raised in a town of 400 people, and is a proud graduate of a rural Maine public school system. After stints in Boston, Brooklyn, and Baton Rouge, Maia currently resides in the Washington, DC, area with her husband (aka Dr. Together), their four medium-sized children, four unruly cats, and a lot of houseplants. In her spare time, she finds joy in leading the local Girl Scout Troop (#togethertroopleader), being a lazy triathlete, and vegan-ish cooking with as few pots and pans as possible.

HEIDI GROSS

Heidi's career spans a variety of educational institutions and roles, including stints at a public boarding school, a small liberal arts college, and a large research university. Her work with The Together Group started by supporting Together Leader public sessions in Chicago, and expanded to include public sessions management, communications oversight, and website development. The joy (and challenge) of editing Maia led Heidi to her current role as managing editor at Brethren Press.

Heidi holds a BS in sociology from Manchester University and an MA in liberal studies from Northwestern University. She is a proud Chicago resident and enjoys trying new restaurants, exploring neighborhoods, and finding pockets in the city that remind her of her rural Indiana upbringing.

INDEX